PSYCHOLOGICAL INSIGHT INTO THE BIBLE

texts and readings

Edited by

Wayne G. Rollins *&* D. Andrew Kille

Foreword by

Walter Wink

WILLIAM B. EERDMANS PUBLISHING COMPANY

GRAND RAPIDS, MICHIGAN / CAMBRIDGE, U.K.

Published 2007 by
Wm. B. Eerdmans Publishing Co.
2140 Oak Industrial Drive N.E., Grand Rapids, Michigan 49505 /
P.O. Box 163, Cambridge CB3 9PU U.K.

Printed in the United States of America

12 11 10 09 08 07   7 6 5 4 3 2 1

Library of Congress Cataloging-in-Publication Data

Psychological insight into the Bible : texts and readings /
    edited by Wayne G. Rollins & D. Andrew Kille ; foreword by Walter Wink.
        p.   cm.
    Includes bibliographical references and index.
    ISBN 978-0-8028-4155-1 (pbk.: alk. paper)
    1. Bible — Psychology.   2. Psychology, Religious.
    3. Bible — Criticism, interpretation, etc.
    I. Rollins, Wayne G.   II. Kille, D. Andrew, 1950-

    BS645.P79   2007
    220.601′9 — dc22

                                                            2007009321

www.eerdmans.com

In Memoriam

Wilhelm Wuellner, collaborator and friend

One of a cloud of witnesses who have recognized

that the Bible and its interpretation cannot be fully understood

without consideration of the nature and habits of the human psyche

Contents

Contents

Contents

xii

Foreword

Between the two of them, Wayne Rollins and Andrew Kille have read just about every book, article, citation, and fragment that deals with the subject of psychological approaches to the Bible. Yet there are those who still deny that such approaches are legitimate and speak of them pejoratively as "psychologizing."

Certainly psychology and theology can decide to have little to do with each other. Psychology deals with things like behavior, cognition, and personal and social development. Theology wrestles with what we might think, preach, and believe. To the extent that our psychologies have degenerated into inhuman objectivism, or our theological reflections into rationalism, to that degree both psychology and theology have pitifully lost their way. And the sad story of twentieth-century psychology is that humans are so often treated as pre-determined robots, with no real freedom for creativity, compassion, or transformation. Be it by Freud or Skinner, graduate schools of psychology have been dominated by scholars and physicians who cannot give a reasonable account of their own kindness, goodness, or love.

Theology can also be destructive. From terror of damnation, to the exclusion of people of other faiths, to the depiction of God as a cruel, abusive parent, biblical theology has all too often crushed the spirit.

But everything changes the moment we see both disciplines as concerned with our becoming human. When psychologists and theologians enlist their considerable gifts for healing, psychology becomes therapeutic and theology becomes redemptive. Is it not the psychological profession that has helped most to set people free from the destructive tendencies of religion? And conversely, is it not the theological profession that has helped to rescue a psychology that had lost its soul? Together they have challenged people to seek the higher self that is their birthright and destiny. Rollins and Kille have documented this painfully slow movement from mutual hostility to mutual interrelatedness.

"Psychologizing" is the term theologians have used to castigate what they regard as the misuse of psychology, and not without grounds. When interpreters of a text read into it concerns that are not there, or where the content of a passage is reduced to nothing but its psychodynamics, we can in all fairness say that psychologizing has taken place. In fact, however, virtually every narrative requires psychological analysis to be understood: *Why* did she do this? Or why did he say that? Psychology is merely one among all the tools that historiography, as a field-encompassing field, gratefully employs.

Psychologizing might lead us to analyze Mary's feelings as expressed in the Magnificat (Luke 1:46-55). However, if we suspect that this hymn derives from tradition and was created by someone else, a legitimate psychological inquiry would lead us to explore what those "others" are expressing and celebrating.

Psychologizing might lead us to develop a personality profile of Jacob from the texts in Genesis, without regard for the effects folk memory and legend may have had on the origins and development of the Jacob traditions. Psychological analysis might yet lead us to explore the psychological dynamics of the story as we have received it. The subject of our inquiry is not some historical person named Jacob, but why and how his story is told, and what the tellers intend the hearers to understand and to experience.

The point of using psychological insights in biblical study is not to map one approach onto the other, to prove that the Bible anticipated contemporary psychological understandings or that psychology is somehow legitimated because it accords with biblical authority. Psychological insights simply are another tool to use when the text determines they might be of use, not as a matter of course.

The efforts of Wayne Rollins and Andrew Kille have not just brought about a thoroughgoing historical synthesis of the literature. In concert with the other writers in this volume and elsewhere (such as Elizabeth Boyden Howes and the Guild for Psychological Studies), they are developing a new kind of exegesis. At their most profound level they show us how to apply psychological insights *to ourselves* as a means of appropriating the text for the task of human transformation. The biblical text, clarified and illuminated by all the tools of critical analysis, now can probe *us*. The subject becomes object, as we ourselves become the focus of analysis. In its objectivity, its alienness and opposition to us, the text can now help us to discover the secrets of the unconscious that have been lost and languishing in the dark corners of our souls.

WALTER WINK

Preface

Everything to do with religion, everything it is and asserts, touches the human soul so closely that psychology least of all can afford to overlook it.

C. G. Jung[1]

Anyone who thinks that . . . religion can be illumined historically and factually without psychological reflection is just as much in error as one who pretends that everything about this religion can be said in this fashion.

Gerd Theissen[2]

The psychological and psychoanalytical analyses of human experience have proven their worth in the area of religion and enable one to detect multidimensional aspects of the biblical message. . . . The aid that can come from this approach to [the historical-critical] method cannot be underestimated.

Joseph A. Fitzmyer, S.J.[3]

In the last three decades of the twentieth century, the field of biblical studies developed a renewed interest in the contribution psychological insight might

1. Carl Gustav Jung, *The Collected Works of C. G. Jung,* trans. R. F. C. Hull, ed. Gerhard Adler et al., Bollingen Series 20 (Princeton: Princeton University Press, 1953-78), vol. 11, par. 72.

2. Gerd Theissen, *Psychological Aspects of Pauline Theology,* trans. John P. Galvin (Philadelphia: Fortress, 1987), p. 398.

3. Joseph A. Fitzmyer, S.J., *Scripture, the Soul of Theology* (New York: Paulist, 1994), pp. 51-52.

make to an understanding of the role of the human psyche or soul in the history of the Bible and its interpretation.

This rebirth of interest in psychology has resulted from changes that have taken place since the 1960s within four spheres: Western culture as a whole, the field of psychology, the field of biblical studies, and the mindset of biblical scholars and psychologists toward one another.

The *change within Western culture* was the phenomenon of the so-called "psychologization of the West." The legacy of Freud and Jung had extended its reach into the streets and introduced a new set of terms and concepts that reflected a change in the way Westerners thought of themselves. The client on the psychoanalyst's couch populated comic strips, TV, and movies. Everyone from bankers to novelists, artists, theologians, and cab drivers found themselves speaking with a psychological accent, making commonplace reference to "repressed desire," "ulterior motives," "complexes," "neuroses," "unconscious drives," and "Freudian slips."

The *change within the field of psychology* occurred with the emergence of new psychological "schools" that began to challenge orthodox Freudian theory and the reductionism, materialism, and positivism of behavioral psychology that had dominated so much of psychological studies from the 1920s to the 1970s and had eliminated religion from the circle of psychological inquiry. These new "schools" include especially object relations, cognitive, developmental, and humanistic psychologies. Their emergence paved the way for the revival of the cordial relations that had existed between psychology and biblical studies prior to the 1920s. That close relationship characterized an era, extending back into the eighteenth century, when "biblical psychology" was a recognized academic pursuit and when the work of Franz Delitzsch, M. Scott Fletcher, William James, and G. Stanley Hall of Clark University, founder of the American Psychological Association, enjoyed an audience of theologians and biblical scholars as well as psychologists.

The *change within the field of biblical studies* took place with the emergence of new forms of biblical criticism that brought new "sister disciplines" to the aid of biblical research to complement the tools of historical and literary criticism that had been the staples of research for a century. In 1977 John Dominic Crossan predicted that "Biblical study will no longer be conducted under the exclusive or even dominant hegemony" of one or two disciplines, but rather "through a multitude of disciplines interacting mutually as a field of criticism."[4] These new disciplines would include rhetorical, canonical,

---

4. John Dominic Crossan, "Perspectives and Methods in Contemporary Biblical Criticism," *Biblical Research* 22 (1977): 41.

feminist, social-scientific, cultural, and psychological criticism, among others, all equipping the biblical scholar to pursue questions about the biblical text, its background, and its history that traditional historical-literary criticism was not prepared to ask or answer.

From these three shifts eventually emerged a fourth: a *change in mutual perceptions between biblical scholars and psychologists.* Biblical scholars began to suspect that their colleagues in psychology might be able to help them understand something more about themselves and the texts they study. They began to appreciate that the Bible is the product of a psychological process in which unconscious as well as conscious factors are at work, as much as it is the product of historical, literary, social, and even revelatory processes. They saw further that these psychological factors were at work in the biblical authors, in the communities they represented, in the stories and materials they preserved, in biblical copyists, translators and publishers, in biblical interpreters and preachers, and in the Bible's long-range effects on individuals and entire cultures, for good and for ill.

Psychologists, for their part, began to see their religious studies colleagues in a new light, and to look beyond the obscurantism, dogmatism, and literalism which had so clouded the view of the Bible in both psychological studies and the culture at large. Carl Jung and Joseph Campbell, literary critics Northrup Frye and Robert Alter, along with a host of world-recognized theologians and biblical scholars, helped psychologists to see that, while the Bible is a record of the past, it is substantially a book about the perennial nature and experience of the human soul or psyche. Though the Bible is not a psychological text, it speaks throughout of the trials, troubles, successes, and victories of the self. They came to understand that it employs a vast array of literary genres — myth and legend, psalm, parable, and sermon — to discern and describe the soul's nature, origin, habits, powers, and destiny. For the first time in decades, psychologists began exploring topics that were also biblical, such as sin, forgiveness, repentance, and conversion.

The purpose of this volume is to introduce the reader to the many dimensions of this newly revived approach to the Bible. Its objective is to provide representative examples of the range of contributions psychological criticism has made over the last century and a half to our understanding of the Bible, of its interpretation and effects, and of ourselves as readers of the Bible.

The book is divided into two parts. Part One consists of five chapters, laying out the theoretical bases for psychological biblical criticism. Chapter 1, "Past, Present, and Future," sketches the historical background and origin of the term "psychology" and recounts the early history of collaboration between psychology and biblical studies prior to the mid-twentieth century. It highlights two pioneers in the field of psychology and biblical studies, Franz Delitzsch and M. Scott Fletcher, and unfolds an agenda for future work in the field. Chapter 2, "The Care and Cure of the Soul," notes that psychology and the Bible have a common parent mission, namely the care and cure of souls. The terms "soul," "psyche," and "self" are examined as they appear across world cultures past and present. Chapters 3 and 4 turn to six different theoretical approaches to psychological biblical criticism: "Freud and Jung" in Chapter 3, and "Behavioral, Cognitive, Developmental, and Object Relations Approaches" in Chapter 4, showcasing the spectrum of insights available through the special perspectives of each. Chapter 5, "Between Texts and Readers," turns to the question, "What happens when a person reads the Bible?" Echoing reader-response criticism, it reminds us that reading is not a one-way street. The chapter explores the question not only of what a text brings to a reader but also of what a reader brings to a text.

In Part Two, "Case Studies and Applications," we turn our attention from theory to application. These nine chapters demonstrate how psychological analysis can be applied to various biblical phenomena. Chapter 6, "Biblical Symbols and Archetypal Images," considers the impressive role of symbols and archetypal images in human experience and the power of biblical symbols to energize, inspire, and project possibilities for the self. Chapters 7 and 8 focus on the psychology of biblical personalities. Chapter 7 covers recent studies of two biblical figures, Ezekiel and Paul, for whom some measure of autobiographical material exists in the Bible. It is possible to make tentative, psychological observations about the person's life and thought "behind the text" based on personal accounts of this sort. For most biblical personalities, however, we have no firsthand, autobiographical information, as, for example, with the portraits of Moses and Jesus. Chapter 8 examines the psychic effect the portrait of a biblical figure like Moses can exercise on its viewers, whether in the text or in sculpture or painting. The chapter also illustrates how the search for the historical Jesus can be aided by attention to the psychodynamics exhibited in the Gospel accounts of Jesus, revealing fascinating observations about the relationships between Jesus and John the Baptist, women, his father, mother, and family, and his disciples, highlighting probable features of the historical figure whose memory lies behind the Gospel accounts.

Chapters 9 and 10 focus jointly on the psychological dynamics at work within biblical narratives. Chapter 9 looks at the texts about Adam and Eve, Jonah, and the Ten Commandments. Chapter 10 explores the texts on the wedding at Cana, the Anti-Christ image, and the theology of Paul. Chapters 11 and 12 present psychological observations on religious experience described in the biblical texts. Chapter 11 considers dreams, prophecy, and healing in Scripture, while Chapter 12 looks at the phenomena of demons and exorcism, glossolalia, and conversion.

Chapter 13 introduces us to the psychological effects that the Bible has had on individuals and communities, noting that, over the centuries, the Bible has exercised both pathogenic as well as profound therapeutic effects on its readers. Chapter 14 returns to the earliest conversations on "biblical psychology," beginning with Tertullian and Augustine, through the Reformers, to nineteenth-, twentieth-, and twenty-first-century biblical scholars. Their goal? To explicate the biblical understanding of the anatomy, powers, habits, pathology, and health of the soul/psyche, not only as an object of academic study but as a prescription for life.

PART ONE

Psychological Approaches to the Bible

CHAPTER 1

Past, Present, and Future

But the book of nature and the book of Scripture are precisely two books which from the beginning were intended to be compared with one another. And if the student of nature asks the theologian or himself as a Christian, How readest thou? the theologian must also in return ask the student of nature, How readest thou?

Franz Delitzsch[1]

It will at once be apparent that Biblical psychology is the description and explanation which the Scriptural writers give of the mental and spiritual constitution of man. It is a historical system of belief or presuppositions which is complete in itself and readily yields to critical examination. It is embodied in a literature which extends over many centuries of Jewish national life, and contains the views of both Hebrew and Christian thinkers concerning man.

M. Scott Fletcher[2]

Psychology as we now know it has its roots deep in the ancient world of the Bible. The name of the field itself is derived from *psyche*, the Greek word for "soul" used in the New Testament, and the development of psychology as an area of study first unfolded in the context of biblical study and theological re-

---

1. Franz J. Delitzsch, *A System of Biblical Psychology,* trans. Robert Ernest Wallis, 2nd ed. (Edinburgh: T&T Clark, 1867), p. 23.

2. M. Scott Fletcher, M.S., *The Psychology of the New Testament,* 2nd ed. (New York: Hodder and Stoughton, 1912), p. 7.

flection. While the Bible is rich with psychological observations and descriptions, they are neither systematic nor scientific. Psychology itself developed as people first sought to develop systems of psychology based on previously unconnected observations of behavior, thought, and personality. Modern psychology as a systematic and scientific field of study did not emerge until the nineteenth century. The year 1879 is generally considered to mark the beginning of modern psychology; in that year Wilhelm Wundt established a laboratory in Leipzig for experimental study.

For nearly two millennia before that time, though, some of the finest philosophers and theologians of the West, including Tertullian, Augustine, Aquinas, and Philipp Melanchthon (who brought the term *psychology* to general use), sought to organize and develop the psychological insights of biblical texts. In 1855, nearly twenty-five years before Wundt, the prolific and highly respected German Lutheran biblical scholar Franz Delitzsch published *A System of Biblical Psychology*, followed by a second edition in 1867. The excerpts from Delitzsch's second edition in the first reading offer a rationale and process for systematic biblical psychology at its fullest before modern psychology.

The end of the nineteenth and early years of the twentieth century encompassed a flowering of psychological study. In the United States, William James had first published his *Principles of Psychology* in 1890 and *The Varieties of Religious Experience* in 1902. His student G. Stanley Hall also studied with Wundt and returned to the United States to found the American Psychological Association in 1892. The first president of Clark University, Hall wrote *Jesus, the Christ, in the Light of Psychology* in 1917.[3] On the Continent, the new theories proposed by Sigmund Freud were introduced to the world in his book *The Interpretation of Dreams* in 1900. In 1912, M. Scott Fletcher published his Oxford dissertation as *The Psychology of the New Testament*, from which the second reading is drawn.

As the twentieth century unfolded, there were many examples of psychological biblical criticism. For the most part, however, these efforts remained spotty and disconnected, often representing a single article by an individual with no sense of how his or her insights might fit into either a psychological or a biblical critical framework. In the later part of the century, there was a revival of interest in psychology and the Bible. No longer did historical-critical methods dominate biblical study, and psychology was developing more useful and precise perspectives. In the third reading, Wayne

---

3. Granville Stanley Hall, *Jesus, the Christ, in the Light of Psychology*, 2 vols. (Garden City: Doubleday, Page & Co., 1917).

G. Rollins maps the field of psychological biblical criticism, identifying key issues and approaches for current and future study.

Reading 1.1   A System of Biblical Psychology

FRANZ DELITZSCH

Delitzsch begins his work firmly rooted in theology. His division of the field of biblical psychology into such areas as "Eternal Presuppositions," "Fall," and "Regeneration" and his suggestion that biblical psychology can help humanity deal with the "last days" may seem odd to modern readers. Nonetheless, he is prepared to incorporate insights from newer empirical research. He raises several questions that remain pertinent today: How should scientific investigation and study of the Scriptures be related to each other appropriately? Is it necessary to be a believer to understand Scripture correctly? How can a biblically based perspective offer a critique of materialistic trends in psychology?

Prolegomena Section II: Idea of Biblical Psychology

The task which I propose to myself is practicable; for under the name of biblical psychology I understand a scientific representation of the doctrine of Scripture on the psychical constitution of man as it was created, and the ways in which this constitution has been affected by sin and redemption. There is such a doctrine in Scripture. It is true that on psychological subjects, just as little as on dogmatical or ethical, does Scripture comprehend any system propounded in the language of the schools. If it taught in such a way, we should need to construct psychology directly from it as little as we do dogmatics and ethics. But still it does teach. . . . Science, moreover, has the duty of bringing to light the materials of doctrine latent in the Scriptures, — of collecting that

---

From Franz J. Delitzsch, *A System of Biblical Psychology,* trans. Robert Ernest Wallis, 2nd ed. (Edinburgh: T&T Clark, 1867), excerpts from pp. 16-25.

which is scattered there, — of explaining that which is hard to be understood, — of establishing that which is doubtful, — and of combining the knowledge thus acquired into a doctrinal whole, consistent and compact.

The formal possibility of the accomplishment of such task is guaranteed by the undeniable unity of character prevailing in the doctrinal materials of psychology placed before us in Scripture. Or are the psychological assumptions and inferences of the biblical writers not in harmony with themselves? We maintain thorough fundamental agreement, without thereby excluding manifold individualities of representation and mode of speech; for in essential spiritual unity the special writers have each their characteristic stamp.

. . . There is a clearly defined psychology essentially proper to the Holy Scripture, which in like manner underlies all the biblical writers, and intrinsically differs from that many-formed psychology which lies outside the circle of revelation.[1] Therefore the problem of biblical psychology may be solved as one problem. We do not need, first of all, to force the biblical teaching into unity; it is one in itself.

The biblical psychology thus built up is an independent science, which coincides with no other, and is made superfluous by no other in the organism of entire theology. It is most closely allied with so-called biblical theology, or . . . with dogmatics. Biblical, or, as may also be said, theological psychology (to distinguish it from the physical-empirical and philosophic-rational science), pervades the entire material of dogmatics, in that it determines all the phases of man's psychical constitution, conditioned upon those facts and relations momentous to the history of salvation which form the substance of dogmatics. But it asserts in all these associations its own peculiarity, in that it considers all that is common to it with dogmatics only so far as it throws light or shadow into the human soul, draws it into co-operation or sympathy, and affords explanations upon its obscurities. . . .

Prolegomena Section III: Method of Biblical Psychology

. . . [T]he matter of psychology divides itself into the following seven heads: 1. Eternal Presuppositions. 2. Creation and Propagation. 3. Fall. 4. Present Constitution. 5. Regeneration. 6. Death and Intermediate State. 7. Resurrec-

---

1. Thus we judge with Schöberlein, in his notice of v. Rudloff, *Studien u. Kritiken* (1860), p. 145, which in appropriate words comes to the defence of biblical psychology; and therefore we have, on scientific ground, the right, which the critic in the *Literar. Centralblatt,* 1855, No. 45, refuses to us, to speak of the Scriptures almost entirely as of one subject.

tion and Perfection. Since psychology after this manner proceeds from eternity, and passing through time turns back again to eternity, there will not be wanting to it a compact unity; but the successful accomplishment of our task will depend on our not losing sight in any wise of the distinction between psychology and dogmatics. Our source is the Holy Scripture, in union with empirical facts which have a biblical relation, and require biblical examination. The Old and New Testament concern us equally; for the Old Testament, which is more directed to the creation and nature, *i.e.* to the origin of things and their external manifestation, gives us disclosures which the New Testament at once takes for granted. The New Testament, on the other hand, affords us, on the ground of the incarnation of the Son of God, far deeper and more accurate knowledge of the nature of God, and of the ethical relations of man to the invisible as to the visible world; and, moreover, it is there that we first learn to understand rightly the beginnings of man in the light of the clearly and specially revealed last things. We must carefully consider this difference of the two Testaments, and in general the progress of the revelation; and we must take pains to distinguish between what Scripture designedly teaches, and what it adopts without close discussion, — as having been ordinarily lawful in antiquity, or prevalent in the Semitic tribes, or in the language of a psychologic view that has become stereotyped — in order to attribute to it its peculiar doctrinal value as it was revealed. Finally, it is not sufficient, by way of adducing proofs, to pick out individual texts from Scripture; but there is necessary, generally, inspection and inquiry into the entire scope of Scripture, that we may not fall back into the faults which made the ancient manner of referring to Scripture proofs, unhistorical, one-sided, and fragmentary. Moreover, we must guard ourselves against the self-deception of interpolating speculative thoughts suggested by Scripture, or physiologic notices foreign to it, in Scripture itself. To interpret into Scripture the circulation of the blood, or the importance of the cerebral system, in place of the activity of the soul, would be just as foolish as to reject such new discoveries because no scriptural statements imply any reference to them. It is proper to revelation to accommodate itself to the degree of cultivation of every age, and to speak, not the language of the school, but the language of life. This observation is just; but it must not be pressed too far. . . . It is just the same with the psychological presuppositions of Scripture. From the standpoint of our present empirical knowledge they may appear unsatisfactory, because, as in the case of what Scripture says on astronomical subjects, they are here or there only gathered from the external form of the phenomenon; but, nevertheless, they are not false: they only become so when the form of the revelation, borrowed from the modes of representation and expression of daily life, is regarded as belonging to its substance. He, for example, who would thus reproach the Scripture, that it always places the soul in immediate relation with the blood, and not with the nerves, would be just as unjust as another would be foolish in reading in Scripture of electricity, magnetism, and such like things, or perhaps of the nervous fluid, abandoned as it is (I do not raise the question how rightly) by modern physiology. Of all these things Scripture can say nothing, since the Holy Ghost speaks there with a human tongue; and human representation and language had not in those times any ideas and words for those things. But we should deeply wrong the Scripture, if we thought that the glory of its psychologic representations must for ever grow pale in the daylight sunshine of the present day, and that biblical psychology is perhaps such as the psychology of Homer — nothing but a fragment of the history of the training of the human spirit, of only antiquarian value! . . . The pathway of knowledge of experimental physical investigation advances from without, inward, and has before it a limit beyond which it cannot now or ever pass. The mode of evidence of the revelation, which gives itself to the internal experience, goes, on the other hand, from within, outward, and has no other bounds than those which it places to itself in accordance with man's attainment in culture and need of salvation.[2] Natural investigation, for example, can at the most tell us how, by means of a purely optical process, the forms of the outer world come in contact with the retina expanded on the background of the eye; but here it must stop: it can go no further; for how, by the further agency of the optic nerve and of the brain, the image comes to representation of this it can never tell us anything. It is absolutely impossible to show how, by means of the brain, irritation of the nerve of sensation is transformed into perception; how thence into the thought-product of perceptions; how thence into the self-consciousness that overrides and penetrates the entire physico-psychical mechanism. . . . But as far as late experimental research has actually revealed to us the secrets of human bodily life, its results agree with the disclosures of Scripture about spirit and soul, — far removed from favouring a materialism which is opposed to Scripture; for, as a late opponent of the folly of the materialistic view of the world has with only too much truth observed, it is not the actual results of physical investigation, but the hypotheses grafted on to them, and arrived at from quite a different source, which demand the denial[3] of ev-

2. "Where is the rule and the measure," cries to us, on the other hand, Noack, in his *Psyche*, vol. iii, 1860, p. 330, "by which this way of evidence of the revelation which gives itself to the internal experience is to be judged? We answer: In the trial of its genuineness, which only the real and genuine one can really undergo, and in the essential harmony of the internal experiences of faithful Christians of all times and of all places."

3. F. Fabri, in his letters against materialism, 1856, and *Evang. K. Z.*, 1857, col. 1069. "Where

ery nobler religious truth, and even of the substantiality and reality of the spiritual altogether.

Our task reminds us not to leave unconsidered many of those results attained by means of the dissecting knife and the microscope; for biblical psychology has not alone to bring out the psychologic aspects of Scripture, but also to show, in opposition to the later science, that, so far as they are well-founded and fairly-balanced presumptions of the revelation of salvation, there is due to them a continually better established claim on the subsistence and authority of our consciousness. In these inevitable references to late physical science, and especially to physiology, we shall make a duty of using the strictest care; and we believe, therefore, that we have no occasion to fear lest any one of the modern philosophers whom we shall name should be able to point out to us that we have not understood him, although he possibly might have to complain that we have not applied what he has said, as he himself intended it. . . . But the book of nature and the book of Scripture are precisely two books which from the beginning were intended to be compared with one another. And if the student of nature asks the theologian or himself as a Christian, How readest thou? the theologian must also in return ask the student of nature, How readest thou? The reciprocity of this question has indeed almost ceased. It tends, moreover, to the honour of theology, that its interest in the book of Scripture is inseparable from the interest in the book of nature, just as it adds discredit to the later physical science, that for the most part it scarcely concerns itself about the book of Scripture, and establishes a yawning gulf between the two divine records. Theology cannot treat it in like manner, for the two books have as their author the one God, from whom the science itself is named. Therefore it cannot refrain from collating the two books, and, moreover, the exegesis of the two books. This also is what is required in the nature of the problem itself, in the field of biblical psychology. But if, in certain cases, a palpable contradiction appears between the interpretation of Scripture and that of nature, we shall be allowed to point out that, for the present at least, the biblical representations are not yet convicted of absurdity. With the materialism of our days, however, we shall concern ourselves little. Biblical psychology may remit the struggle against this barbarism to empirical and philosophical science. There are still many other forms of vigorous opposition between the biblical manner of looking at things and the modern consciousness, and these must impartially be presented to us. On

---

the question is about the fundamental views of a man, from which are built up his moral or spiritual views, there is first of all placed in the scale a factor which lies outside the domain of 'strict demonstration, viz. the *will* of man.'"

this account we shall certainly here and there be constrained to adopt an apologetic tone. And if we apply apologetically something of what has been said by natural philosophers in such a way that what they have not absolutely meant to say shall further the cause of Scripture, we are sorry to give them this cause of complaint, and we console them beforehand with the assurance that it shall not often happen.

... [W]e here upon the threshold make the avowal, that, in order to its right treatment and understanding, biblical psychology presumes above all, that the student has personal experience of that living energy of the word of God which is declared in Heb. iv.12 to divide asunder the inward man with the sharpness of a two-edged sword. Even that just-mentioned natural philosopher[4] has not been ashamed to make the good confession: "Only he to whom it is given to apprehend the highest mysteries of revealed religion in full subjective faith, will be able with satisfaction to himself and to his age to philosophize upon the natural phenomena of the life of the soul." Such also is our conviction. That man only who has returned to the way of repentance and of faith in God in his own experience, is capable of any knowledge about himself which does not stop short at the threshold, and indeed, according to the unalterable law *ex fide intellectus,* is capable of a knowledge, genuine, resting on sufficient and reasonable ground, and truly accurate. Meanwhile we are only here declaring the prerequisite of any intelligent penetration of the substance of biblical psychology, and indeed we hereby desire to impress it upon ourselves as a matter of serious warning. In reference, however, to the well-attested facts of psychical occurrence external to us, there has never perhaps been a time more favourable to biblical psychology, as there has also never been a time that needed it more than the present, which, in features that are constantly becoming more manifest, earns the character of the last days. For the spirit-world, good as well as evil, which in all times has been the background of earthly events, is coming more and more to the front in our times; the end of the Christian era becoming, according to a divine law in the formation of history, ever more like to its beginning. Powerful and awakening invasions of good spirits into the psychical life of men on the one hand, and on the other all kinds of manic, even to the summoning up of the dead, are becoming more and more frequent. We would not be deaf to the preaching of repentance by the former phenomena, nor blind to the pernicious power, of the latter, in which demoniacal influence and human quack quackery are adversely involved. By throwing light from the word of God upon these twofold phenomena, in order to draw from it the power of discerning of spirits as far

---

4. Rud. Wagner, *Der Kampf um die Seele,* p. 113.

as possible, we are satisfying an increasingly urgent necessity of the present day. In the Holy Scripture we have the solution of these enigmas; but they are moreover a living commentary on the Scripture . . . if we would not, to our everlasting disgrace, neglect the consideration of the signs of the times.

Reading 1.2   ## The Psychology of the New Testament

M. Scott Fletcher

M. Scott Fletcher's work at the turn of the twentieth century represents a transitional period, evidencing the earlier theologically based effort to systematize biblical psychology, while drawing more substantially on the emerging field of scientific psychology as a tool for interpretation. Asserting that science and religion deal with different dimensions of human experience, Fletcher nonetheless insists that they must inform each other. He closes his introduction by correlating key terms in psychology with corresponding concepts in the Bible.

Introductory. The Relation of Biblical to Modern Psychology

One of the pioneer expositors of Biblical psychology in modern times, Dr. J. T. Beck, writing in 1843 the preface to his *Outlines of Biblical Psychology,* says, "When at work on my Introduction to the System of Christian Doctrine, I came to see very clearly that for the scientific student, who wishes to define the first principles of Christian Apologetics in a way that will do justice to the teachings of Scripture, a Biblical Psychology is absolutely indispensable."[1] The need for a clear understanding of Biblical psychology was never greater than at the present time. The progress of the historical criticism of the literature of the Bible has thrown its contents into a new perspective, and given to its teaching about human nature a fresh significance. The rise of modern scientific psychology, also, has not only awakened a keen interest in the subject of man's spiritual nature, but has furnished the Biblical student with a new

1. J. T. Beck, *Outlines of Biblical Psychology* (Edinburgh, 1877).

From M. Scott Fletcher, M.S., *The Psychology of the New Testament,* 2nd ed. (New York: Hodder and Stoughton, 1912), pp. 3-22.

instrument of wonderful precision with which to analyse and seek to understand the Scriptural terms which describe the mental and moral nature of man. Only upon a sound Biblical psychology can there be built a sound Biblical theology. Whatever historical criticism can teach us as to the development of thought within the Bible itself, and whatever light modern science can throw upon the constitution of human nature, should help us to understand better what the Scriptural writers say concerning man.

The older books on Biblical psychology appear defective to a modern student just because they lack this historical view and because they interpret the language of Scripture in the terms of psychological conceptions which have been largely superseded. The mechanical and static view of the Bible, which regarded the quotation of any passage from any portion of it as sufficient "proof" of Scriptural doctrine, has given way to a genetic method of study whereby the growth and development of a truth is traced from its birth to its maturity.

The process of "reading into" the psychological language of Scripture the conceptions of patristic or mediaeval philosophy is now held to be utterly misleading, and we require afresh to study the Biblical teaching about man from the standpoint of the Biblical writers themselves. The historical view of the Bible helps us to do this, and modern psychology comes to our aid in the understanding of their meaning. It would be but to repeat the mistakes of the older expositors of systems of Biblical psychology to "read into" the terms of Scripture the ideas of modern philosophy and science. But the purpose of this book is rather to arrive at a knowledge of the psychological conceptions of the New Testament writers, by an inductive study of their teaching, looked at from their standpoint, but interpreted in terms of present-day psychology. Hence it is desirable at the outset to examine and state in outline the relation in which the Biblical psychology stands to modern psychology.

1. Psychology and History

Psychology may be defined briefly as "the science of mind," or more fully as "the science of that which thinks, feels, and wills, in contrast with physics as the science of that which moves in space and occupies time."[2] Professor William James accepts the definition of Dr. Ladd that it is "the description and explanation of states of consciousness as such."[3] It will at once be apparent

2. H. Höffding, *Outlines of Psychology,* translated (from the German edition) by Mary E. Lowndes (London: Macmillan, 1891), p. 1.
3. William James, *Textbook of Psychology,* p. 1.

that Biblical psychology is the description and explanation which the Scriptural writers give of the mental and spiritual constitution of man. It is a historical system of belief or presuppositions which is complete in itself and readily yields to critical examination. It is embodied in a literature which extends over many centuries of Jewish national life, and contains the views of both Hebrew and Christian thinkers concerning man. It doubtless is developed out of prehistoric and primitive reflections; but by the time the first books of the Bible were written, these early ideas had taken more definite shape and were expressed by terms that tended to become relatively fixed.

Within the Bible itself there is evidence that further development of these psychological ideas took place. Still, allowing for such development, the Biblical psychology remains a self-contained and fairly consistent system of teaching about man's inner life of consciousness, and affords a good field for the psychologist in search of historical material. If the N.T. is separated from the rest of the Bible, the deposit of psychological ideas can be studied in detail and as a whole with much greater precision. . . .

The N.T. psychology, when compared with that of the Old, shows signs of having been influenced by three factors — Jewish noncanonical literature, Greek philosophy, and Christian experience — which tended to distinguish it from the earlier Biblical ideas. It affords, then, an excellent example of a historical system which found expression within the limits of a single century and is accessible in a carefully preserved literature.

Modern psychology is a science "still in the making." It takes the subjective facts of consciousness as its first study, but it has to supplement its methods of observation and experiment by considering also the objective facts of mental life seen in animals, children, and savages, and embodied in ancient literature, morals, religion, and art. This is sometimes called objective or sociological psychology. . . . Just as modern psychology has investigated the psychology of the Egyptians or the sacred books of the East as historical forms of thought, so it inquires into the psychology of the Hebrews embodied in the Biblical literature.

The N.T. psychology is of special interest historically to the modern student. It must be remembered that the Gospel preached by Jesus Christ and his apostles stirred the ancient world to its depths. The pages of the N.T. record the earliest effects of that message. Are those effects in the emotional, intellectual, and moral lives of people of no psychological significance as data in trying to obtain a fuller view of the nature of human personality? Into the manifold life of the ancient world Christianity came producing violent agitation in the lives of individuals and nations. New psychic experiences, a new type of character, new moral and social activities emerged. By its historical records or by its casual references to these facts the N.T. affords us psychological material of the highest value in understanding human personality and of the ways it may be modified or developed under fresh conditions of religious life.

2. Science and Religion

Modern psychology looks at man from the standpoint of natural science. Biblical psychology regards him almost entirely as a religious being. If this distinction is observed, the two need not come into conflict, and we shall be free to utilise the results arrived at by scientific psychology in order to understand much that would be otherwise obscure in the Bible. At the same time the religious experiences recorded in the Scriptures afford science additional facts for the contribution which it is making to an independent study of the nature of the religious consciousness. It should be recognised at the outset that the Biblical psychology is not scientific in the strict sense of the word. "Even in the New Testament," says Dr. A. B. Davidson, "there is no Biblical psychology in the scientific sense. The New Testament psychology is not meant to be a psychology of the mind as regards its substance or elements, or even its operations, except on a certain side of these operations. The psychology of the New Testament cannot be pursued further back so as to be made strictly a psychology or physiology of the mind. It remains a description of the mind or its attitudes ethically and religiously."[4] The Scriptures deal primarily with man's relationship to God. The main states of consciousness which it considers and describes are those which arise in connection with its teaching about man's origination from God and his communion with God.

The Biblical psychology is really theocentric. Apart from the conception of the Spirit of God as creating, sustaining, and directly influencing man, the various psychological terms lose their true significance and become the mere vestiges of animistic beliefs, of interest it may be to the anthropologist, but valueless to those who desire to gain through Biblical psychology some truth as to God's continued relationship to man and man's possible fellowship with the Divine. To the religious man the psychological language of Scripture is of the highest importance, for it was fashioned by religious experience and expresses, as no naturalistic system of scientific psychology can ever be expected to do, the influence of God upon the mind of man and the reactions of the soul of man in a spiritual environment.

It must not be hastily assumed, however, that modern scientific psy-

---

4. Abridged from *The Theology of the O.T.*, p. 184.

chology is essentially irreligious because it does not speak the language of the Bible. It considers the facts and processes of the human consciousness as they are in themselves. To do its own allotted work, as a special science, it must free itself from all presuppositions, both of religion and of metaphysics, which seem to offer a short cut to the solution of its problems. . . .

The self-denying ordinance by which psychology is willing to let Metaphysics and Religion settle questions which do not legitimately lie within its province must not mislead us, then, into supposing that scientific psychology is necessarily hostile either to Philosophy or Religion. On the contrary, the work done by psychology is patient roadmaking, whereby Philosophy may have easier access to the mountain-peak of truth from which it can survey experience as a whole in one comprehensive view. If psychology is allowed to do its work thoroughly enough, it may also "prepare the way of the Lord" for the salvation of human souls. . . . In the meantime, the religious psychology of the Bible, expressing in its own appropriate way the facts and experiences which marked the spiritual history of the Jewish people and the yet richer experiences that emerged in Christianity, may be expected to supply the classical terms in which the religious psychology of the future will choose to embody the results of its investigations. Already we find words like Conversion, Sanctification, and Faith, which hitherto have been the exclusive possession of Biblical theology, passing into the current language of modern psychology. But the main terms of Biblical psychology stand strangely alone, in meaning at least, and are often sadly misunderstood amidst the psychological language that has grown up from the days of Aristotle's scientific inquiries to the present day. It is time we more fully utilised the analytical keenness and verbal precision of scientific psychology to study afresh the full meaning of the Scriptural terminology.

3. Terminology — Biblical and Modern

The relation between Biblical and modern psychology is often difficult to determine, owing to their using different sets of terms to denote man's inner life of consciousness. An additional difficulty is created by the fact that, when they use a term in common (e.g. "Soul"), that word is often used with widely different meanings. It is necessary, therefore, as an introduction to what follows, to state and explain the main psychological terms used in modern textbooks, and to see the bearing of these on the terms which occur in the Bible, and especially in the N.T. . . .

Since the critical investigations of Kant (b. 1724; d. 1804) it has been usual to employ a threefold classification of conscious states. The three ultimate modes of consciousness are now named (according to the mental element which preponderates in each) Thinking, Feeling, and Willing. They are sometimes called Cognition, Feeling, and Conation. Under these three heads all the phenomena of the conscious life can be arranged. It must be remembered that each mental element is not separate and distinct in itself, nor can it operate without the co-operation of the other two. . . .

The *thinking* element of consciousness, when viewed alone, is sometimes spoken of as the "Intellect," or "Mind" (in the narrower sense of the word). Under thought or cognition are classified all perceptions and memory, all forms of reasoning and imagination. Its importance for religious psychology is, that by this power men believe, or doubt; they have intuition or apprehension of truth.

The *feeling* element of consciousness begins in such elementary states as sensations; it distinguishes between pleasure and pain, comfort and discomfort, and it includes all emotions, such as joy and sorrow, hope and fear, love and hate. "Toothache is a simple elementary feeling, while sorrow and repentance are feelings which involve ideas and memories."[5] In religion, feeling and the higher emotions occupy a central place, as also in art.

The *willing* element in consciousness, more briefly called "the will," or conation, is the active side of mind. Under this general term are placed all impulses, desires, wishing, striving, and volition. It is the volitional or purposeful quality in human action which lies at the basis of moral character. For both religion and ethics the question of the nature and freedom of the will is of the highest importance.

Behind the threefold activity of thinking, feeling, and willing lies the unity of the ego or self, the subject of these states of consciousness. This self, to whom belong all thoughts, feelings, and volitions, is often called the "soul" in philosophical language. When the soul or ego objectifies itself and knows that it thinks and feels and wills, it attains self-consciousness, which is the essential characteristic of what is called Personality.

The psychological terminology of the Bible is not analytic, but grew out of man's actual experience of life, and especially out of his religious reflection thereon. It has four main terms to describe the various aspects of man's total life. They are Flesh, Heart, Soul, and Spirit. These all occur in their Hebrew equivalents in the O.T. and in their Greek equivalents in the N.T. as the four outstanding psychological terms.

All these words gather round the idea of Life and express some special relation to it. The *Soul* is the *subject of life*. It is the bearer of the individual life,

---

5. Höffding, *Psychology,* p. 222.

what is now called the Ego, or Self. *Spirit*, on the other hand, is the *principle of life* generally, and is therefore regarded, when a constituent part of man, as higher than soul and that which makes man akin to God. The *Heart* is the *organ of life*, and the seat of all thinking, feeling, and willing. The *Flesh* is not merely the body or its material substance. It is *living matter* or the medium of life's manifestation. These words express certain definite psychological ideas, as will appear in the succeeding chapters. In the N.T. some additional terms appear which came into it from Greek thought. What is usually called "Biblical Psychology" is the system of ideas concerning man's conscious life which these terms embody and express. For the elucidation of their meaning the analytical precision of the vocabulary of scientific psychology is very necessary to a modern reader of the Bible.

Reading 1.3 A Psychological-Critical Approach to the Bible and Its Interpretation

Wayne G. Rollins

At the end of the twentieth century, three components were essential to the revival of psychological biblical criticism: describing and mapping the field as a whole, identifying and preserving the largely unknown work already done, and developing a collegial group to showcase new work, discuss issues of common concern and advance the field as a whole. The latter goal was realized with the formation in 1991 of the Psychology and Biblical Studies program unit of the Society of Biblical Literature. In 1993, the chairman, Wayne Rollins, offered the following broad overview of the arenas and challenges for psychological biblical criticism.

What then is the nature and agenda of a psychological-critical approach to Scripture? I would like to submit a definition: The goal of a psychological-critical approach is to examine texts, their origination, authorship, modes of expression, their construction, transmission, translation, reading, interpreta-

---

Wayne G. Rollins, "Rationale and Agenda for a Psychological-Critical Approach to the Bible and Its Interpretation" (Washington, DC: Psychology and Biblical Studies Group, Society of Biblical Literature, 1993).

tion, their transposition into kindred and alien art forms, and the history of their personal and cultural effect, as expressions of the structure, processes, and habits of the human psyche, both in individual and collective manifestations, past and present.

Rollins suggests six specific research areas for psychologically informed exploration: (1) *Forschungsgeschichte,* the history of research in biblical psychology; (2) developing a foundational psychological model; (3) exegesis; (4) hermeneutics; (5) description and analysis of religious phenomena, and (6) *Wirkungsgeschichte,* the ongoing impact of biblical texts on readers and communities.

1. The agenda of a psychological-critical *Forschungsgeschichte* would include, in the first instance, a historical review of the twenty centuries of what Delitzsch called, "Biblical psychology," and which he characterized, not inappropriately, as "one of the oldest sciences of the church."[1] A second item on the historical agenda would be revisiting those early and even mid-20th century works that applied psychological theory to Biblical interpretation and were routinely ignored by mainline Biblical scholarship. . . .

2. *Psychological Theory.* A daunting but necessary assignment for the psychological criticism of Scripture will be working toward a coherent theoretical psychological base for a psychological-critical approach to the text, and advancing a working model of the human psyche, admittedly flying in the face of the difficulties psychologists themselves see, and that Biblical scholars, working in a secondary discipline, fear. . . . David Miell cites five weaknesses in the turn of the century psychological approaches to scripture that soured mainline Biblical scholarship. First, these approaches lacked a systematic and coherent set of well-articulated theories; second, they focused on abnormalities, e.g., the personality of Job, the Messianic consciousness of Jesus, or the conversion of Paul; third, they assumed, naively, that the psychological data supplied in Scripture was historically reliable; fourth, they were guilty of "psychologism," i.e., arbitrary and speculative application of psychological theory to Biblical interpretation; and fifth, they were insufficiently aware of problems of cultural distance and of reductionism.[2]

Although current psychological criticism would no longer be suscepti-

---

1. Delitzsch, *A System of Biblical Psychology,* p. 3.
2. David K. Miell, "Psychological Interpretation," in *A Dictionary of Biblical Interpretation,* ed. R. J. Coggins and J. L. Houlden (Philadelphia: Trinity, 1990), p. 571.

ble to some of the faults Miell cites, it must still be consciously respectful of the problems of cultural distance and reductionism, of "psychologizing," and above all, of failing to attempt a theoretical psychological basis and model of the psyche as its point of departure.

3. *Exegesis.* One of the primary contributions of a psychological critical approach to exegesis resides in its vision of the text as a "psychic event." That is, **it views the text not only as the product of historical, social, and literary processes, but as the product of a psychic process or processes in which conscious as well as unconscious factors are at work in the authors of the text, their communities, and historical settings, as well as in those of the readers, and in which the nature and habits of the psyche are at work in the selection, formulation, organization, and rhetorical orientation of the textual materials.** What we can say with certainty is that the text emerges from conscious and unconscious depths in the author, his personal history, his communal history and the history of the species, albeit realities to which the text itself rarely makes conscious reference. . . .

The question remains, however, whether exegetical access to the unconscious and conscious depths of the text is possible. To date, three routes have suggested themselves: (a) Biblical symbols and archetypal images; (b) the psychodynamic factors at work in Biblical narrative and discourse; and (c) Biblical personality portraits. . . .

4. *Hermeneutics.* One finds consensus in the field of psychological criticism that hermeneutics, as opposed to exegesis, lends itself best to psychological scrutiny, since hermeneutics focuses on the meaning of the text for a living reader whose responses to the text can be observed and measured. A psycho-critical hermeneutic will focus on the catalytic effect that the Biblical text can be seen to exercise on a reader, activating conscience, will, affect, conation, and imagination, and often propelling the reader into a course of creative, moral, or on occasion, destructive action. The task of psychological-critical research is to note such "events" and to develop strategies for their observation and analysis in the attempt to identify what in the text has catalytic force and what in the reader is susceptible to textual overtures.

Two aspects of the text-reader event are of special interest in explaining the psychic effect of text on reader. The first is the plenitude of meaning with which images are produced and perceived by the psyche. A psycho-critical approach to the Biblical text will presuppose that its images rarely if ever convey a univocal meaning. To the contrary they manifest, in Paul Ricoeur's terms, a "surplus" of meaning, or in Wolfgang Iser's perspective, "open spaces." Part of the polyvalent redolence of meaning latent in Biblical language, both for author and reader, are unconscious associations that have either been imported into the text by the author or triggered by the text in the reader, the latter being more accessible than the former.

A second factor at work in the interpretive act is the "psychological type" or type-state of the author or reader that unconsciously qualifies what is written and what is heard. Jung's four-fold typology of thinking, feeling, sensing, and intuiting types finds its analogue in the four-fold meaning Rabbinic and Medieval interpreters found in the text, the literal, allegorical, moral, and tropological. It is also demonstrated in the multiplicity of critical approaches to the text that have developed since 1970. . . .

5. *The psychological description and analysis of Biblical religious phenomena* constitutes a fifth major area of research for a psychological-critical agenda. The task will involve amplifying the work of sociologists, literary critics, theologians, and anthropologists with the insights of psychoanalysis, as well as of social, cognitive, behavioral, and developmental psychology, to explore the phenomena of inspiration, conversion, glossolalia, visions, *enthousiasmos,* demon possession, Biblical dreams, ritual practices (footwashing, eucharist, burnt offering, purification rites) and psycho-spiritual experiential phenomena, e.g., sin, guilt, grace, forgiveness, salvation, redemption, and rebirth. Robin Scroggs writes that "salvation means changes, changes in how we think, in how we feel, in how we act. And that means, or so it seems to me, that psychological intuitions and, perhaps, even explicitly psychological models and terminology can give us insight into what these changes are. . . ."[3]

6. *Wirkungsgeschichte.* Borrowing a phrase from Ulrich Luz, a sixth task on the psychological-critical agenda is the study of the "history of effects" of the Biblical text at the psycho-spiritual level, individually and corporately, pathogenically and therapeutically. In his article "The Study of Religion and the Study of the Bible" Wilfred Cantwell Smith issues a similar call, envisioning a new generation of Biblical scholars specially bred to study what he calls the *Nachleben* or "continuing history" of the text, identifying the forces, for good and for ill, that Scripture has unleashed in its historical wake. To date, the research on the *pathogenic effect of the Biblical text* is barely begun, though work has been done on the Biblical roots of racial prejudice and anti-Semitism, and on the origins of child abuse. The *therapeutic effect* of the Bible, however, has been amply noted, by the kerygmatic proclamations of religious institutions, by psychologists like Jung, who maintained that "religions are psychotherapeutic systems in the truest sense of the word" whose literature provides a description of the individuation process "with an exactness

---

3. Robin Scroggs, "Psychology as a Tool to Interpret the Text," *Christian Century,* March 24, 1982, p. 336.

that far surpasses our feeble efforts," and also by the work of pastoral counselors Donald Capps, Wayne Oates, and Carroll A. Wise who have written on the role of the Bible in psychiatry and pastoral counseling.

———

SUGGESTIONS FOR FURTHER READING

Hall, Granville Stanley. *Jesus, the Christ, in the Light of Psychology.* 2 vols. Garden City: Doubleday, Page & Co., 1917.

Kaplan, Jacob Hyman. *Psychology of Prophecy: A Study of the Prophetic Mind as Manifested by the Ancient Hebrew Prophets.* Philadelphia: J. H. Greenstone, 1908.

Kille, D. Andrew. *Psychological Biblical Criticism,* edited by Gene M. Tucker, 1-37. Minneapolis: Fortress Press, 2001.

———. "Psychology and the Bible: Three Worlds of the Text." *Pastoral Psychology* 51, no. 2 (2001): 125-34.

———. "Reading the Bible in Three Dimensions: Psychological Biblical Interpretation." In *Psychology and the Bible: A New Way to Read the Scriptures,* edited by J. Harold Ellens and Wayne G. Rollins, vol. 1, 17-32. Westport, CT: Greenwood-Praeger, 2004.

Miell, David K. "Psychological Interpretation." In *A Dictionary of Biblical Interpretation,* edited by R. J. Coggins and J. L. Houlden, 571-72. Philadelphia: Trinity, 1990.

Povah, John Walter. *The New Psychology and the Bible.* London: Longmans, Green & Co., 1924.

———. *The New Psychology and the Hebrew Prophets.* New York: Longmans, Green & Co., 1925.

Rollins, Wayne G. "The Bible and Psychology: New Directions in Biblical Scholarship." *Pastoral Psychology* 45 (1997): 163-79.

———. "Psychology and Biblical Studies." In *A Dictionary of Biblical Interpretation,* edited by John Hayes, 337-41. Nashville: Abingdon, 1999.

———. "Rationale and Agenda for a Psychological-Critical Approach to the Bible and Its Interpretation." In *Biblical and Humane,* edited by David Barr, Linda Bennett Elder, and Elizabeth Struthers Malbon, 153-72. Atlanta: Scholars Press, 1996.

———. *Soul and Psyche: The Bible in Psychological Perspective.* Part One: Retrospect, pp. 3-87. Minneapolis: Augsburg Fortress, 1999.

CHAPTER 2

The Care and Cure
of the Soul

The great malady of the twentieth century, implicated in all of our troubles and affecting us individually and socially, is "loss of soul." . . . [T]he root problem is that we have lost our wisdom about the soul, even our interest in it.

Thomas Moore[1]

What shall it profit a whole civilization . . . if it gains knowledge and power over the material world, but loses any adequate idea of the conscious mind, the human self, at the center of all that power?

William Barrett[2]

Our psyche, which is primarily responsible for all the historical changes wrought by the hand of man on the face of this planet, remains an insoluble puzzle and an incomprehensible wonder, an object of abiding perplexity — a feature it shares with all Nature's secrets.

Carl G. Jung[3]

1. Thomas Moore, *Care of the Soul: A Guide for Cultivating Depth and Sacredness in Everyday Life* (New York: HarperCollins, 1992), p. xi.

2. William Barrett, *Death of the Soul: From Descartes to the Computer* (New York: Doubleday, 1986), pp. 164, 166.

3. Carl Gustav Jung, *The Collected Works of C. G. Jung* [henceforth *CW*], trans. R. F. C. Hull, ed. Gerhard Adler et al., Bollingen Series 20 (Princeton: Princeton University Press, 1953-78), vol. 10, par. 526.

Carl Jung once observed that "Everything to do with psychology, everything it essentially is and asserts, touches the human psyche so closely that religion least of all can afford to overlook it."[4] Its corollary is also true: Everything to do with religion, everything it essentially is and asserts, touches the human psyche so closely that psychology least of all can afford to overlook it.

Psychology and religion, including biblical studies, are beginning to warm up to one another after a season of cool distrust throughout much of the twentieth century. Both are beginning to suspect a truth about themselves that was well known up to the twentieth century but eclipsed for five decades in the mid-twentieth century. The truth is that psychology and religion are "womb" mates, much like the biblical twins, Jacob and Esau, who for years were hostile, but after decades of separation found themselves reconciled (Gen. 25:21-26; 33:1-11). For Jacob and Esau the primordial bond was blood and destiny. For psychology, religion, and biblical studies, the bond is a common objective shared for twenty centuries: the *cura animarum*, the care and cure of the soul (Latin: *anima;* Greek: *psyche;* English: soul).

In his essay "The Undiscovered Self," Carl Jung makes a stunning statement about the psyche. "Our psyche . . . is primarily responsible for all the historical changes wrought by the hand of man on the face of this planet."[5] If Jung is right, it means that every human artifact, from the Eiffel Tower, to nuclear weapons, Bach's B Minor Mass, the Great Wall of China, Van Gogh's sunflowers, arthroscopic surgery, the great universities of the world and their disciplines, military torture chambers, the Saturn probe, the concept of a free society, and the entire range of myths, legends, parables, histories, laws and apocalypse in Scripture (not to mention a medicine cabinet full of personal neuroses, obsessions, and fantasies) — all are the "product" of the soul, of the marginless repository of the human psyche. Jung's observation urges a rediscovery of the psyche, with its conscious and unconscious depths, its broad reserves of imagination and spirituality, and its capacity for focused action, as a reality worth serious reconsideration, certainly by psychologists and readers of the Bible, not to mention the culture at large.

The following readings suggest that the common goal of psychology and religion (including biblical studies) is, in the words of James Hillman, the task of "soul-making." Psych-ology, the study of the *psyche,* is never just academic. The goal of contemporary psychology's fifty-some schools is not just understanding the psyche and its habits; its ultimate aim has to do with fixing, healing, and curing the psyche/soul/self.

4. Jung, *CW,* vol. 11, par. 72.
5. Jung, *CW,* vol. 10, par. 526.

Soul-making is also the goal of Scripture. The Bible is a book of the soul, written out of the depths of the soul, addressed to the soul, about the soul, for the soul's health and welfare. The "saving of souls" is its literal objective. It spends its time telling stories of the dysfunctional self; it betrays the pretensions of the proud and superficial; it spells out in stark detail the horrific, destructive capacities of the self. But it also sketches models of the "saved" soul on its pages — in the portrait of the righteous man in Psalm 1, in the mosaic of proverbs that sketches out the image of the wise soul, in the models of justice and mercy in the poetry of the prophets, in the parable of the reinstatement of the prodigal son, and in the apocalyptic portrait in the Book of Revelation of the "saints," clothed in robes of white, who have not lost their souls in the struggle with evil. Both psychology and the Bible, as "womb mates," are constitutionally inclined to recognize the truth, in the words of poet historian Hans Carossa, that "The future of the world is determined by what happens in the human soul."

Reading 2.1   Soul and Psyche: The Bible
in Psychological Perspective

WAYNE G. ROLLINS

Rollins surveys the history of the terms *soul, psyche,* and *self,* all of them current long before the term *psychology* was coined. Though the three tend to be found in different venues — *soul* in religious contexts, *psyche* in psychological circles, and *self* in the culture at large — they point jointly to the same, multifaceted, multi-operational phenomenon of the self with its vast range of conscious and unconscious being.

In an interview in 1955, Carl Jung told of his enjoyment in pointing out to medical students the view of the psyche found in the "old textbook for the

---

Adapted from Wayne G. Rollins, *Soul and Psyche: The Bible in Psychological Perspective* (Minneapolis: Fortress, 1999), pp. 97-104.

Medical Corps in the Swiss army." It offered a description of the brain as a "dish of macaroni, and the steam from the macaroni was the psyche."[1]

Although the "steam model" of the *psyche* largely disappeared from the scene, one still finds an astonishing contradiction in the use, and also in the disuse, of the term *psyche* among psychologists today. On the one hand we find the field of psychology continuing to manufacture psyche-rooted neologisms to describe new activities in the field, e.g. *psycho*metrics, *psycho*dynamics, *psycho*somatic, *psych*iatrist, *psycho*therapy, *psycho*analysis, *psyche*delic, *psycho*social, *psycho*pathology, *psycho*sexual, and *psycho*history. But on the other, we find no effort or apparent desire to define what the *"psych-"* element in these terms might mean.[2] This fact is evident in a walk-through of standard introductory academic psychology texts, histories of psychology, and even texts on the psychology of religion, in which one looks in vain for any reference to the term *psyche*.

A comparable muddle exists with theologians and biblical scholars on the word *soul*. *Soul* appears hundreds of times as a translation term for the biblical words *nephesh, nishamah,* in the Hebrew Bible, and for the Greek word *psyche* in the New Testament (it occurs 105 times). Readers of the Bible seem to have no difficulty understanding the Hebrew Bible when it asks, "Why are you cast down, oh my soul *(nephesh),* and why are you disquieted within me?" (Ps. 42:5) or when the New Testament asks, "What does it profit a person if he gains the whole world and loses his soul *(psyche)?*" But one can be sure that if biblical exegetes were asked to define these terms, telling us precisely what the terms *nishamah, nephesh* or *psyche* refer to psychologically in the experience of being human, they would be as hard pressed as their psychological counterparts.

The aim of this essay is to add some substance to our understanding of the terms *psyche, soul,* and *self,* with a review of the history of each of these terms, their changing meanings, and their use today. I will contend that all three, in the end, refer to the same entity. All three denote the total system of conscious and unconscious life in the human personality. To be sure they are at home in different settings, with nuanced differences in connotation and denotation: *psyche* functions in the psychoanalytic and intellectual communities; *soul,* in religious contexts and more recently in the culture at large, and

---

1. Carl G. Jung, *C. G. Jung Speaking: Interviews and Encounters* (Princeton: Princeton University Press, 1977), p. 262.

2. For example, David M. Wulff's widely used *Psychology of Religion: Classic and Contemporary Views* (New York: John Wiley and Sons, 1991) lists no occurrences of the term *psyche*, though includes ten references to *soul*.

self, both in the culture at large and more recently among professional psychologists; but the phenomenon to which they point is the same.

Psyche in Historical and Contemporary Perspective

Historians of psychology tell us that Aristotle's essay *Peri Psyches (Concerning the Psyche;* Latin: *De Anima)* advanced the "first systematic psychology" in the West, laying "down the lines along which the relationship between various manifestations of soul and mind were conceived" for two millennia.[3] Aristotle, in concert with Greek and Roman successors, collectively provided a detailed analysis of the nature and habits of the human psyche that was not to be improved upon until the eighteenth century. Aristotle defined psyche as the animating principle that catalyzes life in the body and is the source of all the animating functions we associate with being human: reason, will, desire, memory, sensation, perception, learning, motivation, emotion, socialization, personality and imagination — and provided a "systematic psychology" that set the standard for two thousand years.

Furthermore, from the second century c.e. to the eighteenth, Patristic, medieval, scholastic, reformation and enlightenment scholars were engaged in debate over the relative virtues of the biblical understanding of soul/psyche and that of Aristotle, Plato, and the Stoics. It is out of that dialogue that the term *psychology* was born. "Psychology" was introduced to the academic world in 1530 by none other than a biblical scholar, Philipp Melanchthon, in a *Commentary on Aristotle's Peri Psyches.* (Latin: *De Anima).* Melanchthon had fostered the word "psychology" as a way to talk about the "spiritual" faculties of humans, as opposed to animals and angels.

It is this same term, *psyche,* that Wilhelm Wundt, the father of modern psychology, retained as the controlling concept of his "new psychology." Though he warned that he would use *psyche* in a strictly scientific sense, dismissing metaphysical connotations acquired in Western philosophical and religious tradition, he leaves no doubt that he employs its classic sense, namely, to refer to the totality of the psychic life.[4]

Freud and Jung also turned to *psyche* to express the idea of the unified psychic self, freely employing the German *Seele* (soul) as a fitting translation

3. R. S. Peters and C. A. Mace, "Psychology," in *The Encyclopedia of Philosophy* (New York: Macmillan, 1967), vol. 7, pp. 1, 4.

4. Morton Hunt, *The Story of Psychology* (New York: Doubleday Anchor Books, 1993), p. 129.

(though like Wundt, dismissing all metaphysical considerations). In Freud's and Jung's case, however, the concept of *psyche* is enlarged to include the newly highlighted realm of the unconscious.

In the early 1900s the terms *psyche* and *soul* become problematic; an increasingly empirically-oriented environment made it difficult to talk about realities that defy precise, scientific measurement. The roots of this terminological uncertainty can be traced to the influence of the seventeenth-century mechanistic psychology of René Descartes and the rise of British empiricism which led to a "banishment of the intangible."[5] Already in the 1600s, Thomas Hobbes had repudiated the concept of soul (psyche) as "pernicious Aristotelian nonsense," preferring instead to think of psychological phenomena as derivatives of the nervous system and brain. This drive to reduce "psychic" qualities to reflexes in the somatic system came to fullest expression with the advent of behaviorism in the 1920s with J. B. Watson (1878–1958) and his celebrated successor B. F. Skinner (1904–1990). Watson and Skinner eliminate not only *psyche* and *soul,* but add *instinct, consciousness, mind,* and *thinking* itself to the list of casualties, leading to the quip (when Skinnerism began to fade as the premier voice in the field), "Pity poor psychology, first it lost its soul, then its mind, then consciousness, and now it is having trouble with behavior."[6]

The result of this perspectival shift in academic psychology between the 1920s and the 1960s (marked by various schools of thought and driven to no small degree by professional anxiety among psychologists to achieve recognition for psychology as a bona fide scientific discipline) is the virtual disappearance of *psyche* from academic psychological discourse, a loss felt yet today. This shift was evident, as Bettelheim noted, in English translations of Freud that transmogrified Freud's humane language into mechanistic jargon: it rendered *soul (Seele)* as "mental"; *structure of the soul* as "mental apparatus"; *organization of the soul* as "mental organization"; and in many instances completely eliminated Freud's references to soul.[7]

But the ostracizing of *psyche* in academic psychological circles did not go unchallenged. A "correction" set in with two developments in the 1960s and 1970s. The first was "third force" or "humanistic psychology"; the second, a resurgent interest in Freud and Jung. Humanistic psychology (e.g., Abraham Maslow, Gordon Allport, Erich Fromm, Karen Horney) challenged the blackballing of the terms *psyche/soul* on four fronts. First, humanistic psychology

5. Robert C. Fuller, *Americans and the Unconscious* (New York: Oxford, 1986), p. 76.

6. "Psychology," in *The New Encyclopedia Britannica: Macropedia,* 15th ed., vol. 26 (Chicago: Encyclopedia Britannica, Inc., 1989), p. 322.

7. Bruno Bettelheim, "Reflections: Freud and the Soul," *New Yorker,* March 1, 1982, pp. 52-93.

challenged the behaviorist reduction of human nature to neurophysiological causes. Second, it contended that humans are driven ultimately not just by the need for *homeostasis* or inner balance (Freud), but by "final causes" manifested in the "organism's inherent tendency toward . . . Self-transcendence." These "causes" impel humans beyond survival needs and physical needs to higher values, such as self-esteem and competence, and at the highest level, self-actualization, aesthetic pleasure, and understanding, where innate "potentialities, capacities, and talents" are actualized.[8] Third, humanistic psychology repudiated the "cellar view" of the unconscious proposed by Freud, preferring Jung's formulation that the unconscious is not just a repository of the repressed but, more importantly, the source of an intuitive function that guides the organism toward self-actualization. Fourth, humanistic psychology treats the individual as subject as well as object. It takes seriously the approach of William James that welcomed the "facts directly observable in ourselves."[9]

As effective as humanistic psychology was in reclaiming a sense of *psyche*, it fell short of constructing a comprehensive model of the psyche, a task which, as Jung tells us, may in principle be ultimately beyond reach. Jung uses the term *psyche* in its classical sense to refer to the totality of all psychic processes, conscious as well as unconscious, and states that "the reality of the soul is the hypothesis with which I work and my main activity consists in collecting factual material and describing and explaining it." But he adds that "I have neither worked out a system nor a general theory but only postulated concepts which serve as tools, as is usual in any science."[10] . . . "We can nowhere grasp the nature of the psyche *per se* but can meet it only in its various manifestations."[11]

Why does the psyche/soul defy final description? First, it is itself intangible, despite the tangibility of its effects. Second, it is partially unconscious, which by definition means a good portion of it is in hiding and difficult to observe. Third, the instrument we use to observe the psyche/soul is the psyche/soul itself, so that it serves both as subject and object, inviting unavoidable subjective distortion. As James Hillman observes, "The soul can be an object of study only when it is also recognized as the subject studying itself by

8. Fuller, *Americans*, pp. 155, 158-59.

9. Fuller, *Americans*, p. 88; William James, *A Pluralistic Universe* (New York: E. P. Dutton, 1971), p. 196.

10. Gerhard Wehr, *Portrait of Jung: An Illustrated Biography*, trans. W. A. Hargreaves (New York: Herder & Herder, 1971), pp. 153-54.

11. Carl Gustav Jung, *The Collected Works of C. G. Jung* [henceforth *CW*], trans. R. F. C. Hull, ed. Gerhard Adler et al., Bollingen Series 20 (Princeton: Princeton University Press, 1953-78), vol. 15, par. 85.

means of the fictions and metaphors of objectivity."[12] Heraclitus long ago attested to the difficulty of the task: "You could not discover the frontiers of soul (psyche), even if you traveled every road to do so; such is the depth of its meaning."[13]

But Jung contends that even though it is "quite impossible to define the extension and the ultimate character of psychic existence," and even though the *psyche* is "an ineffable totality which can only be formulated symbolically," it is nevertheless real. As an empirical reality it warrants close attention, not only because it is the progenitor of human culture, but also because of its ineluctable role in the destiny of world affairs. Jung writes, "It seems to me far more reasonable to accord the *psyche* the same validity as the empirical world, and to admit that the former has just as much 'reality' as the latter."[14]

Soul in Historical and Contemporary Perspective

The term *soul* has a similar history. It was introduced as an English translation for *psyche* in its Greek context, *anima* in its Latin context, and *Seele* in its German psychoanalytic context. Its past is more complex and problematic than that of *psyche* because of the tendency, especially in English-speaking religious circles, to use it exclusively as a reference to the disembodied self before or after death. The result is that for the first two-thirds of the twentieth century, *soul* was largely absent from the discourse of psychologists and theologians. Though calls for the reclamation of *soul* appeared sporadically in the first two-thirds of the twentieth century, neither academic psychology nor theology was interested, and neither could have anticipated the astonishing resurgence of the term in academic and popular circles in the 1980s and 1990s.

One example is William Barrett's *Death of the Soul: From Descartes to the Computer*.[15] Barrett derides the materialistic, mechanistic reductionism of the physical sciences that would "snuff out this little candle [of soul] as unnecessary and paradoxical." He "recall[s] with Kant . . . that it is the power of mind that creates the systems of mechanics that here seek to extinguish it." He

12. James Hillman, *Insearch: Psychology and Religion* (New York: Scribner's, 1971), p. 18.

13. Phil Cousineau, *Soul: An Archaeology — Readings from Socrates to Ray Charles* (San Francisco: HarperSanFrancisco, 1994), p. 15. Judith 8:14 expresses a comparable opinion from the biblical perspective: "You cannot plumb the depths of the human heart, nor find out what a man [*sic*] is thinking."

14. Jung, *CW*, vol. 11, par. 140; vol. 13, par. 375.

15. William Barrett, *Death of the Soul: From Descartes to the Computer* (New York: Doubleday, 1986).

urges a return to Descartes' dream, which he describes as "the universe as a single machine [that has] there, inside it, at its center, . . . that miraculous thing, his own consciousness, in the light of which he sees and meditates." The book closes with an apt biblical metaphor: "What shall it profit a whole civilization, or culture, if it gains knowledge and power over the material world, but loses any adequate idea of the conscious mind, the human self, at the center of all that power?"[16]

One of the most compelling calls for the reclamation of *soul* is found in the ten essays edited by social scientists Richard K. Fenn and Donald Capps, *On Losing the Soul: Essays in the Social Psychology of Religion.*[17] The editors state that their purpose is "to expand the discourse of the social sciences about the self by reintroducing the word 'soul,'" noting that it has fallen out of use among sociologists and anthropologists (as well as psychologists and theologians). One of the contributors, Bernice Martin, offers an autobiographical response to the question *What is "soul"?*

> "Soul," to my mother and the people with whom I grew up in that working class industrial town, was a word used unself-consciously to mean the ultimate core or essence of the individual's being. . . . People talked of the soul as if it were the irreducible, indestructible part of the person which, perhaps, continued to exist after death. . . . The word . . . suggests to me the possibility of recognizing — hinting at — a level of discourse which accords some ultimate significance to the person beyond what can be said by the expert social scientific disciplines. The metaphysical and theological connotations of "soul" suggest a dimension of the integrity of persons, which is not fully captured by the vocabulary of "self" and "selfhood." The death of the soul is of greater moment than the death of the self.[18]

As striking as the reclamation of soul is among academics, its phenomenal renascence in popular culture in the 1980s and 1990s is all the more remarkable. Just the number of books with the word *soul* in their titles is impressive: Alan W. Jones, *Soul-Making: The Desert Way of Spirituality* (1985); Gary Zukav, *The Seat of the Soul* (1989); Robert J. Drinan, *Stories from the American Soul* (1990); Larry Dossey, M.D., *Recovering the Soul: A Scientific and Spiritual Search* (1990); Thomas Moore, *Care of the Soul* (1991). One of the most comprehensive studies of "soul language" across world cultures is

16. Barrett, *Death of the Soul*, pp. 164, 166.

17. (Albany, NY: SUNY Press, 1995).

18. Donald Capps and Richard K. Fenn, eds., *On Losing the Soul: Essays in the Social Psychology of Religion* (Albany, NY: SUNY Press, 1995), p. 70.

the anthology edited by Phil Cousineau, *Soul: An Archaeology — Readings from Socrates to Ray Charles* (1994), with one hundred and thirty literary selections, including an Egyptian Gnostic myth of the soul's origin, a West African folktale, essays by psychologists, theologians, anthropologists, novelists, mystics, shamans, poets, and philosophers, and selections from sacred texts.

How is one to account for the resurgence of soul at the end of the twentieth century? From the perspective of the history of ideas, the shift can be seen as a popular manifestation of post-modern consciousness and its suspicion of the positivistic and scientistic approach of behaviorism and of radically empirical psychology. From a psychodynamic perspective, the answer may be found in the Freudian concept of the "return of the repressed." It is demonstrated in the return of a long repressed cultural need for a word like *soul* or *psyche* to capture the complex but unified self that most people understand themselves to be, one that cannot simply be reduced to the somatic and physical factors that for so long had been enlisted by behaviorism and empirical psychology to justify the banishment of *psyche* and *soul* from the language.

Self in Historical and Contemporary Perspective

The term *self,* surprisingly, has had a history in psychological circles comparable to that of *psyche* and *soul.* It was periodically rejected by psychologists because it defied empirical description, but reinstated when the need arose for a word to express the concept of the whole person.

Plato, Augustine, Descartes, Kant, and Hume had used the term *self* for that conscious inner agent that observes oneself having experiences. William James, in his 1890 *Principles,* put *self* back on the map with his theory of its four dimensions: *the material self,* which includes body, family, and possessions; *the social self,* consisting of interpersonal sentiments; *the spiritual self,* comprising the "inner" or subjective sense of being, psychic faculties and dispositions; and *the pure ego,* which functions as an inner principle of personal unity. James's most important contribution was the distinction he drew between "self" as subject or knower, which he termed the "I," and "self" as object or known, the "me"; thus he effectively reintroduced the "subjective self" into a conversation from which it had long been excluded.[19]

James's theory, however, was challenged and displaced for half a century

---

19. Hunt, *The Story of Psychology,* p. 157; Michael J. Mahoney, *Human Change Processes: The Scientific Foundations of Psychotherapy* (New York: Basic Books, HarperCollins, 1991), pp. 215-16.

by the materialist views of behaviorism and the rational objectivism of early experimental psychology in the early 1900s. One of his former students, Edward Titchener (1867–1927) of Cornell, was persuaded that "the concept of self should be left out of psychology because it would bring in the realm of meaning, that which . . . lay beyond the purview of psychology as a descriptive science."[20]

By the second half of the twentieth century, however, the term reappeared under the sponsorship of clinical and developmental psychology, the arts, and the humanities. Alfred Adler spoke of the "creative self" as a key ingredient of his "individual psychology." The personality theories of Gordon Allport, Erik Erikson, and Erich Fromm began to speak of "self-concept," "self-attitudes," and "self-esteem." Jung spoke of "Self" as the supreme archetype to which the individual aspires. Rogers and Maslow introduced the notions of "self-actualization" and "self-realization," referring to a unified drive or tendency within the organism to grow and to realize its potentialities. Karen Horney wrote of "Self-analysis" and Heinz Kohut developed "Self Psychology." By the last decade of the twentieth century, *self* had made its return within the guild of academic psychologists. In a chapter on "The Self in Process" in his 1991 volume, *Human Change Processes: The Scientific Foundations of Psychotherapy*, Michael J. Mahoney writes,

> The cognitive, developmental, and emotional (r)evolution(s) have redirected mainstream experimental psychology back "inside" the organism; and the "modern synthesis" in psychology is, in part, an attempt to integrate and transcend inside/outside and mind/body dualisms. What cognitive and life scientists found when they looked inside the most "promising primates," however, was much more than they had anticipated. The recent and ongoing (re)discoveries of emotionality, unconscious processes, and personal meanings are cases in point. But perhaps the single most important (re)discovery of twentieth century psychology has been that of the self, which has (again) become a cardinal concept after a moratorium that lasted over half a century. As Louis A. Sass quipped, "The 'self,' once banished by mainstream psychology to the cloudland of unobservable and irrelevant abstractions, seems to have returned with a vengeance." . . . Whether it is a vengeful return or simply the persistence of a centuries-old mystery, however, self studies are now center stage in psychological laboratories and clinics around the planet.[21]

20. Mahoney, *Human Change Processes*, p. 216.
21. Mahoney, *Human Change Processes*, p. 211.

Academic psychology in the twenty-first century has begun to sense the loss of the *psyche* in *psych*-ology and feel the need for a model of the "self" that will honor the reality of an entity that James had described at the turn of the century and that Aristotle and the biblical tradition had recognized long before.

In summary, the history of psychology and philosophy demonstrate that the three words *psyche* (and its Latin equivalent *anima*), *soul* (German *Seele*; French *âme*), and *self* have surfaced as the terms of choice to refer to the total system of conscious and unconscious life in the human personality, adding credence to the salient biblical question, "What does it profit a person if he gains the whole world and loses his soul *(psyche)*?" (Mark 8:36).

Reading 2.2   Soul: An Archaeology

PHIL COUSINEAU

In this excerpt from the introductory essay in his book, Cousineau, a poet, screenwriter, and adventure travel guide, traces the recurrence of the concept of "soul" across world cultures, languages, and time — from "Socrates to Ray Charles" as the subtitle phrases it. He decries the repudiation of "soul" by late-nineteenth- and early-twentieth-century "scientific reductionism" and "empirical psychology." He celebrates the pan-cultural return of "soul" in the late twentieth century, illustrating the range of soul's virtuosity, from creative genius to lunacy and depression.

> *The philosophy of six thousand years has not searched the chambers and magazines of the soul.*
>
>   Ralph Waldo Emerson

To fathom the unfathomable soul we immediately plunge into mystery. . . . If we're not bewildered by the mysteries of the soul, we're not thinking clearly, to paraphrase the scrawling on subway walls. For the soul's mysteries compress the most profound mythic questions that have always intrigued human

---

From Phil Cousineau, *Soul: An Archaeology: Readings from Socrates to Ray Charles* (San Francisco: HarperSanFrancisco, 1994), pp. xix-xxii.

beings: Where do we come from? Why are here? Where do we go when we die? . . .

From pharaonic Egypt to Delta blues clubs, from the marble-marveled agora of classical Athens to the vast white tundra of Arctic hunters, belief in an uncanny force at the heart of things has been intuited, a sleepstrange feeling rooted in a presence of tremendous impact that circulates through and animates all of nature. . . . Every known culture has taken upon itself the naming of this force, usually after the words for wind, shadow, movement, smoke, strength.

According to the Greek philosopher Diogenes, it was Xenophanes who first equated breath with soul, using the word *psyche* with its colorful associations of coolness, bellows, and butterfly. . . . *Psyche, anima, atman, savira, semangat, nephesh, otachuk, loákal, tunzi, prana, duk,* and *geist* are sacred words used by primal peoples the world over for the surge of life itself, linguistic cousins of what was called *sawol* in Old English, *sawal* by the Anglo-Saxons, *sala* by the Icelandic folk, and eventually, as if stone-polished by the ages, what we now call *soul.* . . .

As the "life-giving principle," in Aristotle's classic definition, soul has bountiful associations: fire and warmth, sexual fertility and inspiration, ecstasy and fantasy, love and madness. As a far-ranging inner landscape, it shares many frontiers, including the realms of dream, imagination, poetry, religion, mythology, death and the underworld. . . .

In the phenomenology of the soul the image of something immaterial and incorruptible that survives after death as ghost or spirit is found throughout history. . . . But with the advent of scientific reductionism and empirical psychology at the end of the often spiritually chloroformed nineteenth century, metaphysical beliefs were scoffed at for being unverifiable, or worse, irrational. Though the "soul" was exiled from so-called rational discourse, even considered a four-letter word in some hermetically sealed circles, the presence is still there, as evident by the curious sense of *being lived* by psychic forces — emotions, dreams, desires — far beyond the realm of rational explanation. . . .

. . . Peculiarly enough, . . . the reality of the soul has also long been expressed by terrified references to its loss, . . . in the harrowing suspicion that a piece of ourselves is "missing," or in the sudden losses of our personal lives, the disturbing disappearance of beauty in our city architecture, the sacrifice of quality to the cult of mediocrity in culture, the vanishing of vitality in business and politics, the trivialization of contemporary life.

. . . As far back as the grievous days after World War II, author Wallace Stegner was saying, "The sickness of our times is not a political sickness; it's a soul sickness." A more familiar litany of descriptions of our fragmented world from any contemporary morning newspaper or evening notebook of a therapist, teacher, or priest would include: a sense of alienation, rootlessness, apathy, burnout, torpor, anxiety, cynicism, the fear of leading an inauthentic life. Every illness has its symptoms, and ours is betrayed by our obsessions, addictions, and violence; our corrosive loneliness, vague purposelessness, and hall-of-mirrors narcissism. Soulless times are often marked by black humor reveling in the self-doubt that our lives are mere movie scripts or, worse, that we're tourists rather than travelers on this road of life. . . .

Novelist Walker Percy said just before he died, "Something has gone wrong with the postmodern world — to the core of meaning itself." And yet, the paradox — one of many surrounding soul — is that these "pathologies," as depth psychologist James Hillman describes them, that entangle us may be the most vivid ways for us to *realize the soul as real.*" . . .

Together, these images outline as if in dark charcoal the meaning-full shape of soul. Identifying what we've tragically lost, sold to the devil, or had violently seized from us can help us recognize why soul describes the elusive element that infuses existence with meaning, vitality, authenticity, beauty, deep desire, real character. Soul is that unmistakable fire that infuses all truly creative endeavors and sends the shiver up the spine, telling us we're in the presence of *lived truth.*

. . . From Socrates, the insatiable seeker after truth, to Ray Charles, the incendiary genius of soul music, the soul-navigating Siberian shamans to Carl Jung in his dream-roving tower at Bollingen, rogue philosophers have observed that the only universe as vast as the one outside is the one inside — one consisting of galaxies of images that have accumulated for billions of years and condensed like stardust in our imaginations.

Ray S. Anderson

Reading 2.3   On Being Human: The Spiritual Saga
of a Creaturely Soul

RAY S. ANDERSON

Taken from a collection of essays entitled *Whatever Happened to the Soul? Scientific and Theological Portraits of Human Nature,* this essay rehearses the question of the biblical author of Ecclesiastes on the nature and destiny of the "human spirit" *(ruach),* a question that has occupied scientific, philosophic, and biblical reflection for centuries. It addresses the question of how "soul" fits with the materialist concept of humanity spun off by molecular biology, clinical psychology, and computer-driven brain scans. In conclusion, Anderson combines theological, scientific, and biblical intuition to arrive at a definition of soul that incorporates the whole person — body and soul, as it were.

The ancient teacher of wisdom in Israel, who called himself Koheleth, was a keen observer of the human condition. As he pondered and probed, he discovered more questions than answers. In a tone that betrayed both relentless cynicism and restless hope, he asked: "Who knows whether the human spirit goes upward and the spirit of animals goes downward to the earth?" (Eccles. 3:21).

Who knows indeed! In former times, we might account for such ignorance as due to lack of scientific knowledge and philosophical precision. But how then would we account for the fact that today, some form of the same question tantalizes our scientists and torments our philosophers? Whether we call it spirit or soul, the question remains: what is it that makes humans both precious and perverse? What gives rise to our deepest religious insights but can also plunge us into the depths of guilt and despair?

Has the concept of a human soul disappeared in the presence of molecular biology, clinical psychology, and computer driven brain scans? Is the disappearance of the soul a consequence of our world "come of age" or is it we who are lost and our souls doing the searching? Perhaps one indication that humans have a soul is that they appear to be the only creatures on earth that are thinking about it! The words of Thomas Moore express this malaise dramatically:

From Ray S. Anderson, "On Being Human: The Spiritual Saga of a Creaturely Soul," in *Whatever Happened to the Soul? Scientific and Theological Portraits of Human Nature,* ed. Warren S. Brown, Nancey Murphy, and H. Newton Malony (Minneapolis: Fortress, 1998), pp. 175-77.

The great malady of the twentieth century, implicated in all of our troubles and affecting us individually and socially, is "loss of soul." When soul is neglected, it doesn't just go away; it appears symptomatically in obsessions, addictions, violence, and loss of meaning. Our temptation is to isolate these symptoms or to try to eradicate them one by one; but the root problem is that we have lost our wisdom about the soul, even our interest in it.[1]

The word "soul" appears almost daily in our newspapers and on the lips of the pundits who peer into the *psyche* of our modern culture. Those who lament the loss of core values in our society warn us that we must recover the "soul" of our people or perish. Strategists who seek to turn their political party back to fundamental principles explain that they are attempting to "recover the soul" of their party. In certain sections of North America the people eat "soul food" and ethnic cultures sing "soul music." The news report of a plane crash reads: "There were 132 souls on board, and all were lost."

This may be why, as a recent survey demonstrated, theologians by and large have abandoned the concept of the "soul" in favor of the "spirit" as the essential core of human subjectivity.[2] Contemporary theologians have become uncomfortable with the concept of an abstract body/soul dualism that has its modern roots in the thought of René Descartes (1596-1650).[3] As a result, many have rejected the concept of the soul as a specific entity residing in the person distinct from the body.[4] Theologians often use the word "spirit" as

1. Thomas Moore, *Care of the Soul: A Guide for Cultivating Depth and Sacredness in Everyday Life* (New York: HarperCollins, 1992), p. xi.

2. Jeffrey H. Boyd, "The Soul as Seen through Evangelical Eyes, Part II: Mental Health Professionals and the 'Soul,'" *Journal of Psychology and Theology* 23, no. 3 (1995): 161-70.

3. Descartes' concept of the soul as an independent constituent of humans, controlling the body which it animates, was called the "ghost in the machine" by Gilbert Ryle, *The Concept of the Mind* (London: Hutchinson, 1949). Commenting on this, Edmund Hill says, "Meanwhile the ordinary Christian, with some reason, will think that he cannot do without the concept of 'soul.' But now it has, most unfortunately and inconveniently and to a large extent through the fault of a Platonized Christianity, become a religious concept, something you believe in or something you don't, like God. And when it comes to making rational sense of the concept the Christian remains stymied, transfixed, paralyzed, mesmerized, fascinated, dumbfounded and dogged by that magisterial sneer — 'the ghost in the machine.'" *Being Human: A Biblical Perspective* (London: Geoffrey Chapman, 1984), pp. 96-97.

4. For example, in G. C. Berkouwer, *Man: The Image of God* (Grand Rapids: Eerdmans, 1962), p. 203: "Scripture never pictures man as a dualistic, or pluralistic being, but . . . in all its varied expressions the whole man comes to the fore. . . . The discussion has especially turned on this point, whether the term 'soul' as used in Scripture has some special religious emphasis in the sense that we must deduce at least some sort of dichotomy. And this is more and more de-

a virtual synonym for "soul" but without the implication, or embarrassment, of having to define or locate the "soul" as a component of human nature.

Can we recover the concept of the soul as an essential aspect of the human person while, at the same time, accepting the discoveries of science as to the apparent correlation of mental activity with brain functioning? Or, to put it more specifically . . . , can we accept a nondualistic, nonreductive physicalist definition of human nature and still use the word "soul" as a distinctive aspect of the human person? . . .

My task as a theologian is to speak to the deeper yearnings and struggles of human existence as much as to bring to those existential human concerns some insights from the Word of God. It is for these reasons that I will use the term "soul" . . . with carefully nuanced and qualified meaning. I use the term "soul" to denote the inner core of the whole person, including the body. By "soul" I mean the personal and spiritual dimension of the self. Thus, the phrase "body and soul" is not intended to suggest that the soul is something that is merely "in" the body, or separate from the body, but the whole person with both an interior and an exterior life in the world.

SUGGESTIONS FOR FURTHER READING

Barrett, William. *Death of the Soul: From Descartes to the Computer.* New York: Doubleday, 1986.

Bettelheim, Bruno. "Reflections: Freud and the Soul." *New Yorker,* March 1, 1982, pp. 52-93.

Brown, Schuyler. *Text and Psyche: Experiencing Scripture Today.* New York: Continuum, 1998.

Brown, Warren S., Nancey Murphy, and H. Newton Malony, eds. *Whatever Happened to the Soul? Scientific and Theological Portraits of Human Nature.* Minneapolis: Fortress, 1998.

---

nied by theologians." So also, Karl Barth, *Church Dogmatics,* III/2 (Edinburgh: T&T Clark, 1960): "We do not [have] a body here and the soul there, but man himself as soul of his body is subject and object, active and passive . . ." (p. 429); Krister Stendahl, "Immortality Is Too Little and Too Much," *Meanings: The Bible as Document and Guide* (Philadelphia: Fortress Press, 1984): "The whole world that comes to us through the Bible, Old Testament and New Testament, is not interested in the immortality of the soul. And if you think it is, it is because you have read this into the material" (p. 196).

Capps, Donald, and Richard K. Fenn, eds. *On Losing the Soul: Essays in the Social Psychology of Religion.* Albany, NY: SUNY Press, 1995.

Hillman, James. *Archetypal Psychology: A Brief Account.* Dallas: Spring Publications, Inc., 1983.

Moore, Thomas. *Care of the Soul: A Guide for Cultivating Depth and Sacredness in Everyday Life.* New York: HarperCollins, 1992.

Rollins, Wayne G. "Bible and the Life of the Soul." In *Jung and the Bible,* 41-55. Atlanta: John Knox, 1983.

Schaer, Hans. *Religion and the Cure of Souls in Jung's Psychology.* Translated by R. F. C. Hull. Bollingen Series 21. New York: Pantheon, 1946 [1950]. Original German edition: *Religion und Seele in der Psychologie C. G. Jungs.* Zurich: Rascher Verlag, 1946.

Swinburne, R. *The Evolution of the Soul.* Oxford: Clarendon, 1986.

Ulanov, Ann Belford. "The Christian Fear of the Psyche." In *Picturing God.* Cambridge, MA: Cowley, 1986.

CHAPTER 3

Freud and Jung

My deep engrossment in the Bible story (almost as soon as I had learned the art of reading) had, as I recognized much later, an enduring effect upon the direction of my interest.

Sigmund Freud[1]

We must read our Bible or we shall not understand psychology. Our psychology, whole lives, our language and imagery are built upon the Bible.

Carl Gustav Jung[2]

No two individuals of the twentieth century have changed the way we understand ourselves, our culture, and our religion more than Sigmund Freud (1856-1939) and Carl Jung (1875-1961). One can hardly open a newspaper without encountering echoes of the new words and phrases Freud and Jung have set circulating in everyday vocabulary: *psyche, the unconscious, psychological complexes, introvert, ego, id, projections, mental blocks,* and *Freudian slips.*

Despite the clinical sound of these psychoanalytic terms, they convey a universal awareness, newly coined in the twentieth and twenty-first centuries,

---

1. Sigmund Freud, "An Autobiographical Study," in *The Standard Edition of the Complete Psychological Works of Sigmund Freud,* ed. James Strachey (London: Hogarth Press and the Institute of Psychoanalysis, 1953-74), vol. 20, p. 8.

2. C. G. Jung, *The Visions Seminars,* vol. 1 (Zurich: Spring Publications, 1976), p. 156; see Edward Edinger, *The Bible and the Psyche: Individuation Symbolism in the Old Testament* (Toronto: Inner City Books, 1986), p. 11.

of the quintessential role of the *psyche* in human affairs and the universal presence of the *unconscious* in all we do, think, want, feel, create, remember, and forget — in religion as well as in the rest of life.

Contrary to popular suspicion, neither Freud nor Jung was out to undo religion or the Bible. They did, however, have an interest in exposing their darker, unconscious sides and their adverse (but also therapeutic) effects. They found themselves fascinated with the mysterious depths of religious texts and symbols, and in fact constructed their own therapies around values inherited from the Bible. For Freud it was *love* and *work;* for Jung it was the *individuation* process — that lifelong trek that takes us from preoccupation with the "I" to identification with a larger Self.

Most people, including Freudians and Jungians, are surprised to learn of Freud's and Jung's investment in the biblical tradition. Théo Pfrimmer tells us in *Sigmund Freud, Lecteur de la Bible* [Sigmund Freud, reader of the Bible], that Freud interjected at least 488 biblical references in his correspondence and writing.[3] He alluded to twenty-one of the thirty-nine books of the Hebrew Bible; he cited the Gospel of Matthew forty-eight times. In addition, Freud made 111 allusions to biblical texts, from Genesis to the First Epistle of John. Freud was also entranced with the cathedrals and biblical art that he found in Rome, Venice, and Assisi. He chose a reproduction of *The Healing of Aeneas and the Raising of Tabitha,* a composite painting by Masaccio and Masolino, to be hung on the wall near his desk in Vienna. The biblical figures Freud was most attracted to were Joseph, Abraham, Jesus, Paul, and above all Moses, especially as portrayed in Michelangelo's sculpture in the church of St. Peter in Chains in Rome. It is worth noting that Freud's last great work was on a biblical theme, *Moses and Monotheism* (1937-39), an undertaking, according to one commentator, that Freud regarded as the first of a "vast work which would apply psychoanalytical theories to the whole of the Bible."[4]

Even more can be said of Jung, in whose life and thought the Bible was a vital presence literally from cradle to grave. No document is cited by Jung more often than the Bible. No cast of characters from any tradition is summoned to the stage of his discourse with greater regularity than biblical figures such as Adam and Abraham, Melchizedek and Moses, Peter and Paul. The degree of Jung's critical interest in the Bible, its worldview, its images and

3. Théo Pfrimmer, *Sigmund Freud, Lecteur de la Bible* (Strasbourg: Protestant Faculty, University of Strasbourg, 1981).

4. H. L. Philp, *Freud and Religious Belief* (New York: Pitman Publishing Corp., 1956), p. 92.

symbols, and its interpretation in the modern world is unparalleled in the life and work of any twentieth-century psychologist.[5]

Freud and Jung, however, do not come to the Bible with the same agenda. Their different approaches were born of the different places in which they found themselves temperamentally and professionally. Freud located his mission in the "lower levels" of the psyche, leaving the "loftier levels" to others. This approach was marked by a relentless "passion for the truth," driven by a determination "not to be deceived" and to "dispense with illusions" that he felt had been intellectually and socially harmful.[6]

Jung, on the other hand, though well aware of the pathologies at work in many aspects of the Bible and its interpretation, came at religion with a more sanguine view, in part motivated by his desire to vindicate the life and work of his father, a pastor in the Swiss Reformed tradition.[7] Jung's psychological research led him to the conclusion that the human psyche is "natively religious" and that the "religious impulse rests on an instinctive basis and is therefore a specifically human function."[8]

Nor was Jung averse to using "God-language," with the understanding that every God-term or God-image is at best an attempt to render in available symbols and images the numinous depths of being. It was Jung's objective to unconceal the truths anchored deep in the soul that are to be found in the creeds, scriptures, rites, and traditions of religion, the meaning of which so many religious practitioners had long since forgotten.

Above all, what drove both Freud and Jung professionally and personally was a commitment to alleviate human psychic suffering and to factor in the role of religion and Scripture in that suffering and in its alleviation. Though the theories of both were amplified and even superseded by schools of psychology and psychoanalysis later in the twentieth century, the questions they raised in the first half of the twentieth century lay the groundwork and provided the conceptual framework for most psychological approaches to Scripture in the second half.

In the readings that follow, we turn first to a description of five contributions of Jungian and Freudian psychology to biblical interpretation, adapted from an article entitled "The Bible in Psycho-Social Perspective" by Wayne G. Rollins. The second and third readings illustrate a Freudian and Jungian reading of the Bible. The Freudian reading comes from Ilona Rashkow, a specialist

---

5. Wayne G. Rollins, *Soul and Psyche: The Bible in Psychological Perspective* (Minneapolis: Fortress, 1999), pp. 446-52.

6. Rollins, *Soul and Psyche*, pp. 34, 41.

7. Rollins, *Soul and Psyche*, p. 49.

8. Wayne G. Rollins, *Jung and the Bible* (Atlanta: John Knox, 1983), p. 119.

in the Hebrew Scriptures and in Judaic and women's studies, excerpted from her two books, *The Phallacy of Genesis: A Feminist-Psychoanalytic Approach* and *Taboo or Not Taboo: Sexuality and Family in the Hebrew Bible*. Rashkow's Freudian-oriented approach to the Bible focuses on the story of the circumcision covenant in Genesis 17 and its psycho-social implications. The Jungian reading is excerpted from Michael Newheart's *My Name Is Legion: The Story and Soul of the Gerasene Demoniac* (2004). It focuses on the "shadow" dimension played out in the figure of the demoniac in Mark 5:1-16. Newheart's approach rests on the Jungian contention that texts are somehow always about the reader as much as they are about themselves.

Reading 3.1   Freud and Jung

WAYNE G. ROLLINS

Though neither Freud nor Jung was a professional biblical scholar, their study of Western European literature, the Bible, religious traditions, cultic rites, symbols, and practices around the world provides a paradigm for a psychological approach to the Bible. Rollins identifies five principles fundamental to such an approach.

Neither Freud nor Jung develops a formal strategy for biblical interpretation, but their lifelong research has provided guidelines and premises for a psychological approach to the Bible and its interpretation. I would like to identify and formulate five of these.

(a) First, Freud and Jung have introduced us to *the unconscious* as a factor at work in every human event and enterprise, including the writing and reading of the Bible. This implies that biblical research must have this factor in mind if one is to understand the full range of dynamics operative in the Bible and its readers.

Wayne G. Rollins, adapted and revised version of "The Bible in Psycho-Spiritual Perspective: News from the World of Biblical Scholarship," *Pastoral Psychology* 51, no. 2 (2002), excerpts from pp. 109-13.

For Freud and Jung the unconscious has several dimensions. One is the *personal unconscious*. For Freud this referred to remnants of personal events, memories, drives, feelings, and emotions that have been repressed, but continue to exercise their effects in conscious life, often in ways that escape conscious notice.

Jung added to this portrait of the *personal unconscious* the concept of psychological type, suggesting that each of us tends to organize our lives around one of four adaptive psychological types: the sensing, thinking, feeling (right and wrong oriented) and intuiting types. As with the four evangelists as well as with four different biblical interpreters, each type refracts its "story" through the lens of the special sensitivity and interest of its own type.

A second dimension is the *historical unconscious*. For Freud this refers to the cultural or racial "memory" that informs and inspires certain cultic acts, such as sacrifice, circumcision, baptism, and sacred meals. In Jung's formulation, the *historical unconscious* consists of remnants of pre-Christian or pre-Israelite consciousness that reside unconsciously in Christian or Hebrew sacred texts. Speaking of the early church, Jung writes, "Everything has its history, everything has 'grown,' and Christianity, which is supposed to have appeared suddenly as a unique revelation from heaven, undoubtedly also has its history. . . . It is exactly as if we had built a cathedral over a pagan temple and no longer knew that it is still there underneath." Jung adds that the presence of pre-Christian factors in Christian texts, unconscious as they are, continue to have their effect, and that as contemporary Western culture has the unconscious stamp of Judaeo-Christianity upon it, so "we are also stamped by what existed before Christianity."[1]

A third dimension of the unconscious, developed largely by Jung, is the *collective or objective unconscious*. Jung describes it as "a sphere of unconscious mythology whose primordial images are the common heritage of mankind . . . its traces can be detected in the images that recur trans-culturally in slightly different guises in symbols, dream narratives, stories, myths, epic narratives, and apocalypses, e.g., in archetypal images of creation, the primordial tree, the sacred mountain, the divine child, the trickster demon, the wise old man, the ominous giant, the wicked queen, and the hero."[2]

(b) Second, Freud and Jung direct our attention to biblical effects, i.e.,

---

1. Carl Gustav Jung, *Psychological Reflections: A New Anthology of His Writings, 1905-1961*, ed. Jolande Jacobi and R. F. C. Hull, Bollingen Series 31 (Princeton: Princeton University Press, 1953), p. 342.

2. Carl Gustav Jung, *The Collected Works of C. G. Jung* [henceforth *CW*], trans. R. F. C. Hull, ed. Gerhard Adler et al., Bollingen Series 20 (Princeton: Princeton University Press, 1953-78), vol. 20, par. 125, 135.

the compensatory function of texts like the Bible for human consciousness. A keystone of Jung's psychology is that the unconscious spontaneously produces images that provide direction in times of individual or cultural crisis. . . . From Jung's perspective, the purpose of these images within the economy of the psyche is to correct the course of the psyche when it has become one-sided or adopts false attitudes. This serves as a corrective not only to the individual psyche, but to the psychic attitude of an entire culture or age when it has become side-tracked or when it forgets its raison d'être.

In the case of the individual these images often manifest themselves in dreams; in the case of an entire culture they are mediated in the forms of great literature, music, or art. Jung writes:

> Herein lies the social significance of art. . . . It is constantly at work educating the spirit of the age, conjuring up the forms in which the age is most lacking. The unsatisfied yearning of the artist reaches back to the primordial image in the unconscious which is best fitted to compensate the inadequacy and one-sidedness of the present.[3]

(c) The work of Freud and Jung also suggests the examination of biblical religious phenomena through the lens of psychological biblical criticism. Though Freud's only extensive commentary on biblical/religious phenomena is in the anthropologically faulted *Totem and Taboo,* his collected works provide hints of other possible lines of research on more solid ground. These would include inquiries into demon possession and hysteria, sexual laws and practices, dreams, and speech as therapy.

Though Jung, like Freud, did not list the full menu of religious phenomena to be psychologically explored in the Bible, he offered psychological commentary on a generous sample of specific instances: ritual practice (foot washing, eucharist, burnt offering, purification rites), mystical experience (visions, dreams, prophecy, photisms, auditions, inspiration, revelation, the inner light, *enthousiasmos*), religious states ("twice-born religion," *metanoia, kenosis,* martyrdom, the experience of sin, guilt, forgiveness, grace, sanctification), religious practices (prayer, glossolalia) and religious experiences (miracles, transfiguration, resurrection). . . .

(d) Another focus for psychological biblical criticism is the analysis of biblical personality portraits. Freud tells us he found himself especially drawn to the biblical figures of Joseph, Abraham, Jesus, Paul, but above all to Moses, as he elucidates in his "love child" essay on "The Moses of Michelangelo"

---

3. Jung, *CW,* vol. 25, par. 130.

(1914). Jung's writings are thickly populated by biblical personalities . . . and he too finds himself consciously (and unconsciously) drawn to the figures of Adam, Paul, Abraham, but especially to the Christ figure, which Jung designates as the "exemplification of the archetype of the Self."

Psychological analysis of biblical portraits of personalities suggests two, possibly three, new lines of exegetical inquiry. The first is simply *character analysis*. This would include, for example, analyzing the psychic habits, strategies, and defenses implicit in the textual portrait of a biblical figure, and commenting on the conscious and unconscious factors that are possibly operative within the psycho-dynamics of the narrative.

A second line of inquiry focuses on portraits of biblical personalities as *models of individuation,* as Moses was for Freud, and the Christ figure or Paul for Jung.

A third possible contribution of a psychological approach to biblical personalities is *psychoanalytic.* Though Jung objected strongly to the Freudian focus on the psychopathology of ancient as well as contemporary authors, he would not deny the benefit that can derive from psychoanalytic observations on literary portraits of biblical personalities. A number of recent studies, especially from a Freudian perspective, have suggested that psychoanalytic observations in the hands of seasoned analysts can provide compelling insight into biblical figures, as in David Halperin's *Seeking Ezekiel: Text and Psychology* (1993) [see Chapter 7 in this volume] or John W. Miller's *Jesus at Thirty: A Psychological and Historical Portrait* (1997) [see Chapter 8 in this volume].[4]

(e) A fifth angle of inquiry that the work of Freud and Jung suggests is the identification and appreciation of the pathogenic and therapeutic elements and effects of Scripture. In conversation with two medical colleagues, both biologists, Freud once compared his work to theirs, saying "you the biological, I the psychological; you at the end of the stars, I at the end of the soul; you with the brightness of the sun, I with the darkness of the unconscious."[5] Freud's special genius of detecting the dark side of the psyche and its capacity for causing mischief even in religious institutions has paved the way for more recent insights into the pathogenic elements in religion and the potentially toxic and caustic nature of some religious texts. Wilfred Cantwell Smith, though not given to identifying his insights as psychological, nevertheless provides a psychological critical observation about the pathogenic potential

---

4. David J. Halperin, *Seeking Ezekiel: Text and Psychology* (University Park, PA: Pennsylvania State University Press, 1993); John W. Miller, *Jesus at Thirty: A Psychological and Historical Portrait* (Minneapolis: Augsburg/Fortress, 1997).

5. Joachim Scharfenberg, *Sigmund Freud and His Critique of Religion,* trans. O. C. Dean Jr. (Philadelphia: Fortress, 1988), p. 88.

of religious texts and "the appalling harm that from time to time scriptures have wrought, the suffering that on occasion they have not only condoned but instigated." Smith comments:

> Scripture served as the chief moral justification for slavery among those who resisted proposals to abolish that institution; and indeed as sanctifying many an oppressive *status quo* against movements for justice. . . . Again, it has served the degradation of women. . . . Another: the mighty force of a scripture's binding a community together has worked to make sharp, and often relentless, divergence between communities. Especially in the case of the Western triad — Jewish, Christian, Islamic — the scripture-based disparagement of those deemed outsiders has been, and continues to be, disastrous.[6]

It will be the task of the psychological critic to take up the mantle of Freud and Smith and bring to consciousness those dark biases in Scripture and its interpreters that cause harm in human affairs both within and outside the communities of faith. It means developing an ear for the pathologies that the Bible can propagate from time to time and the harmful, often unconscious, motives it can be enlisted to serve.

As much as Freud felt obliged to detect the pathogenic in religious systems, Jung felt inclined to find the therapeutic. For Jung, the goal of religious texts in specific and religion in general is the *cura animarum,* the care and cure of souls. In his essay, "The State of Psychotherapy Today," he writes that "religions are psychotherapeutic systems in the truest sense of the word. . . . They express the whole range of the psychic problem in mighty images; they are the avowal and recognition of the soul, and at the same time the revelation of the soul's nature."[7]

For Jung, a primary goal of reading of the Bible through the lens of psychological insight is to come to understand . . . the secret of the therapeutic effect the Bible can have on the human psyche. Certainly this is part of what Jung had in mind when he spoke of the therapeutic power of words:

> Whoever speaks in primordial images speaks with a thousand voices; he enthralls and overpowers, while at the same time he lifts the idea he is seeking to express out of the occasional and transitory into the realm of the ever-enduring. He transmutes our personal destiny into the destiny of

6. Wilfred C. Smith, *What Is Scripture? A Comparative Approach* (Minneapolis: Augsburg Fortress, 1993), pp. 213-14.

7. Jung, *CW,* vol. 10, par. 367.

mankind, and evokes in us all those beneficent forces that ever and anon have enabled humanity to find a refuge from every peril and to outlive the longest night.[8]

Reading 3.2a   Psychoanalytic Literary Theory and the
Hebrew Bible: What Hath Freud Wrought?

ILONA RASHKOW

In this first of three readings, Rashkow explores à la Freud the unconscious factors at work in the Bible, raising the question of what makes the reading of a text psychoanalytic. Is it a matter of tracing Freudian themes or of applying Freudian methods? Is it an exploration of the mind of the author? Or the mind of the characters in the author's stories? Or the mind of the reader? At one time the process of reading the Bible was seen as a straightforward proposition, getting the point of the text. Psychoanalytic theory sees it otherwise.

Sigmund Freud once acknowledged that most of his discoveries about the unconscious mind had been anticipated by the poets of the past. Thus, it should not be surprising that psychology had been used in an effort to explain the origins, character, and effects of literature, including biblical literature.

What makes a reading of a literary work psychoanalytic? . . . To call a reading psychoanalytic or Freudian immediately introduces ambiguity, because such an expression can refer either to the use of Freudian themes or to Freudian methods. That is, an interpretation of a literary work can be called Freudian or psychoanalytic with respect either to the substance of the text (what it reads) or to the interpretive procedures and techniques a reader uses (how it reads).

Generally speaking, there are three points at which psychoanalysis can enter the study of a literary work: examining the mind of the author, the minds and behavior of the author's characters, or our own minds. There is a long tradition of Freudian criticism that examines the text for buried motives and hidden neurotic conflicts that generated the writer's art: in writing *Ham-*

---

8. Jung, *CW,* vol. 15, par. 129.

From Ilona N. Rashkow, *Taboo or Not Taboo: Sexuality and Family in the Hebrew Bible* (Minneapolis: Fortress, 2000), pp. 1-3.

let, for example, Shakespeare was working over the death of his son . . . and in writing *The Gambler,* Dostoevsky was drawing upon the prohibitions placed upon masturbation in his childhood. . . . Because the hazards of examining an author's mind are inversely proportional to the amount of material available on the writer's life and private thoughts, it is never completely safe to guess at the psychic significance of a work of art, even that of a candid living author, and for some major writers (like Chaucer, Shakespeare, and the biblical writers), we have only the most minimal sense of what their private lives may have been. Thus, this form of psychoanalytic literary criticism generally is viewed as mere speculation.

Most of Freud's own ventures into literature were the analyses of literary characters. His initial remarks on the Oedipus complex were literary, involving both Hamlet and Oedipus Tyrannis. Hamlet, according to Freud, is "the hysteric" who delays because he is paralyzed by guilt over Claudius's enactment of his own unconscious wishes. . . . A stream of essays by other analysts followed, mostly on fictitious textual characters. They wrote what might be described as case studies of literature, dealing with those authors or characters whom they categorized as neurotic. Most of them emphasized such analytic themes as the Oedipus complex, . . . schizoid tendencies, latent or expressed homosexuality, guilt, etc., and the roles they played in the works of the writers or among their other literary characters.

Analyzing literary characters has not fallen into as deep a disrepute as concentrating on the writer, in great part because fictional characters are viewed as representatives of life and as such can be understood only if we assume that they are "telling a truth." This assumption allows us to find "unconscious" motivations, albeit in fictitious characters. For example, Abraham's actions and language reveal a great deal about him, despite the fact that all we will ever know is contained in the 1,534 verses of Genesis. . . .

Since authors may not provide much material for the theorists and since characters are not real persons, many scholars have shifted their focus from the interpretation of meanings embedded within a text to the processes of writing and reading. This is true of the French structuralists and post-structuralists (for example, Roland Barthes), psychoanalytically influenced critics (see Norman Holland), and of other proponents of reader-response criticism (such as Stanley Fish, Wolfgang Iser, Hans Georg Gadamer). Rather than attempting to determine objective meanings hidden within a text (meanings a reader needs to extricate) these scholars concentrate on the subjective experience of the reader (interactions between reader/text/author) and the values and premises with which a reader approaches interpretation of a text. As within psychoanalysis itself, their foci are problems of indeterminacy, uncertainty, perspective, hermeneutics, subjective (and communal) assumptions, and agreements.

Until recently, reading the Bible was thought to be a rather straight forward procedure. The goal was to respond properly by trying to understand the text and grasp the meaning. This changed once psychoanalytic literary theory gained wide acceptance within biblical studies.

Of course, psychoanalytic literary theory is no more a conceptually unified critical position in biblical studies than in literary studies generally. The term is associated with scholars who examine the writer (David Halperin), the biblical characters (David Clines, Shoshana Feldman, Ilona Rashkow, Dorothy Zeligs), or the reader (David Clines et al.). Further, the approaches are neither monolithic nor mutually exclusive. But biblical scholars who use psychoanalytic literary theory seem to agree that meaning does not inhere completely and exclusively in the text and that the effects of reading Scripture, psychological and otherwise, are essential to its meaning. Ultimately, this type of literary criticism yields in biblical studies a way of looking at biblical narratives and readers that reorganizes both their interrelationships and the distinctions between them. As a result, recognizing the relationship of a reader to a text leads to a more profound awareness that no one biblical interpretation is intrinsically true. That is, the meaning of biblical narratives is not waiting to be uncovered but evolves, actualized by readers (and interpreters).

Reading 3.2b The Phallacy of Genesis:
            A Feminist-Psychoanalytic Approach

Ilona Rashkow

Rashkow identifies the sense in which her approach is Freudian — an approach, as we shall see, that applies not only to the biblical text and its readers but to Freudian psychology as well.

. . . My theoretical approach is literary, not psychoanalytic, although it is clearly informed by psychoanalytic theory. Unfortunately, the relationship

From Ilona N. Rashkow, *The Phallacy of Genesis: A Feminist-Psychoanalytic Approach*, Literary Currents in Biblical Interpretation (Louisville: Westminster/John Knox Press, 1993), p. 111.

between "literature and psychoanalysis" usually implies a relationship of sub-ordination rather than coordination. Literature is submitted to the "author-ity," to the "prestige," of psychoanalysis. . . . The literary text is considered as a body of language to be interpreted, while psychoanalysis is a body of knowl-edge used to interpret. What I have tried to do throughout this book is to read Freud and the Bible concurrently rather than to provide a hierarchical posi-tioning. That is, I have not been reading the Bible in light of Freud, but rather while reading Freud. Therefore, I hope that I have shown that it is possible to juxtapose Freud and the biblical text without agreeing with all of Freud's views, particularly his views of women. Certainly, I do not consider Freud a biblical scholar. Rather, I appropriate Freud's psychoanalytic approach as an-other tool for biblical interpretation.

Reading 3.2c   Phallocentrism and Logocentrism

ILONA RASHKOW

In this third selection, Rashkow demonstrates how her "reading the Bible with Freud" leads to the unconcealing of a patriarchal, "phallic" agenda that permeates not only the pages of the Bible but Freudian psychology itself. The context of Rashkow's discussion is the inauguration of the covenant of circumcision in Gene-sis 17.

Throughout this chapter[1] I have juxtaposed, rather than hierarchically posi-tioned, Freud's views about female sexuality with those reflected in the Hebrew Bible. Reading Genesis and Freud simultaneously, it seems difficult to distin-guish their respective ideas: "We might lay it down," writes Freud, "that . . . sex-uality . . . is of a wholly masculine character."[2] In biblical narratives, as in Freud, female sexuality is explicitly subordinated to and subsumed by the male.

1. Chapter 5: "Oedipus, Shmoedipus, I Love My Mom!"
2. Freud, *The Standard Edition of the Complete Psychological Works of Sigmund Freud* [henceforth *SE*], ed. James Strachey (London: Hogarth Press and the Institute of Psychoanaly-sis, 1953-74), vol. 7, pp. 135-243.

From Ilona N. Rashkow, *The Phallacy of Genesis: A Feminist-Psychoanalytic Approach*, Literary Currents in Biblical Interpretation (Louisville: Westminster/John Knox Press, 1993), pp. 108-9.

Not surprisingly, Freud's constructs of female sexuality have resulted in varying intensities of dissent. Even analysts as early as Jones write that "men analysts have been led to adopt an unduly phallo-centric view" of female psychosexual development.[3]

More recent feminist critiques of Freud's "Female Sexuality" and the Dora case . . . engage the issue of Freud's preconceptions of femininity. As Christine Froula points out, Freud makes subtle war on woman's desire-language in order to avert its perceived threat to the father's cultural preeminence. . . . This statement could also be applied to the Hebrew Bible. Similarly, Juliet Mitchell points out that psychoanalysis can hardly avoid being phallocentric in a society organized along patriarchal lines: "If psychoanalysis is phallocentric, it is because the human social order that it perceives refracted through the individual human subject is patrocentric."[4]

This criticism also sounds like that voiced by many biblical scholars. As Simone de Beauvoir argues, men have established an absolute human type, the male, against which women are measured. Men are always the definers, women the defined. . . . Certainly, Freud defines female sexuality in terms of the male: "She has seen it and knows that she is without it and wants to have it. . . . As regards little girls, we can say of them that they feel greatly at a disadvantage owing to their lack of a . . . penis, that they envy boys for possessing one and that, in the main for this reason, they develop a wish to be a man — a wish that re-emerges later on, in any neurosis that may arise if they meet with a mishap in playing a feminine part."[5]

Likewise, the Hebrew Bible makes phallocentrism synonymous with logocentrism. Throughout the Scriptures, it is primarily the male characters who have defined "woman" and "man," and in the two-thousand some years of biblical interpretation, it is male-dominated discourse which has "cast in stone" these constructs. The covenant of Genesis 17, symbolized by the circumcised penis, has resulted in the "erection" of a paternal logos through the denial, or misnaming, of female sexual experience. Reconstructing biblical female sexuality reveals the textual struggle of women within and against this patriarchy.

3. Ernest Jones, "The Early Development of Female Sexuality," *International Journal of Psychoanalysis* 8 (1927): 459.

4. Juliet Mitchell, *Psychoanalysis and Feminism* (New York: Random House, 1975), p. xv.

5. Freud, *SE*, vol. 19, p. 252; vol. 16, p. 318.

Reading 3.3   Jung's Story of the Unconscious

MICHAEL WILLETT NEWHEART

Our third reading comes from Michael Willett Newheart's psychological study of the story of the Gerasene demoniac in Mark 5:1-20, the tale of a wildly deranged individual whose demonized shadow side is exorcised in an encounter with Jesus. Armed with the tools of narrative criticism, reader-response criticism, autobiographical criticism, and psychological criticism, Newheart invites the reader to probe the "deep human stories" at work not only in the story of the demoniac, but in the story of Mark the evangelist, the story of the reader, and the story of Newheart himself. Working in the vanguard of psychological biblical criticism, Newheart demonstrates lucidly how the psychoanalytic theory of Freud, the archetypal psychology of Jung, the scapegoat theories of René Girard, and the social-psychological theories of Afro-Caribbean psychiatrist Frantz Fanon help us understand the first-century world of the demoniac and our own. We turn now to his presentation of a Jungian "read" of this dramatic story, which presupposes that texts intrigue us because they speak archetypally, that is, they touch on a truth in our own lives triggered by the exemplification of that truth in one of the story's characters. Newheart will review Diarmuid McGann's Jungian reading of the Gerasene demoniac tale, focusing on the "shadow" side of our selves called to consciousness in the drama of this fractured man in need of wholeness.

With Freud, Jung accepted the reality of the unconscious, but he made a distinction between the personal unconscious and the collective unconscious. The personal is essentially what Freud referred to when he spoke of the unconscious. The collective unconscious, however, is Jung's own term. It is that which we share with all people around the globe. In other words, we have our own personal wells that all connect to one large source of water.

Within the unconscious, both personal and collective, are certain tendencies called "archetypes." . . . Archetypes function in the psyche as instincts do in the body. They produce images that appear in individuals' dreams and in cultural products such as fairy tales, myths, and religious symbols. Three archetypes are the shadow, the anima or animus, and the Self. First, the shadow, which is sometimes referred to as "the dark side," includes everything

---

From Michael Willett Newheart, *My Name Is Legion: The Story and Soul of the Gerasene Demoniac*, Interfaces (Collegeville: Liturgical Press, 2004), pp. 63-67.

one refuses to acknowledge about oneself. What is repressed goes into the shadow. Second, anima and animus are the contrasexual aspects of a person. Anima is the feminine element in the man, and animus is the masculine element in the woman. Third, the Self is the archetype of wholeness. It brings together consciousness and the unconscious. It moves one along to individuation, or self-realization.

. . . Dream interpretation is an important feature of Jungian therapy, even more so now than for Freudians. We look for the archetypal images. . . . If [for example] one dreams about a same-sex figure that seems distasteful or even evil, then that is probably a shadow figure. One needs to be in contact with one's shadow to move toward individuation. . . .

Diarmuid McGann gives an extended Jungian reading of Mark in his book, *The Journeying Self: The Gospel of Mark through a Jungian Perspective.* McGann writes, "Scripture is essential to understanding who we are as a people, and who I am as a person and as an individual."[1] He considers the gospel not just as a story of Jesus but as a "story of me, of who I am and who I am becoming."[2] McGann, then, uses Jungian psychology to relate Mark to a person's inner journey. . . .

McGann meditatively moves through the gospel section by section, viewing each part as a "story of the self." He treats the Gerasene in a chapter entitled "The Shadow." For McGann, Legion is a shadow figure. . . . He says that in our own psyches we must bring together the opposites, such as *persona* and shadow. We project our shadow onto other people, he continues. We must withdraw our projections and integrate our shadow. "The shadow figure comes as a messenger of the unconscious inviting us to pay attention to something bigger than our little ego concerns. The shadow leads us to ourselves, to the deeper self, if we listen attentively."[3]

. . . As he does with each section of the gospel, McGann asks what this story says about the story of the self. He has two points. First, he encourages us to look at our own bodies. They are indicative of disorder or order. They tell us of "our drivenness, our compulsiveness, our destructiveness, our anxiety, etc."[4] The Gerasene was certainly living a disordered bodily existence, as he was living among the tombs and gashing himself. What does my body tell me about myself? "I need to see and feel, and accept the statement that my body is making. Is my body reflecting my conscious life project or is it saying

1. Diarmuid McGann, *The Journeying Self: The Gospel of Mark Through a Jungian Perspective* (New York: Paulist, 1985), p. 9.

2. McGann, *Journeying,* p. 9.

3. McGann, *Journeying,* p. 74.

4. McGann, *Journeying,* p. 78.

something else that I do not wish to hear but need to hear?"[5] Second, . . . he writes, "Under the guidance of the self we are called to recognize the shadow and bring it into the light, to integrate its energies, its values, its strength into our personality, to bring them into our conscious mode of operation and grow into the person we are called to become."[6]

———

SUGGESTIONS FOR FURTHER READING

Miller, David L., ed. *Jung and the Interpretation of the Bible.* New York: Continuum, 1995.

Moore, Stephen D. "Psychoanalytic Criticism [Freud]." In *The Postmodern Bible,* edited by Elizabeth A. Castelli, Stephen D. Moore, Gary Phillips, and Regina M. Schwartz, 187-224. New Haven: Yale University Press, 1995.

Rollins, Wayne G. "Freud and Jung: Psychoanalysis and the Bible since 1900." Chapter 2 in *Soul and Psyche: The Bible in Psychological Perspective.* Minneapolis: Fortress, 1999.

———. *Jung and the Bible.* Atlanta: John Knox, 1983.

Scharfenberg, Joachim. *Sigmund Freud and His Critique of Religion.* Translated by O. C. Dean Jr. Philadelphia: Fortress, 1988.

5. McGann, *Journeying,* pp. 78-79.
6. McGann, *Journeying,* p. 80.

CHAPTER 4

Behavioral, Learning, Object Relations, and Developmental Approaches

The fact that the American Psychological Association currently comprises forty-two specialty-centered divisions barely suggests the incohesiveness of contemporary psychology; each division is in reality a division of divisions, a motley assortment of subgroups the members of which do and believe very different things.

Sigmund Koch[1]

There is no single way to do psychological biblical criticism any more than there is any single psychological theory. Human behavior, thinking, and relationships offer an infinite variety of phenomena for study, and each approach focuses on some segment or another of that variety. Each psychological perspective chooses which behaviors it considers to be significant, how those behaviors are to be described and interpreted, and how they fit together into a model of psychological functioning. The result is that often psychologists themselves disagree profoundly with one another. As Sigmund Koch, a former president of the American Psychological Association, put it:

> Characteristically, psychological events . . . are multiply determined, ambiguous in their human meaning, polymorphous, contextually environed . . . and evanescent. . . . Different theorists will . . . make asystematically different perceptual cuts upon the same domain. . . . The cuts, variables, and concepts will in all likelihood establish different universes of discourse, even if loose ones.[2]

1. In Sigmund Koch and D. E. Leary, eds., *A Century of Psychology as Science* (Washington, DC: American Psychological Association, 1992), p. 17.
2. In Koch and Leary, eds., *Century of Psychology,* p. 93.

What matters for psychological investigation? It might be outward behavior or inner thought processes, dreams, or fantasies. It might be individual self-concepts or family and social relationships. It might be perception or communication or delusion. No wonder that Koch goes on to suggest that it is more accurate to speak of "the psychological studies" than "psychology."

Biblical texts, too, are "multiply determined, ambiguous, and contextual." They are shaped not only by psychological factors but by historical contexts, literary structures, rhetorical intentions, and religious communities. In psychological biblical criticism, it is not sufficient simply to apply a chosen psychological theory to the interpretation of a text. Rather, one seeks the tools that are appropriate to the task of illuminating some aspect of the text, its development, or its interpretation.

When we examine the literature on psychological interpretation of the Bible, we discover that much of the material is grounded in depth psychology, which is concerned with unconscious processes and their effects on the individual. The last chapter dealt with the two most well-known theorists in depth psychology — Freud, and Jung. The Bible, its symbols, and its impact on individuals and culture prove a rich subject for depth-psychological analysis. However, other approaches may help us to see different psychological dimensions of Scripture. In other chapters we will encounter cognitive psychology, which considers the processses of thinking itself (5.2; 12.2; 13.4), and logotherapy, dealing with the creation of meaning (12.1). Here we consider four other approaches: behaviorism, learning theory, object relations, and developmental theory.

Behaviorism became a significant force in psychological studies largely through the work of John Watson and B. F. Skinner. The focus of their attention was outwardly observable behavior and how that behavior could be changed by positive or negative reinforcement ("reward" or "punishment") within the environment. Both Watson and Skinner tended toward radical materialism, denying transcendence or free will; Skinner wrote a book titled *Beyond Freedom and Dignity.* Nevertheless, as we will see in the first reading, some scholars believe that it is possible to reject the radical materialism of classical behaviorism and still use a behavioral perspective to learn something about the Bible.

A modified form of behaviorism, cognitive learning theory, recognizes that stimuli for behavior come not only from the outer environment, but also from within. One can develop an internal standard of desired behavior by observing and imitating external models, thus creating one's own internalized system of reinforcement and inner reward. In our second reading, Gerd Theissen shows how the apostle Paul seeks to discourage his readers in Corinth from associating with the conventionally "wise," and instead to build their inner lives on love.

Psychoanalysis has developed in several new directions since Freud; many of them are far more open to transcendent or interpersonal phenomena. One such approach is object relations theory, which comprehends human beings in terms of their relationships and interactions with others and within themselves. The "objects" of object relations are internalized images of significant figures, especially parents, which continue to affect an individual's self-concept, emotions, and behavior. Our third reading considers some implications of object relations for biblical interpretation.

Finally, developmental psychology takes as its focus the patterns of psycho-social development as individuals move through stages of life. Each individual develops in his or her own unique way, but there are common challenges and stage-specific skills to be gained at each step. Success or failure at mastering a skill at any level will affect how the individual moves into the next stage of development. Our final reading suggests how the story of the Garden of Eden may reflect the stages of human development.

Reading 4.1 Behavioral Psychology and the Bible

EDWARD BOLIN AND GLENN GOLDBERG

This exploration by Edward Bolin and Glenn Goldberg is an example of "affirmative behavioralism." While rejecting the materialist assumptions of "ideological" behaviorism, Bolin and Goldberg nonetheless suggest that there is an affinity between the Bible and some aspects of behavioral psychology.

General Areas of Integration

Behavioral psychology is in general agreement with the Bible since both assert the importance of environmental influence. As behavior theory places a

---

From Edward P. Bolin and Glenn M. Goldberg, "Behavioral Psychology and the Bible: General and Specific Considerations," *Journal of Psychology and Theology* 7, no. 3 (1979): 170-71, 173-74.

major emphasis on environmental factors which influence a person's behavior, so the Bible recognizes the tremendous influence the environment may have on a believer's behavior. Warnings are issued throughout the Old Testament against the Israelites becoming contaminated by pagan environments:

> When you enter the land which the Lord your God gives to you, you shall not learn to imitate the detestable things of those nations. . . . For whoever does these things is detestable to the Lord, and because of these detestable things the Lord your God will drive them out before you. (Deuteronomy 18:9, 12)

This passage not only warns Israel of the environmental threat, but declares God's recognition of that threat and his intention to eliminate it.

Not only does Scripture assume the importance of our environment, but it also affirms the importance of our external behavior. "A point of agreement is reached between contingency management and Christian theology in that both claim behavior is important."[1] Ephesians 5:1-20 lists behaviors which Paul believes are important for the Christian to practice if he is to become an imitator of God. We also see the importance James places on external actions: "Even so faith, if it has no works [an external behavior], is dead" (James 2:17).

Behaviorists claim that the most reliable data is observable behavior, a claim that James also defends: "I will show you my faith by my works" (James 2:18). In this passage, we see that behavior is not only a reliable source of data concerning our faith, but in fact is the criteria. Matthew supports the importance of behavioral data when [Jesus] claims: "You shall know them by their fruits" (Matthew 7:16). Thus, both Scripture and behavior theory assume the importance of external behavior.

Eschatology and Positive Reinforcement

One of the most fertile grounds for integration between theology and behavior theory is that of eschatology and positive reinforcement. Eschatology is "the doctrine of the last things" and deals with the last judgment, the second coming, and the final end time. In describing a coming last judgment, eschatology delineates the ultimate rewards facing mankind. These rewards, which not only provide an incentive for conversion but also a motivation for righ-

1. R. C. Llewellyn, "A Second Look at B. F. Skinner," *Journal of Psychology and Theology* 1, no. 3 (1973): 3-7, p. 6.

teous living, integrate with the behavioral principle of positive reinforcement. Carter and Mohline concur that "the psychology of goals, expectations, [and] rewards . . . parallel and are integrative with their eschatological equivalent."[2] Ellison agrees: "contemporary psychology suggests the effectiveness of using positive reinforcements such as the hope of heaven."[3]

Because of the recent efforts to integrate cognitive and behavioristic approaches, the definition of how reinforcers function has broadened beyond traditional behavioral views.[4] Rotter, introducing a more cognitive element to reinforcement theory, emphasized the individual's subjective expectations about future outcomes and the subjective value of reinforcements in the person's situation.[5] Sheffield deviates from the traditional behavioral stance in his claim that reinforcers are influential because they act as incentives in motivating behavior.[6] Bandura, another learning theorist who includes cognitions, states: "Incentive theories of motivation assume that behavior is largely activated by anticipation of reinforcing consequences."[7]

The properties operating in the social learning view of reinforcement, such as incentive and anticipation, parallel the motives operating in eschatological rewards, namely hope and expectation. Titus 2:13 illustrates how the believer's behavior is activated by anticipation of reinforcing consequences when it describes one as "looking for the blessed hope and the appearing of the glory of our great God and Savior, Christ Jesus.

"The Lord's coming is set before us as the great hope of the Church. . . . The coming of Christ is the great incentive to Biblical Christianity."[8] As the reinforcer in social learning theory is used as an incentive to change the client's behavior, so the Lord's return functions as an inspiration to change the believer's behavior. Anticipating His return induces self-purification (1 John 3:3;

2. J. Carter and R. G. Mohline, "The Nature and Scope of Integration: A Proposal," *Journal of Psychology and Theology* 4, no. 1 (1976): 13-22, p. 13.

3. C. Ellison, "The Foundation of Self-Esteem," In *Self-Esteem*, ed. C. Ellison (Oklahoma City: Christian Association for Psychological Studies, 1976), p. 9.

4. M. Mahoney, "Reflections on the Cognitive-Learning Trend in Psychotherapy," *American Psychologist* 32 (1977): 5-13.

5. J. B. Rotter, "Beliefs, Social Attitudes and Behavior: A Social Learning Analysis," in *Applications of a Social Learning Theory of Personality*, ed. J. B. Rotter, J. E. Chance, and E. J. Phares (New York: Holt, Rinehart & Winston, 1972).

6. F. D. Sheffield, "A Drive Induction Theory of Reinforcement," in *Current Research in Motivation*, ed. R. N. Harber (New York: Holt, 1966).

7. Albert Bandura, *Principles of Behavior Modification* (New York: Holt, Rinehart & Winston, 1969), p. 225.

8. H. C. Thiessen, *Lectures in Systematic Theology* (Grand Rapids: Eerdmans, 1949), p. 444.

2 Peter 3:11); it challenges the backslider to return (Romans 13:11, 12); it encourages watchfulness and constancy (Matthew 24:44; 1 Thessalonians 5:6); and it is a stay during trials and bereavement (James 5:7; 1 Thessalonians 4:16-18)....

Criticisms of Reinforcement

Even though behavior theory relies upon the principles of reinforcement to shape a person's behavior, many Christians believe that a person should be motivated by higher, intrinsically spiritual desires and not by external rewards in this case, eschatological rewards. Many believe that the use of rewards to change behavior is analogous to using a bribe or a power ploy; others claim that reinforcement is ineffective because it cannot change complex behaviors or foster inner-directed responsibility;[9] still others maintain that rewards as a motivator induce selfishness and self-interest.

These arguments fail to recognize that motivation by positive reinforcement is inherent in the social system that God has established. They overlook the fact that behavior is strongly influenced by praise, approval, monetary incentives, and social recognition. That rewards are a primary factor in motivation is apparent in the warning: "Each will receive his own reward according to his labor" (1 Corinthians 3:8). We would not work if we did not receive a salary, yet we do not consider our salary a bribe but merely an incentive. God has created man so that rewards are part of the natural fabric which motivates him.[10]

Hebrews 11:6 establishes God as a positive reinforcer by stating, "He is a rewarder of those who seek Him." It is obvious that God gives rewards, and that they are usually contingent upon appropriate behavior (e.g., seeking Him). In fact, the word "reward" occurs over 100 times in the New Testament and is used most commonly for purposes of operant conditioning. Notice how frequently the emission of correct behavior results in a reinforcement so that that behavior will be maintained: "if any man's work remains, he shall receive a reward" (1 Corinthians 3:14); "if a man perseveres under trial, he will receive the crown of life" (James 1:12); "he who shepherds the flock will receive the crown of glory" (1 Peter 5:1-4).

Heaven itself, along with God's eternal presence, is one of the strongest positive reinforcers Scripture uses to maintain motivation. Notice that the incentive of the heavenly reward resides largely in the fulfillment of human de-

9. T. Gordan, *Parent Effectiveness Training* (New York: Peter H. Wyden, 1970).

10. J. Adams, *Christian Counselor's Manual* (Grand Rapids: Baker, 1973).

sire: the wealth of nations (Revelation 21:26); happiness (Revelation 1:9); no more grief, crying or pain (Revelation 21:4). If there were danger in goodness being ruined, certainly God would not appeal to our pleasure in the heavenly reward. But, in Psalm 16:11 He promises, "In Thy presence is fullness of joy; in Thy right hand there are pleasures forever." The longing for eternal happiness is not to be suppressed so that God can be honored out of some higher, less selfish motive. "Christian hedonism does not put us above God when we seek Him out of self-interest. . . . On the contrary, the one who is actually setting himself above God is the person who presumes to come to God in order to give rather than to get."[11] The Apostle Paul was honest enough to admit that if there were no expectancy of heavenly reward there would be little incentive to maintain his Christian service (1 Corinthians 15:19). If Paul needed more than "higher virtues" to sustain him, how much more do we?

But, if the believer's motivation for conversion and for sanctification is initially controlled in part by the external contingencies of eschatological rewards, this is not to say that righteous living never becomes intrinsically reinforcing. Behavior theory assumes that, through extrinsic reinforcements such as praise, hugging, recognition, and encouragement, a person adopts intrinsic reinforcement such as feelings of pride and approval, feelings which are motivating in and of themselves. Behaviors that have been acquired through reinforcing techniques have a tendency to become intrinsically reinforcing.[12] For the believer, conversion and good deeds are often initially acquired through the attraction of the heavenly rewards. Yet, good deeds have a tendency to become intrinsically reinforcing so that the believer derives satisfaction out of simply obeying God.

Although heavenly rewards are described as a primary reinforcer for believers, this is not to suggest that it is the only primary reinforcer that Scripture provides. For instance, the internal working of the Holy Spirit in a believer's life is also consistent with reinforcement principles of behavioral psychology. Paul states that our experience of the fruit of the Spirit is contingent upon our walking in the Spirit. In addition, abiding in Christ is a strong motivator since we are attracted by His love and the prospect of our joy being made full (incentives which are described in John 15:9-11). The eschatological rewards provide a strong incentive for godly living, yet this is not to deny the motivation that is presently given in Christ and through the Holy Spirit.

11. J. Piper, "How I Became a Christian Hedonist," *His* (1977): 5.
12. D. C. Rimm and J. C. Masters, *Behavior Therapy: Techniques and Empirical Findings* (San Francisco: Academic Press, 1974).

Summary

Behavioral psychology is often assumed to be in direct conflict with Scripture. Questions concerning man's freedom, dignity, self-control, responsibility and motivation have resulted in a hesitancy to accept behaviorism as a viable area of integration. Although these are valid concerns of philosophical behaviorism, they are merely pseudo-issues regarding methodological behaviorism. Methodological behaviorism is not inconsistent with biblical doctrine but, in fact, integrates on many points. The Bible illustrates the use of teaming principles which have been discovered through behavioral research. One obvious parallel between theology and behavioral psychology is that of eschatology and positive reinforcement. The heavenly reward, acting as a strong incentive for Christians, finds similarity in social reinforcers and token economies. Using the properties of praise, encouragement, and comfort, social reinforcers are paired with rewards that await us in heaven to motivate us to good deeds. Likewise, the believer's deeds, functioning as a token economy, can be redeemed in heaven for eternal rewards.

Reading 4.2   Psychological Aspects of Pauline Theology

GERD THEISSEN

In a groundbreaking psychological study of Pauline theology in 1987, New Testament scholar Gerd Theissen, already well known for his sociological studies, turned to psychological perspectives. He sought to look at selected aspects of Pauline theology through three distinctly different theoretical systems: learning theory, depth psychology, and cognitive psychology. Here, he considers 1 Corinthians 2:6-16 in the light of learning theory.

Aspects of 1 Cor. 2:6-16 in Learning Theory

Paul himself describes the reception of revelation as learning. "And we impart this in words not taught by human wisdom but taught by the Spirit" (1 Cor.

From Gerd Theissen, *Psychological Aspects of Pauline Theology* (Philadelphia: Fortress, 1987), pp. 368-73.

Gerd Theissen

2:13). He contrasts two learning processes: the learning process by which one is "socialized" into the world, and an opposed learning process that confers entirely new possibilities of behavior and experience. Paul is aware that these are processes stimulated and influenced from without: one receives either the spirit of the world or the Spirit from God (2:12). Here "spirit" means a formative influence from without.[1] A change takes place within the formative environment. Or, formulated more cautiously, we observe the attempt to free oneself from the existing learning environment (the world and its spirit). But the new environment is by definition not accessible to outsiders. It does not impinge upon the eye and the ear. It is inaccessible to natural "psychic" experience. Despite this inaccessibility we can make some statements about the stimuli, reinforcements, and models that lead to the new learning process.

Paul connects the "perfect" wisdom with a specific social situation. Only among the perfect does he speak wisdom. In 1 Cor. 2:13 *en teleiois* does not mean "to (the) perfect"; for that a simple dative would suffice (cf. Rom. 3:19; 7:1; 1 Cor. 3:1; and many other texts). The words are rather to be understood, like *lalein en ekklesia,* "speak in church" (1 Cor. 14:19), as an indication of the social framework.[2] For each pneumatic discourse there is a situation that stimulates it; Paul gives us a sample of this in 1 Cor. 2:6-16 — the group of the "perfect." He specifies them more precisely in 3:1-3. Harmony is a presupposition of wisdom discourse. As long as conflict and rancor rule, Paul cannot communicate his wisdom.

The homogeneous group of the perfect with its positive emotional climate is not only the stimulus of the wisdom discourse but also its most important reinforcement. Only in this group does the higher wisdom find positive resonance. Paul's inability to communicate (*edunethen* [I was not able] = first-person singular, 1 Cor. 3:1) it to the Corinthians is grounded in the inability of the Corinthians to receive it (*oupo gar edunasthe* [you were not ready] = second-person plural, 1 Cor. 3:2). Paul presents this state of affairs in generalized form in 2:14: the psychic man does not receive what is of the divine Spirit. To him it is foolishness, and he cannot (*ou dunatai*) recognize it, for it must be judged pneumatically. Here one can note a certain imbalance in the estimation of the reinforcing consequences. On the one hand, Paul binds

1. Does Paul understand the "spirit of the world" as a demonic being that blinds believers (thus Johannes Weiss, *Der 1. Korintherbrief* [Göttingen: Vandenhoeck & Ruprecht, 1970], p. 63) or is it a matter of forming an analogy to the Spirit of God?

2. Thus C. K. Barrett, *A Commentary on the Second Epistle to the Corinthians* (New York: Harper & Row, 1973), pp. 68-69. A different position is held by Hans Conzelmann, *Der Erste Brief an Die Korinter,* Kritisch-Exegetischer Kommentar über Das Neue Testament (Göttingen: Vandenhoeck & Ruprecht, 1969), p. 78 n. 31.

the perfect wisdom to positive resonance in the group; on the other hand, he claims that "the spiritual man judges all things, but is himself to be judged by no one" (2:15), as if he were completely independent of the reaction of others, no matter whether they are pneumatics or psychics.

What Paul says in 2:13ff. about the social relationship of pneumatics and psychics has a model in the relationship of Christ to the archons [rulers] of this world. By reference to this model it becomes clear which "reinforcement system" Paul wishes to separate himself from. Just as the pneumatic person moves among those who reject his wisdom and misunderstand him, so too Christ appeared in a world that rejected him. In both cases the wisdom of God was misunderstood. The *oudeis egnoken* [no one understands] (v. 11) and the *ou dunatei gnonai* [they are not able to understand] (v. 14) correspond to the *oudeis . . . egnoken* [none understood] (v. 8). The archons are models of the psychic person who cannot grasp divine wisdom, who even stands opposed to it in hostility. But Christ is the model of the pneumatic who proclaims the same eternal wisdom of God that is the cause of the Christ-event.

But who are the mysterious archons? Whether or not Paul thought of mythic figures in this regard, the recipients of the letter must also have thought of the earthly rulers who were responsible for Christ's crucifixion.[3] They did, after all, know important parts of the Passion tradition, as Paul himself attests (1 Cor. 11:23-26). They probably knew more about the circumstances of the crucifixion than the fact that Jesus was "betrayed" and "handed over" (1 Cor. 11:23), for a tradition of this sort would necessarily have awakened questions about those who betrayed Jesus, handed him over and crucified him.[4]

Yet not only the recipients but the author as well thought of historical rulers in connection with the archons. In Rom. 13:3, the sole Pauline reference apart from 1 Cor. 2:6ff., civil officials are meant by *archontes;* and the train of thought in 1 Cor. 1:18ff. points more to human figures. For divine wisdom is

---

3. Thus Julius Schniewind, "Die Archonton Dieses Äons: I. Kor 2,6-8," in *Nachgelassene Reden und Aufsätze* (Berlin: Töpelmann, 1952); G. Miller, "*Archonton Tou Aionos Toutou* — a New Look at 1 Corinthians 2,6-8," *Journal of Biblical Literature* 91 (1972): 522-28; W. Carr, "The Rulers of This Age — I Corinthians II,6-8," *New Testament Studies* 23 (1977): 20-35; and Ulrich Wilckens, "Zu 1 Kor. 2,1-16," in *Theologia Crucis — Signum Crucis [Festschrift Erich Dinkler]* (Tübingen: J. C. B. Mohr, 1979), pp. 501-37.

4. Luke calls the Jewish authorities that were co-responsible for the execution archons (Luke 24:20; cf. 23:13, 35; Acts 3:14; 13:27). Since the Corinthian community had a tradition of the Last Supper that was related to the Lukan tradition (cf. 1 Cor. 11:23ff. with Luke 12:19ff.), it is reasonable that it was also acquainted in other respects with a Passion tradition with Lukan tinges and that the "archons" were familiar to it on that basis. But this is only a conjecture.

opposed to human wisdom, the wisdom of the wise, of the scribes and of debaters (1:20), of the educated, powerful, and wellborn (1:26ff.). Paul generalizes in view of the situation in Corinth. God will destroy not only the wisdom of the wise (1:19) but absolutely everything that represents something in the world — all the "things that are" (1:28). The association among human wisdom, power, and corruptibility that is established here is presupposed in 2:6ff.;[5] when Paul speaks of the wisdom and the rulers of this world and characterizes them as "transient" (*katargoumenon* [passing away], 2:6, and *katargese* [do away with], 1:28). On the basis of this chain of associations, the archons in 2:6 are primarily earthly rulers — not merely the concrete rulers of Palestine, Pilate and Antipas, but earthly rulers in general, in Corinth and Judea.[6]

The rejection of Christ by these archons corresponds to the rejection of wisdom among human beings. But it is then clear from which system of reinforcement Paul wishes to be independent: it is the system of reinforcement represented by the dominant classes and the leading groups. The assertion that no one can judge the pneumatic is pointed against those who otherwise have the power to judge others. If these powerful people have opposed with hostility the wisdom of God in Christ, and if Christ has overcome their resistance, then Christ becomes a model of behavior and experience that has made itself independent of the negative sanctions of the dominant system of convictions. This is not only a purely formal independence. The wisdom of this world is characterized by its link with social and political power; the foolishness of the

---

5. Precisely the connection of the "archons" with wisdom and power is frequently adduced in favor of a demonological interpretation. Yet these associations are already present in the wisdom literature. (1) H. Lietzmann, *An Die Korinther I.ii*, 4th ed., Handbuch Zum Neuen Testament 9 (Tübingen: J. C. B. Mohr, 1949), p. 17, thinks that it is a characteristic sign of earthly rulers to spread wisdom. But the ideal is that the wise man be king and that the king be wise; cf. Wis. 6:20-21. (2) Martin Dibelius, *Die Geisterwelt im Glauben des Paulus* (Göttingen: Vandenhoeck & Ruprecht, 1909), p. 90, thinks that it would not have been necessary to stress the transitoriness of the rulers with regard to earthly rulers. The earthly rulers of Palestine were probably already deceased by the time of the composition of the Letter to the Corinthians. Yet the sapiential text in Bar. 3:16-19 emphasizes, "Where are the princes of the nations [*archonton ton ethnon*] and those who rule over the beasts of the earth . . . ? They have vanished and gone down to Hades, and others have arisen in their place." Cf. André Feuillet, "Le 'chefs de ce siècle' et la sagesse divine d'après 1 Cor 2,6-8," in *Studiorum Paulinorum Congressus Internationalis Catholicus 1961* (Rome: Pontifical Biblical Institute, 1963), pp. 383-93.

6. A further argument for the interpretation of the archons as men in the citation in 2:9, which serves as biblical proof of the preceding statements. The archons did not recognize the wisdom of God, for it is written that what God has prepared for his elect has not entered the heart of *man*. It will be shown below that the demonic conception is also not entirely unjustified: the earthly archons are in fact shrouded in a mythical aura.

preaching is characterized by its link with a crucified man. If this "foolishness" is recognized as superior wisdom, then the principle of dominance that rules the world is itself called into question. A struggle for power and influence would contradict this perfect wisdom. The divided Corinthians are thus not mature enough for it. They are still "fleshly" (1 Cor. 3:1-3).

Paul still conceals what he opposes positively to the fleshly struggle. At the beginning of 1 Corinthians the accent lies wholly on the fact that a system of reinforcement independent of the old world has appeared with Christ. In the citation in 2:9, Paul implies that this system of reinforcement is operative among those who love God. But none of this is developed. Only later does Paul become more concrete: all pneumatic experience is directed toward love (1 Corinthians 13). In 1 Cor. 3:1, he reproaches the Corinthians as "immature." In 1 Corinthians 13 he shows them the way to maturity: "When I was a child, I spoke like a child, I thought like a child, I reasoned like a child; when I became a man, I gave up childish ways" (1 Cor. 13:11). The *teleioi* [mature, complete] of 1 Cor. 2:6 are those who know the *teleion* [complete, perfect] of 1 Cor. 13:10. What is "perfect" is love.[7]

From 1 Corinthians 13 we thus come to know the new "reinforcement system" of Paul, which is only imperfectly operative even among Christians. One characteristic is striking here. As a rule, Paul motivates love and solitary behavior extrinsically. He appeals to authorities like the law (Gal. 5:14; Rom. 13:8-10) — to moral stimuli, in other words. He threatens negative consequences in case of unloving behavior (cf. Gal. 5:21). He invokes the model of Christ (Rom. 15:7). But in 1 Corinthians 13, he leaves behind all these extrinsic forms of motivation. Love is commanded without reference to an authority. Every allusion to the Old Testament is lacking, as is every appeal to a word of the Lord, or argumentation on the basis of authoritative tribunal. If there is a demand of love — if, in the language of learning theory, there is anything that "stimulates" love — then this occurs through presentation of loving behavior and through nothing else. The same is true of motivation with the aid of positive and negative consequences. No positive consequences are promised. In the end there remain faith, hope, and love. Love is the greatest among them. It is in itself reward for all eternity. Paul does not even promise that it will be "rewarded" by disappearing negative consequences; on the contrary, love bears all, believes all, hopes all, endures all. Once again Paul motivates in a purely intrinsic manner. For this reason be can also renounce all models. He refers neither to himself nor to Christ as models of loving behavior. Rather,

---

7. On 1 Corinthians 13, cf. O. Wischmeyer, *Der Höchste Weg: Das 13 Kapitel des 1. Korintherbriefes*, Studien Zum Neuen Testament, 13 (Gütersloh, 1981).

he speaks of love as of an acting person: "Love is patient and kind; love is not jealous or boastful; it is not arrogant or rude. Love does not insist on its own way; it is not irritable or resentful, it does not rejoice at wrong, but rejoices in the right. Love bears all things, believes all things, hopes all things, endures all things . . ." (1 Cor. 13:4-7). Here love appears as an example of itself. It is its own model. It is from love that one learns what love is. From the perspectives of learning theory, the new reality Paul experienced as overpowering revelation and as "perfection" can be described as intrinsically motivated love: love is experienced as a value in itself. It unfolds itself among the perfect, those who are driven by the Spirit of God, without appeal to external authorities, without reference to reinforcing consequences, without dependence on exemplary models.

In sum, from the perspective of learning theory, Paul wishes to desensitize with regard to the dominant reinforcement system in society through development of the preaching of the cross as "foolishness for the world" and as "wisdom for the perfect." The dominant system is to lose its power over Christians. The preaching is to make one independent from every external judgment. The decisive condition for learning is the model of Christ. In him the impotent is shown as powerful and the powerful as weak. With a view to him one need not be impressed by the claims of the powerful, the respected, and the wellborn. In 1 Cor. 2:6-16, Paul does not yet develop the new "reinforcement system" for the perfect. Only later does he concretize materially what for him is perfect, something that points far beyond the everyday reality of the community: what is perfect is intrinsically motivated love. Only love has completely overcome the reinforcement system based on domination. Only love has emancipated itself from all external authorities, consequences, and models, from all the extrinsic reinforcements whose functioning is inconceivable without power. Such wisdom is for those who are perfect.

Reading 4.3   Winnicott's Squiggle Game
and Biblical Interpretation

RALPH UNDERWOOD

In object relations theory, the concept of "transitional space," proposed by Donald Winnicott, offers a model for understanding how children develop from grandiose egocentricity into the capacity for genuine relationships with others. On the way to learning to recognize others as beings in their own right, children will often take a beloved object — a teddy bear, bit of cloth, or favorite toy — and treat it with special care, endowing it with personality and identity. Significantly, though, others in the child's family will "play along" with the child's identification, treating the object with special care (or, sometimes, disrespect, if a sibling is feeling hostile!). Transitional objects, then, are neither solely the invention of the inner world of the child, nor solely external "realistic" phenomena. They exist in a "transitional space" between these two worlds, mediating between them. Ralph Underwood here suggests that hermeneutics itself is an example of living in transitional space, between the text and the interpreter.

The Squiggle Game: Hermeneutical Model

For many of us it may seem quite a stretch to connect the imagination of the infant with creative reflections on cultural and religious objects. And the distance to biblical hermeneutics may seem farther still. So come one more step with me and consider another phenomenon — not the mental life of the infant but that of an older child interacting with an adult, a kind of halfway spot between the transitional world of the infant and the cultural world of adults.

In London today there is a foundation named the Squiggle Foundation, whose unusual name derives from a game that Don Winnicott played with the children he treated in his psychiatric practice. The squiggle game went something like this. Dr. Winnicott told the patient that he would draw a squiggle, a line or drawing that had no particular meaning, and the child was to draw and make something from this squiggle. Then the child could draw a

---

From Ralph Underwood, "Winnicott's Squiggle Game and Biblical Interpretation," in *Psychology and the Bible: A New Way to Read the Scriptures*, ed. J. Harold Ellens and Wayne G. Rollins (Westport, CT: Greenwood-Praeger, 2004), vol. 1, pp. 144-47.

squiggle, and Winnicott would make something of it. Typically, the psychiatrist would start by closing his eyes and drawing a line. Then the patient would respond by adding a line drawing onto the squiggle in order to give it some meaning. As the child and therapist played this game, reversing roles in turn, they would talk as much as the child wanted. One child, for example, before drawing his response to Winnicott's squiggle, asked about what he could or could not do, and the psychiatrist's response was "There are no rules." On another occasion, the child might begin to tell a story or a dream.[1] Accordingly, a dialogue accompanied the activity of drawing together. When by this means Winnicott began to know a child, he would say, "I do not have a diagnosis of the child, but a diagnosis of my relationship with the child."

To be sure, although this relationship-forming process is play, it has a critical dimension to it. Some problematic process has brought patient and doctor together. The youngster and the adult choose to respond to each other's moves in selective, discerning ways. Still, one can hope that once the game has been played, the psychiatrist can interpret the relationship with the child in a playful spirit.

The squiggle comes from the unconscious and has a primordial quality that reflects the impulse of the moment. The response to the squiggle intends to create a meaningful object, an object that evokes some recognition from both persons. This response is marked by intentionality and creativity. It gives expression to ego qualities.

For an object relations perspective on hermeneutics, I proffer the squiggle game as an analogy for the hermeneutical process. The squiggle game is like the process of developing a relationship with a text and of being in a position to interpret the relationship in a meaningful way. Similarly, hermeneutics emerges out of a process of relationship building such that our interpretations of texts are hunches or declarations about our relationship with these texts. An object relations approach frames hermeneutics as a dynamic relationship between text and readers. Hermeneutics is not simply a task of making a meaning from the text that suits the needs of the readers, nor simply a task of unlocking some a priori meaning ensconced in the text. Rather, hermeneutics is a process in which a unique relationship between text and readers evolves.

A squiggle is symbolic for me of anything in biblical texts that challenges meaningful interpretation, something that says, "What are you going to do with me?" Squiggles are fragments. Responses to squiggles are ways of

---

1. Donald W. Winnicott, *Therapeutic Considerations in Child Psychiatry* (London: Hogarth Press, 1971).

making meaning that in some fashion include the squiggles. No interpretation produces meaning or truth as a complete whole. Rather, responses or interpretations are more or less creative, evoking a liveliness of relationship with a text.

For example, the following is a brief summary of a line of interpretation of some elements in Luke 8:36-39. This interpretation is possible because of contemporary sensitivities and issues. The demoniac falls at Jesus' feet and cries out. The word comes from Greek *anakrazo*, which had a connotation of to choke, and later to cry out. The image that comes to mind is that of an unnatural sound, not the person's own voice at all. Jesus had to subject demons to discourse because they had the power of speech; the person who had thrown himself at Jesus' feet did not. Then it becomes all the more significant at the end of the story that Jesus refuses to allow this person to go with him but bids him tell his story in detail (Greek, *diegou* [imperative form] from *diegeomai* [tell, relate]). What is wondrous in this narrative is that the person now is able to declare God's praise in his own voice among his own people. The legion of demons, the chaotic fragmentation of this person's life, had to be exposed, yet they were not originally part of him. However long ago, they entered his life. The legion of demons was alien and robbed him of his own voice, and when the kingdom of God came near it was time for them to depart, whatever the cost. Note the swine rushing to the lake that scholars cannot locate.

Such an interpretation highlights certain particulars of the text because of their potential significance for readers today who are sensitive to the way that persons struggle with the chaotic, desire to find their own voice, and want to be heard. The interpretation is not objective in the sense of being the one understanding that makes sense for all time and places. On the other hand, it is not merely subjective in the sense of imposing self-serving agendas on the text regardless of its content or context. The interpretation reflects an emerging relationship between text and readers. The text lives for readers and speaks to them.

For another kind of example, one can consider the interpretations of scholars such as Phyllis Trible.[2] Clearly her work is the result of a literary method of analysis, but also it reflects the sensitivities of an age, the kind of questions being raised in a community, and the struggles and gifts of a particular person. One might say that Jacques Derrida,[3] a key figure in the contem-

---

2. Phyllis Trible, *Texts of Terror: Literary-Feminist Readings of Biblical Narratives* (Minneapolis: Fortress, 1984).

3. Jacques Derrida, *Writing and Difference* (Chicago: University of Chicago Press, 1978).

porary deconstruction movement, has set forth an attention-getting squiggle for advocates of hermeneutics. The response of Francis Watson, to cite one example, produces interesting comments on glossolalia texts in the New Testament.[4] Contemporary issues and discussions in communities of discourse create relations with texts that have new problematics and possibilities for understanding.

By providing interpersonal contexts, communities such as communities of faith and communities of scholarship establish systems of checks and balances between imagination and external reality, between creative openness and critical distance. In this sense, hermeneutics is a community as well as a personal undertaking.

Transitional space is the realm of the symbolic. To be in this space entails more than mere openness to other people. Hermeneutics entails a process of negotiating tensions and possibilities between personally primordial texts and culturally primordial texts. Texts open the way to the unspeakable, to what cuts across language and thought, to what can be voiced only in metaphors and stories, known only in silence. Psychologically, the stereotypical view is that interpreting in the sense of explaining is the paternal function, and holding is the maternal function. The two cannot be separated, however. The community locus of hermeneutics — the holding function — is as significant as are the proffered contents of explanation and understanding. Consequently, hermeneutics is a movement from orientation to disorientation to new orientation, as Brueggemann has suggested.[5] When the aliveness of a creative orientation fades, a time of transition, disorientation, and fragmentation ironically comes to the rescue. It is a squiggle game, a way in which trusting and distrusting dance together.

Consequently, hermeneutics is a process that interweaves written and oral processes. The oral is essential and in its fullness involves a bodily presence to one another — despite the Internet — so that we know not only the context of the interpretation but also how people are talking about texts, and how texts move and enliven people. The oral dimension opens up a way for a community of discourse to create a relation with the text and a way to be created by the text. Yet bodily absence and solitude are vital aspects of the interpretive process as well. Through their symbolic power, texts disclose the presence of what is absent.

---

4. F. Watson, *Text, Church and World: Biblical Interpretations in Theological Perspective* (Grand Rapids: Eerdmans, 1994), pp. 89-108.

5. Walter Bruggemann, *The Message of the Psalms: A Theological Commentary* (Minneapolis: Augsburg Press, 1984).

Numerous similarities, then, between Winnicott's squiggle game and hermeneutical process can be noted. Like the squiggle game, hermeneutics is a process of interaction between the primordial and the constructive, between chaos and order, between the deeply emotional and the highly rational. Object relations acknowledges multiple, primitive selves and fragmentation of persons, yet playfully proclaims a paradox in human relations and in the human psyche such that this fragmentation is the essential partner to creativity, including the interpretation of texts. Like the squiggle game, hermeneutics is a process that embodies and forms a relationship between text and person or text and community. Like the squiggle game, hermeneutics takes place in a space in which there is no complete dominance of either objectivity or subjectivity. Like the squiggle game, hermeneutics involves both written and oral communication in the context of community.

Reading 4.4   Developmental Psychology in Biblical Studies

Lyn Bechtel

Lyn Bechtel here suggests that the structure of Genesis 2–4 can be understood in light of developmental theory. Employing an eclectic developmental model, she identifies the fundamental stages of development as infancy, early childhood, middle childhood, adolescence, and adulthood. This selection focuses on Genesis 2 in light of the stage of childhood. The developmental tasks particular to this stage include learning to make choices, developing speech and comprehension, developing friendships, and an early awareness of sexuality.

Developmental Theory and Genesis 2–4

Most interpretations of the Genesis 2:4b–3:24 myth are variation on the "sin and fall" of humanity, in which the human is assumed to be created as a fully grown adult. In that respect and many others, the interpretation does not fit

From Lyn Bechtel, "Developmental Psychology in Biblical Studies," in *Psychology and the Bible: A New Way to Read the Scriptures*, ed. J. Harold Ellens and Wayne G. Rollins (Westport, CT: Greenwood-Praeger, 2004), vol. 1, pp. 122-23, 124-27.

reality. "Sin and fall," however, may not be the most convincing and certainly not the only interpretation. The developmental character of Genesis 1 should point to the interpretation of Genesis 2–4. If Genesis 2–4 is interpreted as a portrayal of stages of human maturation, the story reveals a very sophisticated and multifaceted understanding of life. Humans go from being immature, infertile, dependent infants (2:7-9) and children (2:16-23), to increasingly independent adolescents (3:1-19), and finally to maturing, fertile, interdependent adults (4:1-16).[1] The characters should grow out of their immature understanding of life in the childhood world of the garden and into a mature discernment and acceptance of life in the adult world. Genesis 4:1-16 deals with one of the pitfalls of adult maturation — overcoming self-centeredness and threatened egotistic reactions. The four developmental stages are differentiated by three literary transitions that separate infancy from childhood (2:10-15), childhood from adolescence (2:24-25), and adolescence from adulthood (3:20-24). These literary transitions foreshadow the essential characteristics of adulthood. The three transitions and four developmental stages make human maturation resemble a seven-day week in which days are differentiated yet one day flows seamlessly into the next. A brief introduction (2:4b-6) lays out the time before the birth of humans, and we see the change from infertility to fertility that exemplifies the natural world and foreshadows the human process in adolescence.[2] In what follows, I give a brief description of the creation myth interpreted by drawing on developmental theory and general psychological insights. . . .

Childhood

The development during childhood is essential because without insight from each experience, the child will not have the foundation for the capacity to discern good and bad. With the onset of walking mobility, the child experiences initial socialization into the behavior that is acceptable and unacceptable at this stage in life. The child is now permitted to make simple *choices*. God says, "From the trees in the garden you may certainly eat" (Gen. 2:16). Eating of the

---

1. For a fuller exegesis of Gen. 2–5 as a maturation myth, see Lyn M. Bechtel, "Genesis 2.4b–3.24: A Myth about Human Maturation," *Journal for the Study of the Old Testament* 67 (1995): 3-26; "Rethinking the Interpretation of Genesis 2.4b–3.24," in *A Feminist Companion to Genesis*, ed. Athalya Brenner (Sheffield: Sheffield Academic Press, 1993), pp. 77-117.

2. Claude Lévi-Strauss, *Structural Anthropology* (New York: Basic Books, 1963), stresses that human beings need consonance between their perceptions of social and cosmic levels of experience.

trees is indicative of maturation and is necessary to sustain life in the face of death. It is the first step in understanding death and developing a mature understanding of life. Although God has filled the garden with the potential for maturation and for eventually acquiring adult knowledge, in *childhood* the tree of knowing good and bad (that is, adult discernment) is prohibited because attaining this tree before the child is ready could retard his growth by skipping over essential experiences that form the foundation for a broad intellectual, experiential, and sexual understanding of life. The limitation is *protective* because all children are curious and anxious to grow up and be like their parents. In childhood, all things are possible, *except growing up too fast.* As Rowan Williams, archbishop of Canterbury, points out, the childhood world cannot be stifled or shortchanged. A society that does not protect the childhood world will produce childish and dangerous adults.[3]

As children grow and learn from their experience, however, their possibilities and limitations change. Then God says that if you eat from the tree of knowing, "you will certainly die." The audience assumes that the child will instantly die, but he does not. The audience misunderstands God, which seems to be a human tendency. Although the wise snake tries to correct this misunderstanding of instant death, God's statement remains *ambiguous.* It could imply that as a result of eating from this tree, the child enters adulthood and develops an awareness of the function and inevitability of death. Or it could indicate that upon eating from this tree the human goes through a rite of passage into adulthood. A rite of passage entails the symbolic death of an old, immature perception of life in order to begin a more mature, more intricate level of understanding. That the child lacks the capacity for critical thinking is reflected in his never asking what "you will certainly die" means. He simply unquestioningly obeys.

One of the bothersome aspects of the limitation is that it is never rescinded. The answer lies in the prohibition given by most parents to their young children that they not cross the street alone. Because maturity cannot be imposed, there is no static formula to determine when children are mature enough to cross alone. When they are ready, parents normally remain in the background and watch as their children test their newly acquired autonomy and capacity for discernment. Because few parents ever rescind the prohibi-

3. "We are, or should be, shocked and sickened by pictures of thirteen-year-olds conscripted into an army (as occurred in the Iran-Iraq war and practiced in some of the rebel militias of Africa); by parentless, homeless, criminalized children in the urban streets of Brazil or Guatemala, regularly butchered by police and security forces; by child prostitution and sexual abuse. There is a peculiar horror and pathos in children not allowed to be children." Rowan Williams, *Lost Icons* (London: Continuum, 2002), p. 2.

tion, disobedience affords the definitive break with the past that allows a new capacity to be used.

God declares that being alone is *not good*. Humans need a sense of relationship to the ground, other beings, and one another. Thus, God forms the animals from the ground as "helping companions."[4] Because animals do not bring ego concerns into the relationship and accept people just as they are, they are excellent companions for children learning to relate. In addition, when the child becomes an adult, animals remain helping companions, "co-producing" food to "sustain life" The creation of the animals adds three new capacities: (1) the acquisition of language skills with which to conceptualize, name, and categorize reality; (2) the beginning of identity formation through differentiation of the self from others; and (3) the relational skills with which to foster social identity. In Genesis 1, God conceptualizes and names, which is what the child now does; he is beginning to function in the image of God. As the child categorizes the animals, he becomes aware of the life-preserving domesticated beasts and the life-threatening wild animals, which leads to a "re-sorting" of the animals according to their helpfulness. Because language is one of the chief agents of cognitive development and reasoning, these experiences initiate the capacity for discernment necessary for the tree of knowing.

In the Genesis story, there is no division of childhood into early and middle, unless there is a conceptual division between the creation of the animals and the creation of the woman. Now the child has a deeper existential need — a helping companion to "co-produce" life. Having learned to relate to the animals, the child is ready for gender differentiation, so he can learn to interact with the opposite sex and acquire a social identity. Consequently, God "builds" the woman by putting the man into a deep sleep or symbolic death — demonstrating that new life springs from death.[5] This symbolic death prefigures the symbolic death of the adolescent's rite of passage.

The imagery of God "building" the woman from a rib is fascinating. The Hebrew word for *rib* has an architectural dimension, like Sumerian "rib vaulting" that supports and protects the entire structure, implying symbolically that the woman is built from strength. In addition, in Genesis 6:1-4 women "build" houses, that is, households or dynasties. Thus, when the woman is named, she is called Eve/Life, the Mother of all Life, because she "builds" life. God builds the builder.

---

4. In the Gilgamesh myth, before Enkidu begins to mature and can relate to women, he runs with and relates to the wild animals.

5. In the Gilgamesh myth, sleep is portrayed as the "brother" of death — different yet related.

Because the child has benefitted from his conceptualization experience, he speaks for the first time, declaring that the woman is bone of his bone and flesh of his flesh.[6] In the second wordplay, woman/man *('iššă/'iš)*, the child demonstrates his ability to discern *unity and separation*, which is foreshadowed in Genesis 2:10-15 and 24-25. He comprehends that a man is "flesh and bone;" "formed" from the flesh like clay of the ground, and a woman is "flesh and bone," "built" from a rib/bone.

The woman/man wordplay is peculiar, however. In the *'adam/'adama* wordplay, the word *'adam* can be taken out of the word *'adama,* demonstrating that the human is born from the ground yet always retains unity with it. But here the word woman *('iššă)* cannot be taken out of the word man *('iš);* linguistically the wordplay does not work. Although it demonstrates the differentiated unity between men and women, it does not represent the natural process of men being born from women. However, because the children still lack full understanding of life and the sexual maturity to produce life, the noticeable incongruity in the wordplay points to the need for a change, namely, physical and intellectual maturation. When the man and woman are sexually mature, the wordplay is set right in Genesis 4:1, where a man *('iš)* is born from a woman *('iššă).*

———

SUGGESTIONS FOR FURTHER READING

Behaviorism

Bufford, Rodger K. "God and Behavior Mod: Some Thoughts Concerning Relationships between Biblical Principles and Behavior Modification." *Journal of Psychology and Theology* 5 (1977): 13-22.

———. *The Human Reflex: Behavioral Psychology in Biblical Perspective.* San Francisco: Harper & Row, 1981.

Reynierse, James H. "A Behavioristic Analysis of the Book of Job." *Journal of Psychology and Theology* 3 (1975): 75-81.

Learning Theory

Callan, Terrance. *Psychological Perspectives on the Life of Paul: An Application of*

---

6. Actually, the human's response should have been, "Boy, is she built!"

the Methodology of Gerd Theissen. Studies in the Bible and Early Christianity 22. Lewiston/Queenston/Lampeter: Edwin Mellen, 1990.

Kille, D. Andrew. "Imitating Jesus: Jesus as Model in Cognitive Learning Theory." In *Text and Community: Essays in Honor of Bruce M. Metzger,* edited by J. Harold Ellens, vol. 2. Sheffield: Sheffield Phoenix Press, 2007.

Mitternacht, Dieter. "Theissen's Integration of Psychology and New Testament Studies: Learning Theory, Psychodynamics and Cognitive Psychology." In *Psychology and the Bible: A New Way to Read the Scriptures,* edited by J. Harold Ellens and Wayne G. Rollins, vol. 1, 101-17. Westport, CT: Praeger, 2004.

Object Relations

Dykstra, Robert C. *Discovering a Sermon: Personal Pastoral Preaching.* St. Louis: Chalice Press, 2001.

Underwood, Ralph. "Object Relations Theory and Mark 15:33-39: Interpreting Ourselves Interpreting the Bible." In *Psychology and the Bible: A New Way to Read the Scriptures,* edited by J. Harold Ellens and Wayne G. Rollins, vol. 3, 29-40. Westport, CT: Praeger, 2004.

Developmental

Bechtel, Lyn M. "Genesis 2.4b–3.24: A Myth about Human Maturation." *Journal for the Study of the Old Testament* 67 (1995): 3-26.

Benson, Purnell H. "New Testament Concepts for a Sociopsychological Model of Personality Development." In *Spiritual Well-Being: Sociological Perspectives,* edited by David O. Moberg, 51-71. Washington, DC: University Press of America, 1979.

Lynch, Thomas H. "Corroboration of Jungian Psychology in the Biblical Story of Abraham." *Psychotherapy: Theory, Research & Practice* 8 (1971): 315-18.

Vogels, Walter. "The Inner Development of Job: One More Look at Psychology and the Book of Job." *Science et Esprit* 35 (1983): 227-30.

CHAPTER 5

Between Texts and Readers

It is possible to interpret without observing, but not to observe without interpreting.

Mason Cooley[1]

I have found the Bible, its stories and messages, to be about the most helpful sparring partner that I have had since I was ten years old.

Donna$_2$[2]

What happens when a person reads the Bible? The Bible is a text, and the process of reading it is much the same as reading any text. The process of reading has been compared to a conversation between the author (or, at least, the words of the author) and the reader. Hermeneutics, the study of interpretation, focuses on all the factors that affect the interaction of text, reader, and context.

Early models of interpretation conceived the conversation as being essentially one-way. The author has an idea that he or she wishes to convey to the reader, and, as the reader is not immediately present, writes it down as if speaking to the reader. The reader then reads what has been written and hears it as if it were spoken conversation, and through the words grasps the idea that the writer sought to express.

Few now accept this simple and straightforward model. Even in a one-

1. Mason Cooley, *City Aphorisms,* fifth selection (New York, 1988).
2. In H. Edward Everding Jr., Mary W. Wilcox, Lucinda A. Huffaker, and Clarence H. Snelling Jr., *Viewpoints: Perspectives of Faith and Christian Nurture* (Harrisburg, PA: Trinity Press International, 1998), pp. 51-52.

on-one conversation, we are aware that many things can help or hinder understanding. It is clear that communication is a far more complex and many-layered phenomenon than a one-way "author → text → reader" model can express. Freudian psychology, in particular, suggested that even a conversation is not simple information sharing — there are unconscious factors at work that color what and how we understand from each other, leading Paul Ricoeur to advocate a "hermeneutics of suspicion" as a counter to overly simplistic interpretations.[3]

A frequent objection often raised in applying psychological perspectives to biblical texts is that there is no "psyche" present — a text is not a person, and the ancient author is no longer present to answer questions or explain what was on his or her mind in the writing. It is unmistakable, though, that the process of reading, interpreting, and responding to the Bible does involve at least one very real psyche — that of the reader. Without a reader, a text is literally meaningless; and the moment a reader enters the picture, psychological factors come into play. Along with the unconscious dimensions outlined by Freud, a reader brings perceptual frameworks, cognitive processes, personality factors, social conditioning, and more to the process of reading.

Reader-response criticism, in both literary and biblical studies, focuses on this encounter of reader and text. Seeking to describe and explore the process of reading, reader-response critics often build on covert and vaguely defined models of learning and cognition that are fundamentally psychological. One critic, Norman Holland, consciously bases his approach on Freudian principles. He argues that when a reader reads, he or she unconsciously brings an "identity theme" to the text. In reading, the individual first filters the text's meanings through this identity theme, and then, through fantasy and imagination, strengthens his or her identity. This process, he suggests, explains how it is that different readers find different interpretations of the same text — interpretation is based more on personality than on anything in the text itself.[4]

Holland and Ricoeur caution us to be suspicious of unconscious dimensions in interpretation; still, reading is not a purely subjective process. A reader's psyche does not completely overpower the text. Our ways of expressing the experience of reading suggest that there is, in truth, a conversation partner. We "encounter" a text, are "confronted" by it. It "speaks" to us, and we may find ourselves "wrestling" with it. The biblical text is not simply an object; it is experienced as a presence. Paul Ricoeur describes the encounter of

---

3. Paul Ricoeur, *Freud and Philosophy: An Essay on Interpretation* (New Haven: Yale University Press, 1970).

4. Norman Holland, *Five Readers Reading* (New Haven: Yale University Press, 1975).

reader and text as creating "the world in front of the text," a kind of energy field, if you will, in which a (multidimensional) reader encounters the (potential) meanings of the polyvalent text.[5] This "world in front of the text" is similar in many ways to the "transitional" world described by the object relations psychology of Winnicott and Pruyser described in reading 4.3.

In other chapters of this book we reflect on elements of the text itself that have the potential to affect the reader — symbols and archetypal themes, psychodynamic factors, therapeutic and pathological dimensions. Here we focus on what the reader brings to the process of reading and interpreting the text. In the readings below, we consider unconscious dynamics in interpretation, the role of cognitive frameworks, and the impact of personality type.

Reading 5.1   The Psychology of Biblical Interpretation

CEDRIC B. JOHNSON

In his book *The Psychology of Biblical Interpretation,* Cedric Johnson begins with a consideration of the structures of the mind itself and then traces how such individual traits as cognitive style, perceptual expectations, personal creativity and mental sets, dogmatism, and left- and right-brain phenomena may influence interpretation. Finally, he considers the social-psychological forces at work in the interpreter's relationship to a group or culture. In this excerpt, he discusses the effect of the unconscious psychodynamics of reaction formation, selective attention, and transference.

Personal uniqueness, bias, and the process of how we perceive the world around us can fall under the general title of Personality. There is both semantic and theoretical confusion about the definition of *personality.* I will use the

5. Paul Ricoeur, *Interpretation Theory: Discourse and the Surplus of Meaning* (Fort Worth: Texas Christian University Press, 1976), p. 78.

From Cedric B. Johnson, *The Psychology of Biblical Interpretation* (Grand Rapids: Zondervan, 1983), pp. 42-43, 45-50.

term in a very general sense to indicate the relatively enduring and important characteristics, both conscious and unconscious, observable and unobservable, that exert a strong influence on an individual's behavior.

The behavior I seek to explore is that of biblical interpreters as they engage in the exploration of the meaning and application of Scripture. The biblical data are sometimes distorted through the "spectacles" of our personality.

What causes bias in the way people interpret the data of the world around them? Is it a matter of different perspectives as in the reports of persons who view an accident? Do people have unconscious biases in their perspective? Are there such factors as different cognitive styles where *different* is not necessarily wrong?

The Unconscious

Part of this bias may stem from what has been termed "the unconscious." . . . Sigmund Freud (1856-1939) compared the mind to an iceberg with conscious processes represented by the tip. Most levels of awareness operate unconsciously; they are like the rest of the iceberg below the surface.

. . . What can Freud say to biblical interpreters? The answer could well be: "Be cautious about the impact of your unconscious processes on the application of meaning." Unconscious processes are manifested in reaction formation, selective attention, and a transference relationship with the text. We will consider each of these in turn.

Reaction Formation

One of the functions of the unconscious mind is the management of certain anxious thoughts. The mind uses various devices to deal with anxiety; these are described by psychodynamic theorists as unconscious defense mechanisms. A person may distort reality in attempting to reduce anxiety. One such defense is *reaction formation,* which may take two forms: (1) the person may fight actively against the thing that provokes anxiety; (2) the reaction of the person is just the opposite of what he/she is really feeling. A homophobic person who actively crusades against homosexuals may be defending against his or her own homosexual impulses. The crusader for prohibition could be defending his or her unconscious fear of substance abuse, or impulse control.

To suggest that every time a person had a strong feeling or behaved aggressively in a certain direction, he or she was attempting to reduce anxiety with a reaction formation would be reductionistic. However, one wonders about the motivation of persons who overreact. Believing that an attitude of overreaction to homosexuality, for example, would not affect one's interpretation of Scriptures that deal with homosexuality would be naive, and to say that the person is manifesting a reaction formation defense against the fear of homosexuality is unwarranted. We may suspect a reaction formation in the person who says, "God could not be opposed to anything so fulfilling as homosexual love," or who proceeds to explain away all comments in the Bible against it. Such a person could be defending against the anxiety-provoking thought that homosexual behavior is in fact a dysfunctional expression of one's sexuality.

Selective Attention

Selective attention is another aspect of the psychological unconscious. Shevarin and Dickman point out that, "Inherent in all the major models of attention is the assumption that at least part of the cognition related to attention takes place outside of awareness."[1] Ongoing psychological processes are affected by these beyond-the-awareness cognitions. Evidence for the latter comes from experimental studies rather than clinical observations. The fact that a person attends to one issue and neglects another has wide support. The issue under discussion at this point relates to unconscious influences on selective attention. We need to be aware of ex post facto decisions that rule absolutely *why* a person has interpreted a passage of Scripture in one way and not another. After-the-fact psychological explanations can be notoriously inaccurate and open to hindsight biases. David Myers writes:

> In our psychological society a speculative psychology-of-the-gaps pops up everywhere to explain human behaviors not yet explainable scientifically. Oedipal interpretations of homosexuality, existential theories of the popularity of Star Wars, and psychodynamic explanations of Richard Nixon's enigmatic behavior are offered to a public that can hardly be expected to discriminate psychology's hunches from its established facts.[2]

The problem with psychodynamic concepts such as selective attention, the unconscious, and reaction formation is that they are not subject to many types of scientific investigation.

1. Howard Shevarin and Scott Dickman, "The Psychological Unconscious: A Necessary Assumption for All Psychological Theory," *American Psychologist,* May 1980, p. 423.
2. David G. Myers, *The Inflated Self* (New York: Seabury, 1980), p. 105.

Note that, at this stage in modern American culture, to say that a phenomenon is unscientific is tantamount to saying that it is absolutely wrong. The word "science" exercises the kind of authoritative sway that the Christian religion did during the Puritan era of American history. Richard Gelwick writes: "Events and ideas have combined to convince the modern world that the objective ideal of knowledge is the method of science and hallmark of truth, even though it is not practiced in science nor capable of establishing truth."[3]

Even behaviorists cannot maintain a scientific position that includes total objectivity. They have chosen a methodology that responds only to observable behavior and refuses to make inferences about unconscious motivation. There are environments other than the laboratory where unconscious processes can be observed. The relationship between the patient and his or her psychotherapist is one such context.

The Text and Transference

Psychotherapists describe the unconscious and stereotyped ways by which a person relates to the authority symbol or person as transference.[4] Such an interpersonal perceptive distortion causes a person to relate to an authority "as if" the relationship were part of an early childhood conflict. Some therapists recognize and utilize the "as if" quality of the relationship between them and their patients as a part of the psychotherapeutic process. Often the patient transfers to the therapist feelings that the patient experienced towards a significant authority figure in childhood. Just how certain therapists utilize the transference phenomenon is not my immediate concern, but the results of transference must be noted. A developmental perspective helps us understand transference. A child learns the experience of trust in the first six months of life. If, for some reason, the child was deprived of a nurturing relationship with the primary care giver during that period, the experience of trust in later life becomes severely disturbed. As an adult, such a person may be inhibited in intimacy, doubt the best intentions of others, distrust authorities (including the Bible) and generally feel insecure. They relate to the authority "as if" it were the care giver from the past. Such a patient, deprived of childhood experiences of trust, may distrust his or her therapist.

3. Richard Gelwick, *The Way of Discovery: An Introduction to the Thought of Michael Polanyi* (New York: Oxford University Press, 1977), p. 15.

4. The idea that a person can experience a transference relationship with the text of Scripture was first presented to me by a student, Lee Erickson, in 1980.

Different childhood experiences of authority produce different adult conflicts. Some adults manifest a passive surrender to superior power. They have a series of unquestioning responses to authority symbols and persons. A classic Candid Camera television show illustrated such compliance to authority symbols. A traffic signal was placed in the middle of a sidewalk near a busy shopping center. A number of parcel-laden persons would stop on the sidewalk when the signal was red. There was no logical reason for their behavior except for their unquestioning compliance with a symbol of authority — the traffic signal.

The fact that the Scriptures are authoritative in their meaning and in our lives needs to become a part of the mind set of all believers. However, the term "authority" provokes different images and responses in different people. Psychotherapists recognize that some people have problems with authority. Of these, some become very compliant in the presence of an authority, others rebel against symbols and people of authority. The Bible is authoritative, but for some people it evokes the wrong image of authority. They have an unconscious response to the Scriptures as if they are being taught by authority figures from their past. They are not relating to the Bible like the Bereans in Paul's day, who "examined the Scriptures every day to see if what Paul said was true" (Acts 17:11). Their reflexive response sometimes distorts the true meaning of Scripture.

Consider the effect of transference on biblical interpretation. One person may respond to the Scripture rebelliously because it tells him or her to behave in a certain manner. Another person may respond with unquestioning compliance to the scriptural applications of an authority figure (e.g., the preacher). In both instances, compliance and rebellion, the real meaning of the Scripture could be distorted by an unconscious transference relationship.

No matter, then, how a person chooses to approach the phenomenon of unconscious motivation, we all approach our world with a unique legacy of learned responses. Whether we call these "unconscious responses," or see them as aspects of our person that we choose to ignore, they can impact the process of biblical interpretation.

Transference is not the only manifestation of reflexive responses to past events. We all have painful events in our past that impinge on the present. Take for instance the development of our feelings toward the term "father." For some the term evokes feelings of warmth, affection, and acceptance. When they come to the Scriptures and read that God is their father, they have a positive response. However, for others the term evokes a negative response. J. B. Phillips recognized such interpretative distortions in his excellent book, *Your God Is Too*

Small.[5] God may be viewed as a policeman who is out to get us. The genesis of such distortions is often to be found in a person's developmental history. Take the case of the Christian woman who views God as a distant and judgmental parent. Her developmental history reveals such a relationship with her father. During her teenage years her father became afraid of the incestuous thoughts he was having. Instead of dealing with his thoughts he defended himself against them by distancing himself emotionally from his daughter. The child experienced this defensive act as personal rejection. When she became a Christian she transferred this fear to her heavenly father. Her interpretation of Scripture was therefore distorted through such an unconscious response. One can only wonder about the events in a person's past that lead to an overemphasis on such things as the holiness or the love of God. Could not whole systems of theology have been impacted by such unconscious transference?

Reading 5.2   Viewpoints: Perspectives of Faith
            and Christian Nurture

H. EDWARD EVERDING JR. ET AL.

Edward Everding and his colleagues asked students at Iliff School of Theology in Denver a series of questions about their interpretation of the Bible and its authority, their understanding of truth, and their interpretation of tradition. From the responses they identified four basic cognitive orientations that shaped the students' faith and understanding. The four perspectives are denoted as "A, B, C, and D," but for the sake of discussion, they are personalized as "Affiliating Al," "Bargaining Betty," "Conceptualizing Charles," and "Dialectical Donna." While most individuals will, in fact, display a mixture of the four types, the study shows vividly how personality factors can affect interpretation of the Bible.

This reading is based on students' responses to 2 Timothy 3:14-17:

But as for you, continue in what you have learned and firmly believed, knowing from whom you learned it, and how from childhood you have known the

---

5. J. B. Phillips, *Your God Is Too Small* (New York: Macmillan, 1953).

From H. Edward Everding Jr., Mary W. Wilcox, Lucinda A. Huffaker, and Clarence H. Snelling Jr., *Viewpoints: Perspectives of Faith and Christian Nurture* (Harrisburg, PA: Trinity Press International, 1998), pp. 24, 29-30, 32-33, 40-41, 42-43, 49, 51-52, 58-59.

sacred writings that are able to instruct you for salvation through faith in Christ Jesus. All scripture is inspired by God and is useful for teaching, for reproof, for correction, and for training in righteousness, so that everyone who belongs to God may be proficient, equipped for every good work.

The students were asked "What do you feel stands out for you in this biblical text?" and "What do you think is the main point of the text?"

Perspective A: Affiliating Al

Al's Interpreting Style

When Al interprets 2 Timothy 3:14-17, he tends to focus on abstract meanings or guidelines that are personal, true, and authoritative. Al_1 (male, age 21) focuses on the abstract and generalized meaning of "usefulness." *What do you feel stands out for you in this biblical text?* "That the scriptures are useful." *Why is that particularly significant to you?* "That they are useful, well, because I am studying to be a minister and I should hope that they are useful in some way."

Al_2 (female, age 43) applies the text in an abstract but uncritical way, indicating an understanding of authority as external and absolute ("God's plan"). *What do you think is the main point of the text?* "For me the main point is not that the Bible has been divinely inspired or some such thing. You can also take the knowledge that you are going to get, because that is where we are in seminary and do something with it because that also is God's plan for us."

Al_3 (female, age 37) abstracts meaning on the level of personal inspiration and support. His response also seems to understand scripture as an external authority. *What stands out for you in this biblical text?* "I think the text is an inspiration to teachers of the scripture, Bible scripture, to reach others, and also a support of teachers in trying times, that they might have to reflect back on scripture for their own support." . . .

Summary[1]

Al's faith perspective sees a right or wrong world, a true or false world. The group with which he identifies sets the norms for determining the absolute truths of the Bible and the correct past traditions that he can pass on to oth-

---

1. In the original, these sections are titled "Summary and Table" and include detailed tables of the attributes of each orientation, which have been omitted here for the sake of space.

ers. The content that takes center stage for Al's normative group could be literary-critical biblical scholarship, pietistic evangelicalism, feminist theology, or any number of other subject areas. The illustrations from our research data reflect the influences of the learning environment of a "liberal" graduate school of theology that values new information and critical thinking. That is, these students were expected to change and, for the most part, they adapted to that expectation. For example, Al_2 has become very aware of "my blacks and whites," and Al_6 knows that "I'm going to have to have some type of form" with which to think differently.

Although the structure of our thinking forms the essential framework for meaning, content also plays a significant role in enhancing (or restricting) the broadening, enriching faith potential for each perspective. Content includes not only ideas, images, and concerns, but also the covert and implicit expectations and norms of the environment in which one's thinking takes place. Whatever the content, Al identifies truths as those personal guidelines, examples, and doctrines which provide an abstract but clear set of directions for what he can interpret from the Bible and apply to his life. Some Als may see themselves grounded in absolute truths that they uncritically and tacitly apprehend, whereas other Als see themselves as alive to a world of abstract ideas that enable them to soar beyond a concrete and literal world of biblical interpretation. . . .

Perspective B: Bargaining Betty

Betty's Interpreting Style

When Betty interprets 2 Timothy 3:14-17, she tends to focus on the message, guidelines, or instructions that she feels are useful and workable, but she does not assume that these are necessarily applicable to anyone else. Her way of thinking rejects explicit, absolute understandings of the Bible, because she recognizes diversity within it or within interpretations of it, but she may still long for a hidden absolute as something consistent that can be relied upon.

$Betty_1$ (male, age 21) holds an external view of authority ("the things that have to be done") but bases the differences of interpretation she finds upon "the way a person feels." *What do you think is the main point of the text?* "If you take all these things, all these things will fit together and you'll have the closeness to God that's desired by most everyone." *Are you saying you agree or disagree with the text?*

I agree with the things that have to be done, but I disagree with the fact that they have to be just that, I guess. I don't feel it takes into consideration the real feeling of the person, that sort of thing, and I think that's an important part of it, too, the way a person feels. He may have a legitimate reason why he feels that way; and why would I argue with him if he truly believes that way? Maybe he feels he's gotten close to God the way he is.

Betty$_2$ (male, age 29) interprets the text in terms of an abstract concept or message ("foundation") that is applicable to one's experience and that should be instructive. *What do you think is the main point of the text?* "Basically, I would say that it wants you to know that what you have learned in the past is very important. . . . You established a foundation to this point, and you should use that foundation throughout the rest of your life." *What do you feel about the text?* "I agree with it because I see that is what has happened in my life. It has been affirmed in my life." *Would you summarize what you think the text is all about?*

The foundations are very important, and you should continue to build upon [them]. It also uses all the tools that you learned in that growing-up period to, again, add to your life. You shouldn't discount them even though some of them are bad and some of them are good. Basically, the point is that the Bible is something that is constantly in use, one of those tools. It is something that should be used.

Betty$_3$ (male, age 32) rejects the Bible as infallible or absolute. She is aware of its "contradictions" and inconsistencies. Yet she thinks it can still provide "unfailing" guidance, which for her is an implicit absolute. *What do you think is the main point of the text?* "I agree that what you have learned is very important in the Christian context. . . . Let it be your guide as you go on in becoming truly the man of God." *Do you agree or disagree?* "I agree with the portion that says don't abandon what you have learned. The inference there is that what you have learned is good, and one should never abandon what he has learned that is good. The disagreement is also the inference that the Bible is infallible, that the Bible cannot be questioned or refuted." *Why do you disagree?* "I am not a biblical scholar, but the formation of the Bible, for example, from all that was written in early Christian history was, at best, a haphazard process. The Bible offers many contradictions. My feeling is that if the Bible was divinely inspired, there would not be so much inconsistency in it." *Can you summarize what you think the scripture is all about?* "The text is encouragement. It is encouragement in saying that what you have been doing is good. . . . Keep at it, but also move forward, that you have more to learn. But never lose sight of the fact that the Bible is an unfailing guide to lead you into righteousness, that the, Bible is an index of how one becomes right with God." . . .

Summary

Betty's perspective of faith demonstrates her ability to perceive, understand, and accept multiplicity. This is perhaps the distinguishing feature of perspective B. This interpreting style identifies what is useful or workable for the interpreter, but it is not necessarily applicable to anyone else. Betty is a bargainer in the sense that the Bible may have ultimate authority for her, but she will not impose that understanding on anyone else. She will explore various traditions (including religious traditions other than her own) with interest, respect, and self-reflection. Biblical images, messages, guidelines, and meanings are pondered in terms of their meaningfulness for Betty, and although she might suspect or hope that there is an unshakable truth to be discovered, she will not impose evaluative criteria on someone else's meaning. That's the bargain! . . .

Perspective C: Conceptualizing Charles

Charles's Interpreting Style

When Charles interprets 2 Timothy 3:14-17, he analyzes it and presents his conclusions in abstract concepts of meaning.

Charles$_1$ (male, age 22) analyzes the function of faith and contextualizes as "a problem of language" the possible meaning of scripture as inspired. He assumes responsibility for his own learning by evaluating the text's consistency with other parts of his experience. *What do you feel stands out for you in this biblical text?* "The faith that you have already gotten inside you is the guiding principle, and that scripture, however inspired it may be, should be used to instruct others for salvation for faith in Jesus Christ. I think scripture has been inspired by God. Of course, you get into a problem of language. But I think it should be used in context, in relation to the faith you already had inside you." *How do you feel about the text?* "I could . . . see how it is useful for my own belief that I have learned and internalized, because I read it and I can identify with it. If it said something else, I'd have to think on that and say, 'Well, is that consistent with the way I feel about it and the way I think, in context with other scriptures as well?' I'd have to analyze it."

Charles$_2$ (male, age 27) reasons analytically from the evidence to a conclusion that he describes using concepts of "growing" and "completeness." He continues to examine the text for other possible meanings, focusing on the ideas it conveys. *What do you think is the main point of the text?* "I'd be hard put to pick out one main point, because on the one hand the author is encouraging the reader to continue from what you have learned, and yet he also goes on to say that scripture will help you continue to grow. It will help you be complete. I suppose those really aren't two different points, but maybe subpoints of the idea of continue to grow to become more complete." *How do you feel about the text?* "I almost got a feeling of . . . the idea of look out for things that are wrong and stuff like this. But as I read on, there's so much talk about growth and teaching, the idea of learning — that sort of got rid of that [initial] feeling. It's more of a positive, very alive type of thing that the writer is trying to encourage, not a closedmindedness."

Charles$_3$ (male, age 33) analyzes what he concludes is the writer's main point and then differentiates his own position, based on literary and historical criteria. *What do you think is the main point of the text?* "The main point, it seems to me, is that the scripture is primary, that it is really all we need, that it is of utmost importance." *What do you think it is all about?*

> I wouldn't take the writer's view of the scripture as kind of the final word or the only word of God. I think scriptures are very important and something that I hold dear to myself, but I think that all the scriptures are not inspired by God, and that we can experience and find God outside of scriptures. So I guess what I would do with the text is to see it as a kind of an injunction for me or as a reminder to me of the importance of scripture. . . . I think much of the Bible is myth, poetry, some of it not very inspired poetry, and I think a lot of it is nationalistic literature, history of a people as they have come to understand themselves, and so I think that [it] is good for study and so forth, but I am not sure that it is inspired or that it could be called profitable.

Charles$_4$ (female, age 38) draws a distinction between his own understanding of the text as "inspired" and a common appropriation of it as "the divine word of God." Then he cites criteria for a rational methodology that searches for a more accurate interpretation. *What do you think is the main point of the text?* "Well, I think this is probably prooftexting for many by saying that the Bible is the divine word of God and it should be regarded accordingly and it is all of . . . equal value. . . . I think that is the way it is used. That is not where I come out personally. Well, I think the scriptures are inspired, but I don't believe they are dictated by God. . . . There are a good many inconsistencies." *What do you think the text is all about?* "Well, I would say from my own point of view, we do need to study and know scripture, but that includes knowing when it was written, the circumstances of who wrote it, why they wrote it, when they wrote it, a good many other things that have to do with where it came from and what it means. And simply to say that it is all the word of God is not accurate." . . .

Summary

The search for rationality characterizes Charles's perspective of faith. He understands himself as a reasoning and reflective being who takes responsibility for his own growth and creation of meaning. He interprets biblical texts by analyzing images and abstracting concepts that are consistent, clear, and coherent. This might involve using critical procedures developed by various academic disciplines to demythologize symbols and stories in order to obtain interpretations that are appropriate for his contemporary context.

In his search for rational meaning, Conceptualizing Charles also struggles with how people have been confronted by God within the context of different communities and traditions. The determination of authority for Charles is basically an internal, rational process, so he analyzes traditions for their validity and chooses to endorse or transmit those he reasons to be most adequate. Although Charles can assess and understand the rational validity of concepts and theories other than his own, he will often dichotomize those understandings by contrasting and polarizing opposing viewpoints. . . .

Perspective D: Dialectical Donna

Donna's Interpreting Style

When Donna interprets 2 Timothy 3:14-17, she analyzes it and dialogues with it for the disclosure of images, ideas, and new meanings that can be integrated into her self-understanding and personal commitment. Donna$_1$ (female, age 33) demonstrates this very effectively with her critical self-awareness of different, almost contradictory meanings she can discover in a single text. *What do you think is the main point of the text?* "I guess, for me, that by being aware of what we have learned and from whom we learned it and what the instructions are — they are valuable and therefore, we may be complete if we follow those things and act on them." *Do you agree or disagree, and why?*

There are a few phrases in it [that] I have trouble with. Yet, when I go beyond just my first reaction to them, I at least can appreciate even those. . . . The phrase that first struck me wrong was "for reproof." I heard that as being critical. "You aren't doing it right. That is the way you ought to do it." Yet, when I go beyond that, I think of the essence of discipline and discipleship and appreciate that as a part of [it]. That is the way I would interpret "for reproof, for correction."

Donna₂ (female, age 38) makes reference to a similar dialectic that she experiences with the Bible as a "sparring partner." *What do you feel stands out for you in this text?* "I guess that although I am not a believer in biblical inerrancy or that kind of thing, I have found the Bible, its stories and messages, to be about the most helpful sparring partner that I have had since I was ten years old. I have been going back and forth since that time and find it to be a very helpful dimension." *How do you feel about the text? Do you agree or disagree?* "The concept of canon is important to me, so just because I don't particularly like one passage, I would not prefer that it be cut out of the Bible. I would rather that it be there and scratched me occasionally. Maybe at some point it will be helpful."

Donna₃ (female, age 34) analyzes and integrates both abstract ("as a learner") and personal ("my understanding") meanings from the text. She enlarges her interpretation to include several types of communities. *What stands out for you in this biblical text?* "I think as a learner I am engaged in learning continually, and I learn as a member of a specific faith community and as a member of another kind of community, which I guess I would call a societal community. All of those different areas of my life integrate to give me a sense of being a part of all human endeavor." *Please summarize what the text is all about.* "I think the text is calling on me to consider the validity of the roots of my tradition, my own understanding of ministry of service and what I think it is all about . . . and how I go about using that tradition as a part of my understanding of what ministry is."

Donna₄ (male, age 31) also describes interpretation as an interactive relationship with a text that is fluid ("malleable") but coherent ("foundation," "structure"), not haphazard. *How do you feel about the text?*

Well, to me it has a really nice flavor, probably because of my childhood and background. There were times when I thought it was pretty ridiculous to participate in some of the things that I was taught, and yet the older I got, the more I was [convinced] that it was really sound stuff, solid foundational stuff with which I could build in my own structure — all those persons who were in my life who helped me lay a foundation, you know, who have given me that foundation so that I can continue to learn in what I have been taught, what I really believe. It has become very malleable, the structure. It changes, depending on my life situation, but the foundation stays the same, so I've got a really good feeling about it. . . .

Summary

Donna's perspective of faith integrates feeling and reasoning with personal commitment. It is important to her to examine and articulate her location in a pluralistic and relativistic world. In her movement toward integrative thinking, she embraces ambiguity, complexity, and paradox as much as rationality. Donna cherishes dialogue with the Bible and with other persons as subjects or partners with whom she discovers new meanings. Within the larger context of communities and traditions, she experiences a personal confrontation with God through her engagement with diverse images, stories, and analysis of biblical texts.

Dialectical Donna understands herself in both continuity and discontinuity with traditions. The past is part of her, yet she takes responsibility for evaluating her past in terms of the aspects of her traditions that she will appropriate into her present commitments. Similarly, the Bible has authority for Donna, but she weighs its authority along with other kinds of authorities as she determines where she will stand within a relativistic world and within her community of faith. Truth is what Donna is committed to today, based upon how she examines data, what has been tested in history and community, and what makes sense of her particular personal and social life situation. . . .

Reading 5.3   Personality Type and Scripture

LESLIE J. FRANCIS

Founded originally on the model of personality described by C. G. Jung, the Myers-Briggs Personality Inventory identifies how individuals experience the world around them, organize their perceptions, and respond. Personality types are identified in relation to four sets of polarities: Introvert-Extravert (energy directed inwardly or outwardly), Intuitive-Sensing (preferring "the big picture" or individual details), Thinking-Feeling (evaluating by logical or relational standards), and Judging-Perceiving (preferring openness or closure). In the last reading, Leslie Francis comments on the implications of the Myers-Briggs personality types for one special type of biblical interpretation — preparation for preaching.

Personality Type and Preaching

The Myers-Briggs Type Indicator provides information about the individual's orientation (introversion or extraversion), perceiving process (sensing or intuition), judging process (thinking or feeling) and attitude towards the outer world (judging or perceiving). The crucial information for the preacher, however, centres on the two processes, that is to say on the two distinctions between sensing and intuition (the perceiving process) and between thinking and feeling (the judging process).

According to the theory, every individual needs to draw on all four functions of the two processes: sensing and intuition, thinking and feeling. But at the same time one of these four functions is preferred and becomes dominant. The four dominant functions of sensing and intuition, thinking and feeling, when dominant, approach the world in very different ways. These different approaches will be attracted by very different perspectives in preaching.

At its basic level, the sensing type needs to respond to facts and information, to details and clearly defined images. The intuitive type needs to respond to challenges to the imagination and arresting ideas, to theories and possibilities. The feeling type needs to respond to issues of the heart and to the stuff of human relationships. The thinking type needs to respond to issues of the head and to the stuff of logical analysis.

From Leslie J. Francis, *Personality Type and Scripture: Exploring Mark's Gospel* (London: Mowbray, 1997), pp. 9-10.

Of course, left to their own devices preachers will emphasize their own type preference. The preacher who prefers intuition will preach a message full of fast-moving ideas and imaginative associations. The sensing types in the congregation will quickly lose the thread and accuse those preachers of having their heads in the air and their shoes high above the ground. The preacher who prefers sensing will preach a message full of detailed information and the close analysis of text. The intuitive types in the congregation will quickly tire of the detail and accuse those preachers of being dull and failing to see the wood for the trees.

The preacher who prefers feeling will preach a message full of human interest and of loving concern for people. The thinking types in the congregation will quickly become impatient with this emphasis on interpersonal matters and accuse those preachers of failing to grasp the hard intellectual issues and the pressing challenges and contradictions of the faith. The preacher who prefers thinking will preach a message full of theological erudition and carefully argued nuance of perspective. The feeling types in the congregation will quickly become impatient with this emphasis on theological abstraction and accuse those preachers of missing the very heart of the gospel which cries out for compassion, understanding and human warmth.

SUGGESTIONS FOR FURTHER READING

Francis, L. J. *Personality Type and Scripture: Exploring Mark's Gospel.* London: Mowbray, 1997.

Francis, L. J., and P. Atkins. *Exploring Luke's Gospel: A Guide to the Gospel Readings in the Revised Common Lectionary.* London and New York: Mowbray, 2000.

————. *Exploring Matthew's Gospel: A Guide to the Gospel Readings in the Revised Common Lectionary.* London: Mowbray, 2001.

Holland, N. *Five Readers Reading.* New Haven: Yale University Press, 1975.

Oates, W. E. *The Bible in Pastoral Care.* Philadelphia: Westminster, 1953.

Rashkow, I. N. "Intertextuality, Transference and the Reader in/of the Biblical Text." In *Reading Between Texts,* ed. D. N. Fewell, 57-73. Louisville: Westminster/John Knox, 1992.

PART TWO

Case Studies
and Applications

CHAPTER 6

Biblical Symbols and
Archetypal Images

Because there are innumerable things beyond the range of human understanding, we constantly use symbolic terms to represent concepts that we cannot define or fully comprehend. This is one reason that all religions employ symbolic language or images.

C. G. Jung[1]

It has always been the prime function of myth and rite to supply the symbols that carry the human spirit forward, in contrast to those other constant human fantasies that tend to tie it back.

Joseph Campbell[2]

The year 1912 is most likely the birth date of depth psychological analysis of religious symbols, myths, and archetypal images. It was the year Jung published *Symbols of Transformation*. Overriding the caveats of Freud, Jung decided to descend into the heart of what Freud had called "the black tide of mud of occultism," namely the world of myths, stories, rituals, legends, and iconography of Christianity and Judaism, but also of Gnosticism, Babylonian religion, the oriental mysteries of Buddhism and Hinduism, and native American religion.

Jung began to see affinities between "religious" images and stories and those that spontaneously surfaced in the dream work of his clients. He came

1. Carl G. Jung, *Man and His Symbols* (New York: Dell Publishing, 1971), p. 21.
2. Joseph Campbell, *The Hero with a Thousand Faces* (New York: Pantheon Books, 1949), p. 11.

to realize that the language of the Bible, the sacred words of liturgy, and the symbolism of the Mass shared characteristics of symbols everywhere. They are the by-products of the human psyche bent on capturing realities that defy definition and that submit to discussion only in metaphorical form. Jung also began to reflect on their heuristic or constructive function in the life of the psyche.

Jung made a fundamental distinction between symbols and signs. Signs like "EXIT" or "$2.95 PER POUND" or "NO PARKING" are not symbols. They are the product of the conscious mind, bent on making one point very clearly and as unambiguously as possible. Signs can in time become symbols; symbols can revert to being signs; but the two do not function with the same effect in the human psyche.

When an image converts from the status of sign to symbol, something happens. "Wall Street" becomes more than a busy street in Lower Manhattan. "Jerusalem" becomes more than just another Middle Eastern capital. The "cross" becomes more than a Roman instrument of torture. And the "stars and stripes" and the "black swastika on a red field" become more than just national flags. Symbols don't send a single, simple, instant message. Symbols, unlike signs, are "alive" and somehow carry with them a piece of the living reality they represent.

The function and effect of symbols is not to inform the mind but to awaken consciousness. And as dream symbols emerge spontaneously from the unconscious to compensate for human consciousness, calling our attention to elements in our lives that consciousness has ignored, so the symbols produced in the literature or music or art or religion of a culture are enlisted in the task of transforming cultural consciousness and, at their best, introducing values and truths the culture has ignored and "needs to hear."

The secret of the power of symbol for the human psyche is that it gains a hearing from more than the rational and conscious side of the self. Far from being simply a visible icon that speaks to consciousness, it becomes a "psychic fact," capable of triggering the senses, arousing feelings, awakening intuitions, and stirring the deeps.

The glossary of biblical symbols is immense. There are geometric symbols, like the cross (1 Cor. 1:17) and the square (Rev. 21:16). There are numerical symbols, such as the ubiquitous numbers seven, twelve, and one; symbolic colors are found in the Bible, black for the mournful (Jer. 4:28), red for blood and violence (Rev. 6:4), and white for ritual purity (Ps. 51:7). Symbols of the human body, often applied as metaphors for God, include the voice (Isa. 6:8), the right and left hand (Matt. 25:33), and the face (of God) (Ps. 11:7). Animal symbolism ranges from the great beast to the serpent, the dove, and the lamb.

Natural symbols include the mountain, wind, sea, seed, harvest, the deep, and the rock. Sociocultural and household images abound, such as the symbols of the cup, the door, the shepherd, the garden, father, mother, temple, priest, king, and the shepherd's staff.

Jung identified a special class of symbol he called "archetypal images." Archetypes are primordial images that constitute a common heritage of humankind. Jung found them operative in what he called the "collective" or "objective [universal] unconscious." They are typical forms that appear spontaneously around the world, independently of tradition, in myths, fairytales, fantasies, dreams, visions, and the delusional systems of the insane. Joseph Campbell described these archetypal images as "a cast of inevitable stock characters that have played through all time, through the dreams and myths of all mankind, in ever-changing situations, confrontations, and costumes."[3]

One excellent example of these universally recurrent forms is the image of the "hero," which Joseph Campbell finds in various guises from Assyria, Babylon, Greece, and Rome, to Cambodia, Indonesia, Honduras, Argentina, and the Bible.

The Bible is filled with such stock figures of the psyche, from the image of a primordial garden with its primordial human pair, to the serpentine trickster figure, the tree of life, the sacred mountain, the wicked queen, the divine child, and the coming great age, to cite just a few. Walter Wink observes that such classical images appear

> so frequently in widely scattered mythic traditions that we are justified in regarding [them] . . . as a standard component in spiritual development. The very pervasiveness of such stories . . . is evidence that we are dealing with something fundamental to the spiritual journey itself, and not merely with etiological legends invented to "explain the origin of things."[4]

The psychological expeditions of Jung and Freud into the land of biblical symbols and archetypal images have enabled us to address questions previously unanswerable to biblical scholars, namely, how we can account for the catalytic effect of the Bible on the human heart, will, and mind. They also help solve the riddle why painters, novelists, poets, filmmakers, playwrights, and sculptors turn to Scripture for their subject matter. They also provide a clue as to what is so compelling to the human psyche about the Exodus jour-

3. Joseph Campbell, ed., *The Portable Jung* (New York: Viking Press, 1971), p. xxxi.
4. Walter Wink, "On Wrestling with God: Using Psychological Insights in Biblical Study," *Religion in Life* 47 (1978): 142.

ney, the story of Job, the Christ figure, the image of the prodigal son, or the lurid array of apocalyptic images of doom and ecstasy in the Book of Revelation.

Jung theorized that archetypal images emerge spontaneously in the human psyche to come to its assistance when it is in crisis, when it is at a crossroads, unsure of its next step. In such a situation, the right image, the right story, the right voice presents images of possibility that provide a way forward, energizing will and imagination. Symbols and archetypal images have power, as Jung observes:

> Whoever speaks in primordial images speaks with a thousand voices; he enthralls and overpowers, while at the same time he lifts the idea he is seeking to express out of the occasional and transitory into the realm of the ever-enduring. He transmutes our personal destiny into the destiny of mankind, and evokes in us all those beneficent forces that ever and anon have enabled humanity to find a refuge from every peril and to outlive the longest night.[5]

In the readings that follow, we will turn to discussion of some of these images, with an essay on water symbolism in Christian baptism, a survey of the plethora of archetypal images that populate the pages of the Bible, and a discussion of an unusual portrait of Christ in terms of the archetype of the "holy fool."

5. Carl Gustav Jung, *The Collected Works of C. G. Jung*, trans. R. F. C. Hull, ed. Gerhard Adler et al., Bollingen Series 20 (Princeton: Princeton University Press, 1953-78), vol. 15, par. 129.

Reading 6.1   Water as a Religious Symbol

PATRICK HENRY

Patrick Henry is one of the first among New Testament scholars to include a chapter on the role of psychological studies in biblical interpretation. In this chapter he cites the observations of cultural historian Mircea Eliade and the commentary of Freudian-oriented Richard Rubenstein on the psychological significance of water symbolism in the rite of baptism.

In a curious sixth-century Byzantine treatise there is an account of an emergency baptism in the desert. A [man] . . . who has joined some Christian refugees from war falls desperately ill, and asks to be baptized. No water is available, so one member of the group pours sand over the man's head and pronounces the trinitarian formula ("I baptize you in the name of the Father, Son, and Holy Spirit"). The illness abates, the man recovers, and when the refugees get back home they ask the bishop whether the baptism was valid. There is no problem with the lay status of the one who did the baptizing; from very early times the church recognized the right of lay persons to perform the sacraments in emergencies. But the use of sand is another matter. The bishop gathers his clergy, and after a long discussion they agree that the baptism was not valid. The man . . . is taken to the nearby Jordan River, where he is properly baptized and becomes a Christian.

At one level this story is quaint, but at another level it suggests a religious instinct on the part of the bishop and his clergy that finds resonance across barriers of time and place and culture. Water symbolism is one of the most basic of all religious forms of expression. In a chapter of nearly thirty pages on "The Waters and Water Symbolism" in his book *Patterns in Comparative Religion,* Eliade gathers a wide range of evidence to support his sweeping contention that "in cosmogony, in myth, ritual and iconography, water fills the same function in whatever type of cultural pattern we find it; it precedes all forms and upholds all creation."[1]

According to Eliade's analysis, the "dying and rising with Christ" in the Pauline characterization of baptism implies more than even the cessation of

1. Mircea Eliade, *Patterns in Comparative Religion* (New York: Sheed and Ward, 1958), p. 188.

From Patrick Henry, "Water, Bread, Wine: Patterns in Religion," in *New Directions in New Testament Study* (Philadelphia: Westminster, 1979), pp. 208-12.

life and the renewal of it. Baptism involves a return to the beginning of things, to the chaos over which the Spirit of God brooded (Gen. 1:2), and from which order was created. Speaking of water symbolism generally (that is, not with specific reference to Christian baptism), Eliade says:

> Immersion in water symbolizes a return to the pre-formal, a total regeneration, a new birth, for immersion means a dissolution of forms, a reintegration into the formlessness of pre-existence; and emerging from the water is a repetition of the act of creation in which form was first expressed. Every contact with water implies regeneration: first, because dissolution is succeeded by a "new birth," and then because immersion fertilizes, increases the potential of life and of creation.[2]

There is of course much water imagery in the New Testament. In addition to various baptisms there is also the living water referred to in the Gospel of John (4:7-15), and "the river of the water of life, bright as crystal, flowing from the throne of God and of the Lamb" in the book of Revelation (22:1). From Eliade's point of view, the best place to look for the nature of early Christian experience would be not the primitive kerygma (preaching), but rather the symbols, such as water, which relate Christian experience to a wide range of religious data.

Attention would focus not so much on Paul's doctrine of justification by faith as on the imagery of 1 Peter, which is considered by a growing number of scholars to be an early Christian baptismal sermon altered slightly into the form of a letter. The text addresses its hearers: "Like newborn babes, long for the pure spiritual milk, that by it you may grow up to salvation" (2:2); here is what Eliade would call the true note of initiation — a return to the beginning, a starting from scratch, a genuine *starting*, for salvation is presented as a process of growth. Later in 1 Peter we have the earliest expression of what would become in later centuries a much-used image for baptism: in Noah's ark, eight persons "were saved through water. Baptism, which corresponds to this, now saves you" (3:20-21). With Noah, God started the world of living things all over again, so the imagery here also points to Eliade's understanding of water symbolism. . . .

Rubenstein, in his analysis of Paul's interpretation of baptism, draws a somewhat smaller circle than Eliade does. The Freudian has a more restricted theory of the origins of religious images than does the historian of religions.

> Perhaps the central insight of psychoanalysis is that all the "higher" productions of the human psyche — such as art, myth, and religion — are

2. Eliade, *Patterns*, pp. 188-89.

ultimately objectified expressions of the organism's developmental vicissitudes and its strivings for bodily gratifications within the emotional matrix of the nuclear social unit, the human family. Psychoanalysis has sought to uncover the organic, developmental, and familial realities underlying the symbolism of religion. Paul's bodily "materialism" and his persistent tendency to utilize the metaphors of paternity, fraternity, and filiation in his religious thought expressed a similar insight intuitively. The very crudeness of Paul's images testifies to their emotional honesty and their overwhelming power. The crudeness also makes it possible for depth psychology to comprehend Paul's theology in terms of its own symbolism.[3]

This is only a fragment of the impressive pattern of Freudian meaning that Rubenstein finds in Paul, but it relates particularly closely to Eliade's findings. If for Eliade the meaning of baptism is the return to creation in a cosmic sense, for Rubenstein its meaning is a return to creation in a very personal sense.

Paul was able to associate the death and Resurrection of Christ with the experience of the newly baptized Christian because he understood intuitively and gave theological expression to the identity of womb and tomb in the subliminal consciousness of mankind. By his association of baptism with Jesus' death and Resurrection, he was able to bring to consciousness some of mankind's oldest and most profound responses to water.[4]

Rubenstein cites Eliade as support for his view, and there is of course a fair degree of correspondence between them. But the close ties of the Freudian interpretation to the central myths of familial relationship make Rubenstein's enterprise quite different from Eliade's. Rubenstein, before he is through discussing baptism, will have gone on to say that "Baptism promises escape from the hostility of the Divine Infanticide; baptismal rebirth thus involves the hope for a noninfanticidal Parent" (that is, a parent who will not seek, either actually or symbolically, to kill the child); and, beyond that:

In the course of psychoanalysis, fear of the father is usually uncovered first. Fear of the mother is older and less subject to therapeutic amelioration. If baptism involves the hope for the noninfanticidal Parent, the rite

3. Richard Rubenstein, *My Brother Paul* (New York: Harper & Row, 1972), pp. 26-27.
4. Rubenstein, *My Brother Paul*, p. 57.

carries with it the assurance that the believer, after his return to the watery womb, has been rescued and need no longer fear his original mother.[5]

Rubenstein certainly does not argue that Paul had figured all of this out. Psychoanalytical interpretations of texts seldom if ever claim to be reporting what was going on in the author's conscious thought. The terminology Rubenstein applies to his understanding of Paul is thoroughly uncommon in the field of New Testament study; literary criticism more generally has become accustomed to such ways of speaking, and in that field, techniques for judging the particular applications of the Freudian approach have been developed. It will be a while before New Testament scholars figure out just what to make of Rubenstein's book, and even more, of his whole manner of approach. But the strangeness of the effort should not in itself get in the way of appreciating Rubenstein's central argument. He attributes Paul's genius to his intuitive capacity to "make manifest the unmanifest," that is, to bring to the surface of powerful symbolic expression the hidden dynamics of the human unconscious. "Paul was able to express some of the deepest and most archaic emotional strivings of mankind because he was able to give objectified expression to his own unconscious mental processes."[6]

Reading 6.2 Biblical Archetypes and the Story of the Self

Wayne G. Rollins

Expanding on Jung's thesis that "There are as many archetypes as there are typical situations in life,"[1] Rollins presents a catalogue of biblical archetypes, organizing them in two classes: first, archetypal persons, places, and things, and second, archetypal processes in terms of which biblical writers interpret their world.

5. Rubenstein, *My Brother Paul,* pp. 66-67.
6. Rubenstein, *My Brother Paul,* p. 29.
1. Carl Gustav Jung, *The Collected Works of C. G. Jung,* trans. R. F. C. Hull, ed. Gerhard Adler et al., Bollingen Series 20 (Princeton: Princeton University Press, 1953-78), vol. 9.1, par. 99.

From Wayne G. Rollins, *Jung and the Bible* (Atlanta: John Knox, 1983), pp. 77-85.

Archetypal Persons, Places, and Things

This class represents figures that humans everywhere perceive as recurrent types. When we meet new persons we often perceive them in terms of these types and react accordingly. When we hear stories about these figures, we respond with the emotions we associate with these types.

The hero is the most psychologically powerful figure to appear in the art, literature, and storytelling of the world. Joseph Campbell's classic title, *The Hero with a Thousand Faces,* makes this plain. Drawing on ancient sagas, stone reliefs, oral traditions, and wall paintings, from as far away places as Assyria and Babylon, Cambodia and Indonesia, Honduras and Argentina, Greece and Rome, he finds the hero, again and again, in a thousand guises.

We know his story well. Anyone of us can construct it on demand: the twelve labors of Hercules, the tale of Gilgamesh, the travels of Odysseus, the lives of Moses and Abraham, the story of Jonah, the Way of the Cross. All relate to the three-fold pattern: "the departure" following a challenge or call; "the trials"; and "the return" — to everyone's astonishment. Not all heroes survive physically, nor are they all crowned. But all are tempered and not found wanting. The hero can appear as a warrior or lover, a prince or priest, a patriarch or prophet, male or female, a god or a human. But whenever his story is told, we listen. . . .

Archetypes of the masculine and feminine. The way we perceive men and women is affected by archetypes of the masculine and feminine. The masculine archetypes include the kind father as well as the ogre; the friendly dwarf and the ominous giant; the noble knight and the devilish trickster; the divine child and the youth savant; the wise man and the wizard; the saint and the sinner; the sage and the slayer of dragons; the frog with the prince inside and the tyrant king with a self-destructive demon inside.

The feminine archetypes manifest a parallel range: the nourishing mother and the cruel mother (more often than not, a "stepmother"); the lovely princess and the wicked queen; the wise old woman and the witch of the North; the heroine in armor and the Huntress; the virgin and the Earth Mother; Cinderella and the femme fatale.

Archetypes of the "inner self." We have noted earlier the four archetypes of the "inner self" Jung found most conspicuous: the persona, the anima/animus, the shadow, and the ego. Others might be added: the archetype of "flesh and spirit," often found at war with one another; the archetype of the androgyne, expressing the sense of a primordial unity of the sexes; the archetype of the "four humors," or in its modem Jungian version, the "four functions": thought, feeling, sense, intuition. They constitute a cast of figures recurring in literature touching on the inner life: morality plays, sermons, religious allegories, even psychoanalytic theories.

Archetypes of the "other." The Latin term *alienus* and the Greek term *barbaros* indicate the tendency to view a person of another tribe, religion, language, system, dress, custom, or land, in one of two stereotypical ways. One of the stereotypical reactions to an "other" is suspicion or fear. The central figure in Camus' *The Stranger* exemplifies this archetype. By the simple fact of his difference, he evokes a hostility that destroys him. Catholics and Protestants, Jews and Gentiles, whites and blacks have been seized by such archetypal feelings.

A second stereotypical reaction to the "other" is quite the opposite. It tends to see in the "other" a God-sent gift. "Do not neglect to show hospitality to strangers," the author of Hebrews writes; "for thereby some have entertained angels unawares" (Heb. 13:2). We find the same theme in Greek and Arabic culture. It even occurs in the American South in Peter Jenkins' autobiographical *A Walk Across America*. Taken under the wing of young, curious blacks in Murphy, North Carolina, Peter is introduced, with beard, Malamute, and backpack, to their mother, Mary Elizabeth. She, after a long but "loud" silence of studying and watching Peter as he eats his first meal in their trailer, tells him, "You don't know me yet, but I want ta tell ya something. . . . I believe in God. And I think He sent you here ta test aw' faith. So, from now on, if you want to, you can stay with us."[1]

Archetypes of the cosmos. The word "cosmos" comes from a Greek root that means "structure" or "organization." Archetypes of the cosmos represent those typical ways in which persons through the ages have tended to formulate that structure. Has there ever been a culture that at one time did not think of its world in terms of a heaven above, the earth in the middle, and a realm of the demonic or dead below? Or has there ever been a culture that did not somewhere in its past divide the skies into zodiac-like constellations of stars that were seen not as mere lights but powers that affected human destiny? Even when "up" and "down" disappeared in the light of the space age, there were radio telescopes, space probes, and UFO watches still directed "out there" as the place from which "higher intelligence" could be expected.

Archetypes of the holy. The central archetype that springs up virtually everywhere, in every age, and at one time or another in every heart, is the holy archetype or God archetype. Though often expressed in spatial or temporal images, the God archetype urges us to think in terms beyond space and time, everywhere and yet nowhere, named and beyond naming, all good and yet finally encompassing all evil as well, the one and the many.

---

1. Peter Jenkins, *A Walk Across America* (New York: Fawcett Crest, 1979), p. 143.

Like the "hero archetype," the holy archetype can be imaged in myriad forms. The trinitarian formula suggests three categories of God images.

The holy can be imaged as spirit. This archetypal tendency urges us to consider the holy beyond humans and nature, rendered in images at best abstract: "the eternal," "the Platonic ideal," "the Logos" or "Word," "the Name," "heaven," "Being itself," or the *"mysterium tremendum et fascinosum."* It envisions the divine as beyond human structures, moving freely in and among us, invisible, incorporeal, yet bathing all it touches in ineffable power and light.

The holy can be imaged as a transcendent being with personal attributes. This archetypal tendency urges us to image the divine as transcendent but personal: a father, judge, master, creator, redeemer, with a face to turn toward us in blessing, an eye to observe our ways, an ear to hear our petitions, a strong arm to lift us up and guide us, and a voice to speak his word to his prophets. Though transcendent, he knows our nature and we are created in his image.

The holy can be imaged in incarnational terms, as God become human flesh. The experience of the early church catalyzed the most radical expression of this archetype, imaging God as become human, with a family, hometown, with arms, hands, eyes, ears, and a body of flesh, who ate, drank, wept, talked, became thirsty and fatigued, argued, taught, and after approximately thirty years of life, suffered and died as a public enemy. Judaism and Islam have resisted the expression of this archetype in such a radical form, restricting their portraits of God's immanence to images of prophets and teachers who are bearers of his word. Like Christianity, they have allowed that the holy can "descend" to touch special persons, places, or objects at special times, but they have avoided the absolutized image of the God-human union manifest in the Christian tradition.

The holy can be imaged in terms of nature, i.e., natural phenomena and creatures of the earth, sea, and sky. Christianity, Judaism, and Islam in general have resisted this archetypal tendency. To be sure, they will admit to images of the divine moving in wind or star, earthquake or storm; and we do hear in Scripture of a "whale," a lion in his den, or even the earth (Rev. 12:16) moving to do God's bidding, and of God's spirit descending in the form of a dove. But, in general, a theological consensus has developed to allow no sacred animal [with the rare exceptions of the "dove" and the "lamb"], stream, rock, or any other natural phenomenon into the imaginal repertory of the holy among the "religions of the Book." In fact, as a symptom of their disdain of the natural, they have tended to reserve natural and animal imagery for the demonic or Satanic: the dragons Leviathan and Rahab, the beast with 666 upon its forehead, and the talking serpent in the garden.

Archetypal Processes

The archetypal tendencies within us structure our perceptions of the world not only in terms of types of persons, places, and things in our inner and outer worlds, but also in terms of processes.

The conflict between good and evil. In every culture at every level we find evidence of an archetypal preoccupation with the conflict between good and evil. It can be imaged in a thousand forms, but all are variations of a single perceptual motif, that life engages us in a battle between the light and the dark. Examples are the stories of the Lord subduing Leviathan in the Hebrew Scriptures, or of the Messiah overcoming the beast in Revelation, or of St. George subduing the dragon, David doing in Goliath, or of Robin Hood and the sheriff, or of the "white hats" and the "black hats" in Westerns, or of the Sons of Light and the Sons of Darkness in the writings of Paul and the Dead Sea Scrolls. In the heart of the London Zoo stands a tall statue in white stone, depicting a bare-chested male in mortal combat with a wild animal in attack position on its hind legs. The statue's power resides, not in its report of a famous fight between a man and an animal, but in its capacity to arouse in the viewer an archetypal openness to subduing the fiercest of forces, without or within.

Planting, growing, and harvesting. A compact parable in Mark's Gospel images the archetypal perception of planting, growing, harvesting as an analogue to the life process:

> The kingdom of God is as if a man should scatter seed upon the ground, and should sleep and rise night and day, and the seed should sprout and grow, he knows not how. *The earth produces of itself,* first the blade, then the ear, then the full grain in the ear. But when the grain is ripe, at once he puts in the sickle, because the harvest has come. (Mark 4:26-29, italics added)

The story in itself turns on the phrase, "the earth produces of itself," leading to the archetypal perception that the earth is a gracious mother (Latin *mater,* whence English "matter"), without whose rhythms and patterns we would not be sustained for a moment. But as a parable it occasions another archetypal insight, celebrated in Thanksgiving festivals and harvest ceremonies, that we live as part of a process in which we play at best a minuscule role, seeding, planting, perhaps watering a bit, but for the rest only waking and sleeping while the divine mysteries in nature move on.

Death and resurrection. The literature and art of the world reflect archetypal consciousness of another aspect of the divine mystery in life, namely death and resurrection. The subject matter is not just physical death and physical resurrection, but a pattern of being, in which what appears to be ir-reparable loss is supplanted by unimaginable gain: being hopelessly lost and then found, being hopelessly ill and healed, being hopelessly locked into a de-structive pattern of living and then forgiven and released. The stories of the prodigal son, of the man blind from his youth, of the lost sheep, of the con-version of Paul, of the Exodus and Exile, of the Second Coming and the Last Day, and countless others, express this archetypal realization. Its liturgical an-alogue is found not only in the Easter celebration at the end of Holy Week, but in the ancient rite of baptism, which has at its heart the archetypal theme voiced in the words of Paul: "We were buried therefore with him by baptism into death, so that as Christ was raised from the dead by the glory of the Fa-ther, we too might walk in newness of life" (Rom. 6:4).

Experiencing life as history. Whenever one digs into the religious and philosophic traditions of the world, one finds a story, picture, or metaphysical model that reveals where time began, when it began, where it is heading, and what stages are in between. From Hesiod and his golden and silver ages, to Hegel with his historical sequence of thesis, antithesis, and synthesis, to the book of Revelation with its millennial schemes, we find expressions of the ar-chetypal perception that history is real, and that the life story of humanity, of nations, and the world is neither pointless nor shapeless. It respects a pattern of "ages," "epochs," "times and seasons," "millennia," or cycles that spell out a macrocosmic pattern within which the microcosm of our own time can and does play a role.

The Archetype of Archetypes: The Self

In his autobiography, Jung states that by 1920 he "began to understand that the goal of psychic development is the self . . ." and that "the self is the princi-ple and the archetype of orientation and meaning."[2] In David Cox's words, Jung concluded that the Self is a "sort of archetype of archetypes."[3]

The Self for Jung is, as noted earlier, not the ego. It is the Self with a large "S"; large not referring to one's ego but to the reality of a Self that is larger than ego.

The ego is the center of consciousness that thinks, plans, directs, and

---

2. Carl Gustav Jung, *Memories, Dreams, Reflections*, trans. Richard Winston and Clara Winston (New York: Vintage Books, 1963), pp. 196, 199.

3. David Cox, *Modern Psychology: The Teachings of Carl Gustav Jung* (New York: Barnes and Noble, 1968), p. 153.

prides itself on these accomplishments. It is most visible in full form between childhood and middle age. It is the archetype of one's "subjective identity," with which we are wrapped up during the first half of life when we face the task of differentiating who we are. In the second stage of life, the Self begins to emerge more clearly into consciousness, with another task in hand. Not differentiation, but integration and acknowledgement of all the parts of the self, even those the ego could never quite own up to: the persona, the shadow-side, the contra-sexual side, all one's attitudes and functions, not just one or two. The Self is the archetype of one's "objective identity"[4] in the sense of recognizing the broader reality of which we are part.

In Jung's own language, "the self designates the whole circumference which embraces all of the psychic phenomena in man. It expresses the unity and wholeness of the total personality. . . . Only partly conscious . . . , it embraces what can be experienced and what cannot or what has not yet been experienced."[5] Whatever the human's wholeness, or the Self, may mean per se, empirically it is an image of the goal of life spontaneously produced by the unconscious, irrespective of the wishes and fears of the conscious mind. It stands for the goal of the total person, for the realization of the person's wholeness and individuality with or without the consent of the will. "The dynamic of this process is instinct, which ensures that everything which belongs to an individual's life shall enter into it, whether he consents or not, or is conscious of what is happening to him or not."[6]

What images emerge in our art, literature, and dreams to express this archetypal perception of the Self? We have spoken of the mandala which as a squared-circle in infinite variations expresses the inclusive as well as centered quality of the Self. "Hero stories" are also images of the Self, baiting the imagination and will to "win" our Selves, even at personal cost. Wise figures in fables and proverbs, like the tortoise and the ant, tutor us in truths about the Self from childhood. Poetry nourishes us with visions of the Self: "Two roads diverged in a wood and I, I took the road less traveled by." Parables abound with them: the pearl of great price; leaven hidden in a loaf; a mustard seed, so small in its beginning and so magnanimous in its maturity. The Gospels constantly return to the subject: "You are the salt of the earth; you are the light of the world," or,

---

4. Edward Edinger, *Ego & Archetype — Individuation and the Religious Function of the Psyche* (Boston: Shambala, 1992), p. 3.

5. Gerhard Wehr, *Portrait of Jung: An Illustrated Biography*, trans. W. A. Hargreaves (New York: Herder & Herder, 1971), p. 49.

6. Carl Gustav Jung, "Answer to Job," in *The Collected Works of C. G. Jung*, trans. R. F. C. Hull, ed. Gerhard Adler et al., Bollingen Series 20 (Princeton: Princeton University Press, 1953-78), vol. 11, par. 459.

"What does a man gain by winning the whole world at the cost of his true self? What can he give to buy that self back?" Above all, God-images mirror the Self, as an expression of the immensity of the mystery from which we are born, the heights to which we might aspire, and the depths we may have to plumb for the Self to come into its own. At the head of the list, in Jung's perspective, is the image of Christ, who Jung says "exemplifies the archetype of the Self."[7]

Reading 6.3   Jesus the Holy Fool

ELIZABETH-ANNE STEWART

Elizabeth-Anne Stewart introduces the archetypal image of the Holy Fool as a "familiar figure in whom we recognize some truths about our own humanity." The Holy Fool archetype is the model of one who consciously steps out of culturally accepted patterns to point to a higher truth, even at the risk of mockery and jeering. Stewart's book offers a feast of examples, ranging from the dramatic "foolishness" of the Hebrew prophets to Paul's self-confessed role as "fool for Christ" (1 Cor. 4:10), from the clown paintings of Georges Rouault to Dostoyevsky's Prince Myshkin, from St. Francis and Mother Teresa to the Holy Fools of Russian Orthodoxy and Etty Hillesum's "interrupted life" at Auschwitz. In this excerpt Stewart provides the psychological "reasoning" behind the imaging of Jesus as a Holy Fool who, in the words of Paul, plays out a foolishness "wiser than men" (1 Cor. 1:25).

Fool as Archetype

The fool, as archetype, has ancient roots and many cultural manifestations; it is also known by many names — clown, trickster, jester, buffoon, joker. It springs up in oral traditions, in the earliest sacred texts, in legends, folklore, and fairy tales with such regularity that one might ask, "What is so quintessentially appealing about this figure? How has it succeeded in grasping the imaginations of peoples everywhere? How can this archetype reveal anything significant about

---

7. Carl G. Jung, "Christ, a Symbol of the Self," in *Personality and Religion: The Role of Religion in Personality Development,* ed. William A. Sadler Jr. (New York: Harper & Row, 1970), p. 136.

From Elizabeth-Anne Stewart, *Jesus the Holy Fool* (Franklin, WI: Sheed & Ward, 1999), pp. 35-37.

the person of Jesus? As we explored the concept of psychological archetypes, we saw that "archetypes pre-exist in the collective psyche of the human race."[1] The fool, then, is a familiar figure in whom we recognize some truth about our own humanity. Often existing outside the norms of society, the fool is not far from the center of human experience. Richard Boston sees the fool as one whose role is to be the focus of laughter and who, in turn, makes us laugh, often becoming, like Jesus, a scapegoat figure.[2]

Through the antics of the fool, we find vicarious release for much we have repressed within ourselves. When we dare to "put on" the fool, the release is, of course, more complete though it is possible to cross the boundaries of ethical behavior into excess and debauchery. It is infinitely safer to watch the clowns in the circus ring than to put on a clown's costume and all the license this represents. Again, there is a need to stress here that it is the redeemed side of the fool which is applicable to this study of Jesus as Holy Fool. Though Jesus was a breaker of rules and taboos, an agent of chaos, his intent transcended the desire to be a catalyst of laughter and his behavior never degenerated into lewdness or cruelty. Boston lists the attributes of the typical fool as "gluttony, erudition, stupidity, sexuality, cunning, shiftlessness, malice, deceit, and truth-telling."[3] It is the wisdom of the fool and the truth-telling of the fool which are relevant here.

Fools can exhibit a depth of wisdom that seems incongruous. Given the professional fool's task of entertaining others and of being the butt of others' jests, it is startling to realize how close to the mark the fool's observations can be. It is as though the outwardly outrageous dress and behavior obscure from the casual observer the fool's ability to perceive, critique, and speak truth. One is left wondering if the fool is really a sage *incognito,* and if the trickster is the shadow of the fool. Who is really wise? The jester dressed in motley or the king who wants to be humored, in every sense of the word? Jesus — wearing the simple garb of a Mediterranean peasant — spoke the truth to those who thought he was possessed; ironically, they themselves were emotionally, imaginatively, and morally deficient, in spite of their claims to status and religious monopoly.

Fooling can also be existentially dangerous. Who would trade places with the circus clown catapulted across the ring from a fiery cannon? Or with the clown whose clothes catch fire while he or she is attempting to save a burning house? Or with the clown riding high above us on the high-wire, bravely peddling a dilapidated unicycle in serious need of wheel alignment?

1. Robert Johnson, *Inner Work* (New York: Harper & Row, 1986), p. 27.
2. Richard Boston, *An Anatomy of Laughter* (London: Collins, 1974), p. 93.
3. Boston, *Anatomy,* p. 93.

Or with the clown who enters the lions' cage, grasping only a mop and bucket as security? While we may laugh at the *auguste*, victim of slapstick humor, or at the white-faced clown who argues with ring master and public, while we may be mesmerized by equestrian comedy or acrobatic comedy, the truth is that the dividing line between the comic and the dangerous is thin. The illusion before us may seem to be carried out with the sleight of hand of a magician, but one false step, one error of judgment and the "near miss" could well become tragedy. Sitting in the safety of our seats, we feel the thrill of the drama unfolding before us, but seldom know what risks are being taken in the name of entertainment. In the passion narratives, Jesus the Holy Fool submits to slapstick which is ultimately death-dealing: for him, there is no safety net, no last minute reprieve, no *deus ex machina,* no standing ovation. There is only the laughter of mockery and the silence of the tomb.

SUGGESTIONS FOR FURTHER READING

Bregman, Lucy. "Symbolism/symbolizing." In *Dictionary of Pastoral Care and Counseling,* edited by R. Hunter, 1248-50. Nashville: Abingdon, 1990.

Clift, Jean Dalby, and Wallace B. Clift. *Symbols of Transformation in Dreams.* New York: Crossroad, 1984.

Harding, M. Esther. "The Cross as an Archetypal Symbol." In *Carl Jung and Christian Spirituality,* edited by Robert L. Moore, 1-15. New York: Paulist, 1988.

Jung, Carl Gustav. "Approaching the Unconscious." In *Man and His Symbols.* New York: Doubleday, 1964.

———. "Christ, A Symbol of the Self." In *Aion: Researches into the Phenomenology of the Self,* edited by William McGuire et al., 36-71. Princeton: Princeton University Press, 1959.

Miller, David L. *Christs: Meditations on Archetypal Images in Christian Theology.* New York: Seabury, 1981.

Moore, Robert, and Douglas Gillette. *King, Warrior, Magician, Love: Rediscovering the Archetypes of the Mature Masculine.* San Francisco: HarperSanFrancisco, 1991.

Newheart, Michael Willett. "Johannine Symbolism." In *Jung and the Interpretation of the Bible,* edited by David L. Miller, 71-91. New York: Continuum, 1995.

CHAPTER 7

Biblical Personalities:
Ezekiel and Paul

Exalted prophet though he was, to Ezekiel probably belongs the distinction of having embarrassed more exegetes than any other inspired author of the canon.

Ned H. Cassem, S.J, M.D.[1]

The letters of Paul seem very personal and self-revelatory. Perhaps for this reason, psychological analysis of Paul has been irresistible for many of his interpreters.

Terrance Callan[2]

The Bible is full of memorable personalities. They laugh, grieve, lash out in anger, fall in love, and struggle with the whole range of conflicts inherent in human living. It is no wonder, then, that as soon as psychological investigations began to shed light on human behavior, people sought to apply psychological theories and explanations to the people of the Bible. Indeed, some of the earliest examples of psychological criticism involved analyses of the personalities and quirks of such figures as Moses, the prophets, Jesus, and Paul.

There remain significant obstacles to such analysis. For the most part, those early investigations suffered from the implicit assumption that the Bible was a historically reliable source of bibliographic material. Or, conversely,

1. Ned H. Cassem, "Ezekiel's Psychotic Personality: Reservations on the Use of the Couch for Biblical Personalities," in *Word in the World,* ed. R. Clifford (Cambridge, MA: Weston College Press, 1973), p. 59.

2. Terrance Callan, *Psychological Perspectives on the Life of Paul: An Application of the Methodology of Gerd Theissen* (Lewiston/Queenston/Lampeter: Edwin Mellen, 1990), p. 137.

they adopted a skeptical attitude toward the biblical texts and suspected that the writers were, consciously or unconsciously, concealing truths about the characters that could be recovered only by "reading between the lines."

In Chapter 5, we mentioned Paul Ricoeur's idea of the "world *in front of* the text," the relationship between reader and text in which interpretation takes place. We can further distinguish two other interrelated dimensions of the text: the world *behind* the text and the world *of* the text. The world *behind* the text includes the personalities of the authors and their historical and cultural contexts, as well as the factors that contributed to the writing, preservation, and transmission of the texts. The world *of* the text encompasses literary qualities of the written text — language, structure, narrative, plot, and characterization.

Psychological analysis of biblical figures faces a number of challenges: the tendency to confuse the world of the text with the world behind the text, a failure to recognize the cultural meaning of symbols and behaviors, anachronistic application of modern conceptions to ancient people and situations, and making overstated claims based on tiny fragments of unverifiable information.

Psychological criticism has much to offer in dealing with the world *of* the text. The reason biblical figures are so lively and inspire such curiosity and wonder is that they are "true to life." The power of texts to move us depends in part on how characters come to life in them. By treating biblical materials as reliable biographical accounts, however, some psychological critics ignored the fact that the Bible is a literary document with its own conventions of description, narration, and dialogue that are far different from modern biographies. Believing they were studying the historical figures *behind* the text — the author or people described — critics used psychological methods in an attempt to do historical research. In effect, they sought to put biblical figures "on the couch," and dealt with those personalities as if they were clients in therapy.

The conventions and forms of biblical literature are not those of our contemporary era. The Bible does not present psychological case histories or even "straight" biography — it is written "from faith to faith," that is, by people who are seeking to communicate a religious message, not a consciously psychological one. Psychological realities are inescapable, in that wherever there are human beings there are psychological dynamics at work, but those realities will manifest themselves differently in different contexts. It is therefore essential to understand behavior in the context of the historical and cultural context of the time, and not to assume direct parallels to modern life. For example, the cultures of the Bible were communal and based on systems of honor and shame, while our modern Western culture is guilt-based, focused on the individual. Behaviors that would seem pathological in our culture might well have been conventional and expected in the ancient world.

Ultimately, we must resign ourselves to the fact that any psychological analysis of a biblical character must remain to some extent tentative. In dealing with a client, the contemporary therapist always has the option of checking his or her perceptions with the individual. It is possible to ask, "What did you mean by that?" and "How does that make you feel?" Clearly, there is no possibility of such a conversation (except in our imaginations) with someone in the Bible.

Occasionally, though, we suspect that something of the world behind the text, especially of the personality of the author, may be discernible in the text before us. Either because of the extent of material from one writer — for example, the apostle Paul — or because of strikingly distinctive elements in the text that seem utterly beyond the expected — for example, in the book of Ezekiel — it may be that something can be said about the authors themselves. In this chapter we will look at studies of Ezekiel and Paul, from whom we believe we have some measure of autobiographical material. In the next chapter, we will explore how a psychological approach might be applied to personalities for whom we have *no* direct information. With care, and remaining sensitive to the issues of literary convention, cultural differences, and the fact that insights cannot be verified with the individual himself, we may yet gain important insight into these biblical personalities.

Reading 7.1 Seeking Ezekiel

DAVID J. HALPERIN

The prophet Ezekiel has attracted much attention due to the descriptions of his unusual and even bizarre visions and behavior. In *Seeking Ezekiel* David Halperin offers a critique of previous psychological approaches to Ezekiel before presenting his own careful interpretation. In this passage, he considers the psychological dynamics that lay behind Ezekiel's muteness and paralysis (Ezek. 3:25-27).

From David J. Halperin, *Seeking Ezekiel: Text and Psychology* (University Park, PA: Penn State Press, 1993), pp. 207-15.

Our analysis of Ezekiel 16 and 23 has shown us a man overwhelmed by sexualized rage against females. He perceives them as powerful and cruel, sexually rampant, seductive and treacherous. Seldom does he openly express his anger against any human woman.[1] Rather, he displaces his feelings onto personifications of Israel, Judah, and Jerusalem; and, in deeper disguise, onto the Temple (Ezekiel 8). His rage prevents him from mourning his wife's death. But he has no conscious awareness of this and must imagine himself blocked by Yahweh's command. It goes almost without saying, however, that the roots of his anger must lie in a human relationship; most plausibly, his relationship with his mother.

We have seen traces of an even more deeply buried rage, directed against the male figure who is likely to have been the worst of his abusers. Given Ezekiel's association of this male figure with his God, we can understand why he found it safer to turn most of his wrath against the female; indeed, to identify himself with the male and under this guise to take his revenge on the female.

Even the female, in her original form, was an unacceptably dangerous target. Ezekiel's religious culture taught him that his rage against his mother must be ferociously repressed. "He who curses his father or his mother shall surely be put to death" (Exodus 21:17). The stronger the impulse to curse, the more stringent must be the repression. It would be hard to imagine a more effective way to repress a curse than with muteness.

But the blocked impulse had a way out. Hidden behind the ultimately powerful male, Ezekiel might dare to proclaim his rage and loathing — provided that its female object is suitably disguised. He must make absolutely

---

1. Only, to my knowledge, in 13:17-23: Certain self-proclaimed "prophetesses" have stitched together some sort of paraphernalia, with which they entrap other people's vital forces *(nefashot),* "killing people who ought not to die and keeping alive people who ought not to live." Yahweh, indignant at this, promises to intervene, tear up the women's traps, and set the victims free. "I will . . . save my people from your clutches; they shall no longer be prey in your clutches, and you shall know that I am YHWH" (verse 21, in Greenberg's translation [Moshe Greenburg, *Ezekiel 1–20, A New Translation with Introduction and Commentary,* Anchor Bible 22 (Garden City, NY: Doubleday, 1983]). These women surely cut a rather pathetic figure; especially if we suppose with Zimmerli that verse 19 intends to say that they perform their sorceries in exchange for "handfuls of barley and bits of bread." Walther Zimmerli, *Ezekiel: A Commentary on the Book of the Prophet Ezekiel* (Philadelphia: Fortress Press, 1979-83). But, for Ezekiel, they are mistresses of life and death, whose sinister power over God's people can be broken only by God himself. The terrifying image of female power, which was Ezekiel's childhood burden, will do much to account for his perception of them. Greenberg remarks that the language of 13:17-23 recalls Proverbs 6:26, which carries us back to the "strange woman" and the complex of terrors with which Proverbs surrounds her.

clear that his words are not his own, that he cannot be held responsible for them. "When I speak with you, I will open your mouth, and you will say to them: Thus says the Lord Yahweh" (3:27).

Let us grant that 3:26 and 27 contradict each other. The one represents Ezekiel as dumb and therefore unable to reprove. The other has him speaking the words — reproofs, presumably — of Yahweh. But we may resolve the contradiction without recourse to editorial tinkering, by recalling Freud's story of the borrowed kettle. Eager to deny that he had damaged his neighbor's property, the borrower "asserted first, that he had given it back undamaged; secondly, that the kettle had a hole in it when he borrowed it; and thirdly, that he had never borrowed a kettle from his neighbour at all."[2]

Ezekiel, driven to deny that he could ever have cursed his *(ex officio)* loved and revered mother, uses a similar strategy. First, he protests, he is absolutely without speech and therefore cannot possibly curse her. Second, the harsh words he speaks are really Yahweh's, and he cannot be held responsible for them. Third, they are really not directed against his mother at all — as he asserts by the symbolic disguises and displacements of his rage. This threefold protest, to be sure, smacks of the comical. But it can nonetheless aptly describe Ezekiel's unconscious reasoning. The ways of the comic and the processes of the unconscious, Freud has shown, lie very close together.[3]

In this way, Ezekiel's conflicting claims that his dumbness was both absolute and intermittent become psychologically intelligible. The "double-think"[4] involved was a necessary response to the otherwise unbearable pressure of contradictory demands.

Once we have allowed that this pressure might to some extent distort Ezekiel's memory of his disability, we may permit ourselves to wonder if it did not work another, fairly slight, distortion. Is it possible that, even apart from his proclamations in Yahweh's name, his dumbness was not always absolute? That, like Aronson's intermittently mute and paralyzed patient, he may at times have been able to communicate in a whisper? This conjecture is not indispensable. Yet it will certainly make living with a seven-year dumbness eas-

---

2. Sigmund Freud, *The Interpretation of Dreams,* translated from the German and edited by James Strachey (New York: Avon Books, 1965), pp. 152-53; Sigmund Freud, *Jokes and Their Relation to the Unconscious,* translated from the German and edited by James Strachey (New York: W. W. Norton, 1960), p. 205.

3. Sigmund Freud, *Jokes and Their Relation to the Unconscious.*

4. Leonard Shengold uses Orwell's word frequently to describe the psychological defenses of those who have endured intolerable childhood abuse. His book, *Soul Murder,* may perhaps orient us to what Ezekiel may have suffered. See Leonard Shengold, *Soul Murder: The Effects of Childhood Abuse and Deprivation* (New Haven: Yale University Press, 1989).

ier to imagine. No doubt, Ezekiel was entirely mute much of the time. But perhaps it was only in anticipation (3:22-27) and in retrospect (24:25-27, 33:21-22), driven by the need to deny any expression of his hostility, that he conceived himself as always entirely mute.[5]

Exodus 21:16-18, as we have seen, prescribes death for striking as well as for cursing one's parents. Here, perhaps, we have the clue to one meaning of Ezekiel's paralysis. As he made himself mute in order to repress his childhood urge to curse his mother, so he made himself immobile in order to repress a childhood urge to strike her.[6] Like the urge to curse, the urge to attack forced its way out, in an attenuated but unmistakable form. Lying helplessly on his side (4:4-8), Ezekiel nonetheless bares his arm in what is obviously a threatening gesture directed against the mother city. (The commentators agree on this understanding of 4:7.)[7]

Given this underlying motivation for Ezekiel's paralysis, it is understandable that he may have unconsciously exaggerated its severity. It may originally have been to some extent intermittent. He will have found it inconvenient to remember, and will therefore have forgotten, the times when it was relaxed. We may therefore grant the essential reality of Ezekiel's long-term immobility, without having to take at face value his apparently fantastic claim of having lain continuously on one side for 390 days, forty on the other (4:5-6).

Ezekiel's explanation, that he lay on one side to bear the iniquities of Israel and on the other to bear the iniquities of Judah, is to be considered a *post hoc* rationalization of his behavior. It nonetheless preserves a distorted echo of his real motive: to restrain himself from committing what he perceived to be unbearable iniquity.[8]

---

5. "Patients who present with one form of conversion voice disorder very likely have experienced other forms." Arnold E. Aronson, *Clinical Voice Disorders: An Interdisciplinary Approach*, 2nd ed. (New York: Thieme, 1985), pp. 141-45. The reader may object that I have earlier criticized Greenberg, Garfinkel and Davis for refusing to take Ezekiel's claims about his experience at face value. Now I seem to be doing the same thing. But the degree of distortion of reality posited by my hypothesis and that posited by theirs, are of different orders of magnitude.

6. "Unconscious denial of anxiety related to aggressive impulses is apt to be associated with feelings of weakness or numbness." Frederick J. Ziegler and John B. Imboden, "Contemporary Conversion Reactions. II. A Conceptual Model," *Archives of General Psychiatry* 6 (1962): 279-87.

7. R. E. Clements, *Isaiah 1–39*, New Century Bible Commentary (Grand Rapids: Eerdmans, 1980); Greenburg, *Ezekiel 1–20*; Zimmerli, *Ezekiel: A Commentary of the Book of the Prophet Ezekiel*.

8. The play on the words "bear iniquity" is valid in Hebrew as well as English with Ezekiel's *tissa' 'et 'awonam . . . wenasa'ta 'awon bet yisra'el . . . wenasa'ta 'et 'awon bet yehudah*, compare Cain's protest, *gadol 'awoni minneso'* ("My iniquity [or 'punishment'] is great beyond bearing," Genesis 4:13).

Can it be coincidence that Ezekiel's contemporary, the author of Psalm 137, calls upon himself a curse that strikingly resembles what Ezekiel actually experienced?

The psalmist dreads — which is to say, unconsciously desires — that he might forget the mother city, that he might set his own satisfaction above her. He therefore begs that his right hand, which might strike her, may itself "forget" (how to act, presumably). His tongue, which might curse her, is to stick to the roof of his mouth (137:5-6).[9]

To "forget" Jerusalem is an expression of hostility. But it may be protective at the same time. For an abused child, repression of memory may be the only way to restrain feelings he cannot tolerate. The psalmist, we may imagine, desperately wants to forget his unbearable rage and pain. He calls upon paralysis and dumbness to enforce his repression.

This conjecture requires us to assume that the psalmist shared with Ezekiel, not only the adult trauma of exile, but certain childhood traumas as well. The two men dealt with their feelings in different ways. The psalmist directs his rage at his "bad mother," and his longing for revenge, toward the "daughter of Babylon." For her brutality toward helpless children, he assures himself, she will be cruelly punished.[10] He turns his yearning for a good mother toward his idealized Jerusalem.

For Ezekiel, by contrast, the "bad mother" is Jerusalem, which he hates with fanatic intensity (chapters 16, 22). His "good mother" is perhaps the fantasy city and Temple sketched in chapters 40–48. The real (= bad) Jerusalem spread her legs for all passers-by (16:25). But the ideal Temple will open her "gate" only to Yahweh, and to the "prince" — surely the infant Ezekiel — who sits nourishing himself within (44:1-3).[11]

---

9. His language is very close to Ezekiel's: *tidbaq leshoni lehikki* (Psalm 137:6), *uleshonekha 'adbiq 'el hikkekha wene'elanta* (Ezekiel 3:26). I have adopted the most conservative interpretation of the difficult *tishkah yemini* ("may my right hand forget," without any direct object). Many scholars prefer to translate verse 5's second *skh* (not the first) as "wither," on the basis of a supposed Ugaritic cognate. See A. A. Andersen, *The Book of Psalms*, New Century Bible (London: Oliphants, 1972), p. 899; David Noel Freedman, "The Structure of Psalm 137," in *Pottery, Poetry, and Prophecy: Studies in Early Hebrew Poetry* (Winona Lake, IN: Eisenbrauns, 1980), pp. 311-12. This interpretation will suit my hypothesis still better.

10. "O devastated daughter of Babylon, happy is he who pays you back for what you have done to us. Happy is he who seizes and smashes your little ones against the rock" (verses 8-9). *What you have done to us* (understand, *to me*) is the key phrase, which makes intelligible the feelings that underlie this gruesome curse.

11. The traditional Christian expositors who saw in 44:1-3 a prophecy of the Blessed Virgin (see G. A. Cooke, *A Critical and Exegetical Commentary on the Book of Ezekiel* [Edinburgh: T&T Clark, 1951]; Wilhelm Neuss, *Das Buch Ezechiel in Theologie und Kunst bis zum Ende des XII*

Yet both Ezekiel and the psalmist found themselves unconsciously wishing for dumbness and paralysis, to help them control their terrifying rage. Ezekiel, unluckier than his fellow exile, was able to make his wish come true.

So far, I have explained Ezekiel's dumbness and paralysis as protective measures. They held back his urges to avenge himself for his childhood wounds. They consequently had the effect of repressing the memory of these wounds.

In Chapter 4, however, I proposed a different interpretation, no less oriented toward Ezekiel's childhood experience. I suggested that Ezekiel's immobility reenacted his infantile helplessness, whereas his dumbness repeated his experience of crying out for care and being ignored. (If I cry and no one responds, surely it is because I am unable to make a sound?) Ezekiel's conversion symptoms will then have manifested what Leonard Shengold calls the "mysterious compulsion to repeat traumatic experiences," in the expectation that "this time the contact will bring love instead of hate."[12] They serve as an extreme illustration of Kinzl's observation: in hysterical patients, "functional aphonia has the effect of making something undone, of a regression to infantile dependence."[13]

These two interpretations do not exclude each other. On the contrary, if Freud was right that "a hysterical symptom develops only where the fulfilment of two opposing wishes . . . are able to converge in a single expression,"[14] their simultaneous presence is precisely what we would expect. Ezekiel's dumbness and paralysis served at once to reenact his early traumas, and to repress expression of the hate and rage that these traumas provoked.[15]

I do not exclude the possibility that Ezekiel's symptoms may have had still other functions. Like Edward Tauber's patient, Ezekiel may have used his

---

Jahrhunderts [Munster: Aschendorff, 1912]) were surely wrong in detail but right as to the essentials. Significantly, this same gate later becomes the source of Ezekiel's river of life (47:1-12, especially verse 2). I pursue this line of thought a short distance in the Excursus. I hope others may be encouraged to follow it further. (Julie Galambush, *Jerusalem in the Book of Ezekiel: This City as Yahweh's Wife* [Atlanta: Scholars Press, 1992], now offers some relevant observations.)

12. Shengold, *Soul Murder*, pp. 26, 28, 99. Lenore Terr gives many examples of how this "mysterious compulsion" can manifest itself. See Lenore Terr, *Too Scared to Cry: Psychic Trauma in Childhood* (New York: Harper & Row, 1990), pp. 235-80.

13. Johann Kinzl, Wilfried Biebl, and Hermann Rauchegger, "Functional Aphonia: A Conversion Symptom as a Defensive Mechanism against Anxiety," *Psychotherapy and Psychosomatics* 49 (1988): 31-36.

14. Freud, *The Interpretation of Dreams*, pp. 608-9.

15. Somewhat like the hypnoid state Shengold describes in one of his analytic patients; which, he says, "both warded off and repeated the past." Shengold, *Soul Murder*, p. 143.

dumbness to seal his intimacy with a father-God who did not speak in the ordinary sense of the word.[16] But the two complementary interpretations I have proposed are the primary ones. Together, they are certainly adequate to explain how Ezekiel's symptoms came into existence.

But how did the symptoms end? Ezekiel's paralysis seems to have faded after he had finished expiating "the iniquity of the house of Judah" (4:6). His dumbness was more persistent. We may guess that, of the two repressions that of speech was the more important. Ezekiel could no longer strike his mother. But he could, if he did not check his impulses, defame her memory.[17] His muteness therefore continued to oppress him, until external circumstances brought him relief.

How did this happen? Let us recall, once again, that Ezekiel's strategy for attacking his mother involved identifying himself with the father (Yahweh speaks with Ezekiel's voice). He was then free to persecute the female, in the guise of the righteously inflamed male.

When we consider that Ezekiel worked this strategy out with Jerusalem and the Temple as his representations of the female, we can understand that which properly puzzled Yehezkel Kaufman: the unparalleled ruthlessness of Ezekiel's prophecy of doom. "Isaiah steadfastly believed in Jerusalem's inviolability. . . . Jeremiah promises to the very last that if the city will submit to Nebuchadnezzar there will be no fall or exile."[18] "Alone among the prophets, Ezekiel foretells the unconditional destruction of Jerusalem. His prophecy of the destruction of city, temple, and monarchy has no accompanying call for repentance." (Kaufman adds, with greater perspicacity than he can have realized: "His fierce antipathy toward Jerusalem . . . leads one to suspect some personal provocation is involved.")[19]

City and Temple fell. A fugitive brought the news to Ezekiel's community. In that instant, Ezekiel must have leaped to the conclusion that his self-identification with the paternal tyrant had been successful. In defiance of the devout expectations of an entire nation, Yahweh had shown beyond doubt that he shared Ezekiel's savage hatred of the woman/sanctuary. He who had threatened death for striking or cursing one's mother, now had proved with his actions that such murderous expressions of rage were no crime after all. Ezekiel's guilt was absolved, his fear of punishment relieved.

16. Terr, *Too Scared to Cry.*

17. The Mishnah, contrasting the prohibitions of striking and of cursing one's parents, makes a similar point (Sanhedrin 11:1).

18. Yehezkel Kaufman, *The Religion of Israel: From Its Beginnings to the Babylonian Exile* (Chicago: University of Chicago Press, 1960), pp. 403-9.

19. Kaufman, *The Religion of Israel*, pp. 428-32.

It would be too much to claim that Ezekiel now allowed himself to become consciously aware of his feelings. On the contrary, in 25:1-7, he disowns his glee over the fall of the Temple by projecting it onto the "bad boys" of Israelite tradition, the Ammonites (cf. Deuteronomy 23:3-6). These wicked heathen will be punished, Yahweh solemnly promises, "because you said, Aha! [*he'ah*] over my sanctuary when it was profaned, and over the land of Israel when it was devastated, and over the house of Judah when they went into exile . . . because you clapped your hands and stamped your feet and rejoiced with all your soul's contempt over the land of Israel" (25:3, 6).

We cannot deny that the Ammonites may indeed have celebrated the news of Jerusalem's destruction. Yet other passages in the Book of Ezekiel leave little doubt that the sadistic euphoria expressed here was, in reality, Ezekiel's own. He it was who cried "Aha!" (*'ah*), clapped his hands and stamped his feet (6:11), while howling damnations against the land of Israel (6:2-3, 7:2) and the soon-to-be-profaned sanctuary (7:20-24).[20]

Now he had a clear sign that his murderous wishes had divine approval. The unconscious anxieties these wishes had aroused must have been greatly soothed. The elaborate mechanisms he had used to guard against them were no longer required. "Then my mouth was opened, and I was dumb no more."

This denouement, as we have seen, did not come unexpected. The death of Ezekiel's wife had inspired him with the conviction that he would be able to speak freely once he learned of Jerusalem's fall. The event proved that his conviction had been justified. How did this happen?

On the basis of our argument so far, it is easy enough to formulate an explanation. Jerusalem and the Temple were the screen *par excellence* onto which Ezekiel displaced his image of the hated and hateful female. But he must also have displaced something of this image onto his wife. When she abruptly died, and he understood this to be an act of God, he will have responded much as he later responded to news of the destruction. Unconsciously, he must have been aware that his feelings for his wife were linked with his feelings for the Temple. So we must understand the woman-sanctuary equation of 24:15-27. And we must translate his assurance, that "Ezekiel shall be a token for you" (24:24), into the underlying reality. His reac-

---

20. I can see no reason to suppose that *'ah* in 6:11 and 21:20 means anything different from *he'ah* in 25:3, 26:2, 36:2 (Greenburg, *Ezekiel 1–20*, pp. 135-37). Ezekiel attributes similar outpourings of *Schadenfreude* to Tyre (26:7), Edom (35:10), "the enemy" (36:2), and an unspecified "they" (36:13). All of these remarks, especially the last, can be interpreted as conveying Ezekiel's own feelings. "You [feminine] eat human flesh, you have deprived your peoples of their children" (*'okhele 'adam 'at umeshakkelet goyayikh hayit;* 36:13). We are by now familiar with Ezekiel's child-eating females.

tion to his wife's death was a token for *him,* foreshadowing how he would react to news of the Temple's fall.

But, if so, why did he not begin to speak as soon as she died? We must recall that his feelings toward her were far more ambivalent than his feelings toward the Temple. His love for the individual woman countered his hatred for the displaced image of the Female. His emotional paralysis at her death followed, as we have seen, from this ambivalence.

This was hardly a situation likely to relieve Ezekiel's anxieties and release his repressions. His wife's death may indeed have indicated to him that Yahweh hated the Female, and thus helped ease his guilt over his own hatred. But it also had the effect of provoking more guilt, that he should feel joy and satisfaction at the death of that specific female. . . . Further, as a token of the divine will, the death of a human being is far more ambiguous (and therefore less reassuring) than God's devastation of his own sanctuary.

The death of Ezekiel's wife therefore could not itself "open his mouth." But it did allow him to anticipate that his mouth would be opened at some future time, when another mother-representation, which he hated with a hatred more nearly pure, would meet her end.

The situation came to pass. He responded as he had expected. The unconscious had prophesied of its own workings. Its prophecy, not unnaturally, came true.

How permanent was Ezekiel's "cure"? Most psychoanalysts, I imagine, would be pessimistic. Ezekiel's dumbness was his desperate yet indispensable device for coping with a painful and deep-rooted conflict. A fortuitous external event like the fall of Jerusalem might provide some relief. But, without any true resolution of the conflict, the relief could only be temporary.

It is hard to imagine that Ezekiel could have resolved his conflict without some measure of insight into its reality. It is harder still to think of any way he could have achieved that insight. It will follow that the dumbness must sooner or later have returned, or been replaced by some other conversion symptom serving the same function.

Reading 7.2   Psychological Perspectives on the Life of Paul

TERRANCE CALLAN

We saw in Chapter 4 how Gerd Theissen used depth psychology, cognitive theory, and learning theory to analyze aspects of Paul's theology. Inspired by Theissen's example, Terrence Callan goes further, applying methods derived from psycho-biography to discern a portrait of the apostle himself. In this selection, Callan discusses the tensions between competition, boasting, and humility in Paul's self-expression.

A. Paul the Competitor

1. Pre-Christian Period

In Paul's brief references to his life before becoming a follower of Jesus, he gives us reason to believe that comparison of himself with others and competition with them was an important element of his personality at that time.[1] In Gal 1:14 he explicitly compares his pre-Christian self with his contemporaries and says that he surpassed them — "I advanced in Judaism beyond many of my own age among my people, so extremely zealous was I for the traditions of my fathers." The same thing emerges almost as clearly in Phil 3:4-6 where Paul argues that he has greater reason for confidence in the flesh than others do (v. 4). After mentioning his circumcision on the 8th day, he enumerates in v. 5 some foundations for confidence in the flesh which are his by virtue of birth, i.e., being of the people of Israel, of the tribe of Benjamin, a Hebrew of the Hebrews.[2] Then in vv. 5-6 he lists three reasons for confidence in the flesh

---

1. Or at least this is how Paul saw himself at the time he wrote. For a discussion of the way the retrospective point of view influences Paul and Augustine, see Paula Fredriksen, "Paul and Augustine: Conversion Narratives, Orthodox Traditions, and the Retrospective Self," *Journal of Theological Studies* 37 (1986): 3-34.

2. According to Beverly Gaventa 'a Hebrew of the Hebrews' is generally interpreted to mean one of three things: (a) Paul and his family were Jewish rather than Gentile, (b) they spoke Aramaic or Hebrew, or (c) they were not Hellenized but used Jewish language and customs. Gaventa argues that 'b' is most likely. Beverly Gaventa, *Paul's Conversion: A Critical Sifting of the Epistolary Evidence* (Duke University dissertation, 1978), pp. 270-72.

From Terrance Callan, *Psychological Perspectives on the Life of Paul: An Application of the Methodology of Gerd Theissen* (Lewiston/Queenston/Lampeter: Edwin Mellen, 1990), pp. 16-24, 36-39.

which are his own achievement: "as to the law a Pharisee," i.e., a member of an observant group of Jews; "as to zeal a persecutor of the church," i.e., so ardent that he took the extreme step of persecuting; and "as to righteousness under the law blameless," i.e., a perfect Jew.[3]

Not only do these passages tell us that Paul compared himself with others and competed with them: they also tell us that Paul's competition took the form of outdoing others in zeal *(zelos)* for Judaism (cf. also Acts 22:3). This word and its cognates have been studied by A. Stumpff.[4] According to Stumpff the basic meaning of *zelos* is "the capacity or state of passionate committal to a person or cause," which can be a good or a bad quality. When it is a good quality, this passionate commitment is 'zeal' or 'enthusiasm'; as a bad quality it is 'contention' or 'jealousy.'[5] But when *zelos* was used to translate *qn'h* and its cognates in the Greek translation of the Hebrew scriptures, it took on new meaning. Most strikingly, it was frequently imputed to God in the sense of 'jealousy,' indicating God's exclusive claim on, and commitment to, Israel.[6] And then, in dependence on this usage, *zelos* was occasionally imputed to men with the implication that they are "representatively . . . filled by this holy zeal for the maintaining of the divine glory. . . ."[7]

According to Stumpff, Paul uses *zelos* in this last sense in the passages we are considering.[8] If so, then it may be that Paul's striving to excel, taking the form of surpassing zeal, was authorized and strengthened by being identified with the zeal of God himself. This would help to explain the otherwise

---

3. As we can see from these passages, comparison of oneself with others is intrinsically competitive; when used positively it is designed to show that one is at least equal to others. Paul seems to show an awareness of this when he recommends in Gal 6:4 that each test his or her own work so as to have a reason to boast in oneself, not another. Likewise in 2 Cor 10:12 Paul says that he will not compare himself with his opponents. But he goes on to criticize them for measuring themselves by themselves and comparing themselves with themselves, which seems to be what he is recommending in Gal 6:4. On the rhetorical use of comparison see Hans Dieter Betz, *Der Apostel Paulus und die sokratische Tradition: Fine exegetische Untersuchung zu seiner "Apologie" 2 Korinther 10:13*, Beitrage zur historischen Theologie 45 (Tübingen: Mohr [Siebeck], 1972), pp. 119-20; Christopher Forbes, "Comparison, Self-Praise and Irony: Paul's Boasting and the Conventions of Hellenistic Rhetoric," *New Testament Studies* 32 (1986): 1-30, especially pp. 2-8. Betz points out that Paul's critique of comparison in 2 Cor 10:12 is similar to the critique of comparison in the popular philosophy of the day (*Der Apostel Paulus*, pp. 120-21).

4. A. Stumpff, "*zelos ktl*," *Theological Dictionary of the New Testament*, trans. and ed. Geoffrey W. Bromiley (Grand Rapids: Eerdmans, 1976), vol. 2, pp. 877-88.

5. Stumpff, "*zelos ktl*," pp. 877-78. In the negative sense *zelos* is similar in meaning to *phthonos*.

6. Stumpff, "*zelos ktl*," pp. 879, 884.

7. Stumpff, "*zelos ktl*," p. 884; cf. 878.

8. Stumpff, "*zelos ktl*," pp. 880-81, 887.

surprising fact that Paul was a persecutor. Identification with the zeal of God might lead to actions which would be unlikely as actions of a mere human being. Such identification is explicit in the case of Phineas, the prototype of religious zeal. After Phineas has killed Zimri and the Midianite woman as they lay together, God says that Phineas was zealous with the zeal of God (Num 25:11). . . .

2. Christian Period

It seems clear that one result of Paul's conversion was that he became critical of his own propensity to compare himself with others and compete with them. It is probable that this is so because such competition is an expression of self-reliance, and in his conversion Paul was profoundly convinced that righteousness was a free gift and could not be earned. Consequently he eschewed self-reliance and with it competition. This is fairly explicit in Phil 3:3-11. After enumerating his reasons for confidence in the flesh in vv. 4-6 (as we have seen), Paul goes on in v. 7 to say that whatever gain he had, he counted as loss for the sake of Christ. And then in v. 9 he says that he has given up trying to establish his own righteousness by keeping the law, and now looks for righteousness which comes through faith (in Christ). Thus Paul simultaneously turns his back on self-reliance and on competition with others in the effort to establish his own righteousness.[9]

However, it is also clear that even as a Christian Paul did continue to rely on himself and compete with others despite his arguments against doing so. A particularly illuminating example of this inconsistency is found in 1 Cor 15:10.[10] Paul says

> By the grace of God I am what I am [i.e., an apostle], and his grace toward me was not in vain. On the contrary, I worked harder than any of them

9. This is commonly recognized as a theme of Paul's theology: cf. Rudolf Bultmann, *Theology of the New Testament* (New York: Scribner, 1951, 1955), §23. In *Paul and Palestinian Judaism: A Comparison of Patterns of Religion* (Philadelphia: Fortress, 1977) and *Paul, the Law and the Jewish People* (Philadelphia: Fortress, 1983), E. P. Sanders has argued (correctly, I believe) that Paul's objection to Judaism is most basically that Jews have rejected Christ, not that Judaism essentially entails self-righteousness. However, in making this argument, I think Sanders may underestimate the degree to which Paul retrospectively (perhaps depending excessively on his own experience) analyzes the Jewish failure to believe in Jesus as springing from self-reliance. Of course, Paul is also critical of Gentile self-reliance.

10. Gerd Theissen also notes this inconsistency in *Psychological Aspects of Pauline Theology* (Philadelphia: Fortress, 1987), p. 34.

[i.e., the other apostles], though it was not I, but the grace of God which is with me.

After first claiming that he worked harder than any of the other apostles, Paul corrects himself and says that it was not his doing, but the grace of God. From this we can see that Paul did not want to rely on himself and compete with others after his conversion. But the passage shows just as clearly that despite this desire Paul did continue to rely on himself and compete as a Christian, since he does claim to have worked harder than the other apostles. And it suggests that Paul is partly unconscious of this continuing self-reliance and competition because the statement is also a misstatement, a slip of tongue or pen, which Paul corrects.[11] Finally, this passage also shows that insofar as he was aware that he continued to rely on himself and compete with others, Paul could allow for this by attributing it not to himself, but to the grace of God, i.e., by identifying his striving with the action of God's grace in him. Thus both before and after he became a Christian, Paul identified his efforts with the action of God in him; however, this was not in the former case, as it was in the latter, a way of allowing for such effort despite a critical attitude toward it.

If we look only at Paul's final statement, 1 Cor 15:10 is simply one expression of his well-known view that human effort, his own and others', does have a place in Christian life as a response to the free gift of righteousness.[12] This stands in a dialectical tension with Paul's critique of self-reliance, but is not inconsistent with it. But 1 Cor 15:10 also shows that Paul's pre-Christian attitude of self-reliance expressed in competition, persisted in him unconsciously and that it was inconsistent with his critique of self-reliance. Insofar as Paul becomes conscious of it (as he does in 1 Cor 15:10), he can allow for it by identifying it with the action of God in him. But insofar as it remains unconscious, it makes Paul inconsistent with himself.

11. In this passage a verb in the first person singular *(ekopiasa)* is followed by *ouk ego . . . alla*. There is a formal parallel to this in 1 Cor 7:10. In Gal 2:20 a verb in the first person singular *(zo)* is followed by *ouketi ego . . . de*. We find another sort of correction in 1 Cor 1:16. All of these may point to differences between Paul's conscious and unconscious attitudes. In each case Paul's first statement would reflect his unconscious attitude and the correction, his conscious attitude. G. Theissen gives a different psychological interpretation of 1 Cor 15:10 and Gal 2:20, seeing them as examples of religious restructuring of causal attribution (*Psychological Aspects*, pp. 35-36).

12. On this see William A. Beardslee, *Human Achievement and Divine Vocation in the Message of Paul*, Studies in Biblical Theology 31 (Naperville, IL: Allenson, 1961), especially pp. 41-65. That Paul in general allows for human effort by identifying it with the action of God is suggested by 1 Cor 15:58 where Paul urges the Corinthians to abound *(perisseuo)* in the work of the Lord, knowing that in the Lord their toil is not in vain, and by such descriptions of Christian life as "walking in the spirit" (Gal 5:16) and "putting on Christ" (Rom 13:14).

The picture of Paul which emerges from 1 Cor 15:10 is confirmed by a variety of themes running through his letters. These show that despite his critique of self-reliance and competition, as a Christian Paul continued to rely on himself and compete unconsciously, and that insofar as he was conscious of it he authorized it by identifying with God and/or Christ.[13]

a. Use of Athletic Imagery   In a number of places Paul applies the image of athletic competition to himself[14] and others (1 Cor 9:24-7; Gal 5:7). V. C. Pfitzner argues that Paul's point in using this image is not to approve or promote competition.[15] However, even if it is not his conscious intent, the use of such imagery, which is intimately connected with rivalry and self-assertion,[16] seems to show that Paul unconsciously saw himself and other Christians as self-reliant and competitive.

b. Fear of Failure   In connection with several of these uses of an athletic image Paul expresses concern that he may have run in vain (Gal 2:2; Phil 2:16) or be found wanting (*adokimos* — 1 Cor 9:27). Similarly, Paul is elsewhere concerned that he may have labored in vain (Gal 4:11; Phil 2:16; 1 Thess 3:5), boasted in vain (2 Cor 9:3-4) or be found wanting (*adokimos* — 2 Cor 13:6). This concern may be expressed obliquely when Paul denies that the grace of God toward him has been in vain (1 Cor 15:10; cf. 15:58) or that his work has been in vain (1 Thess 2:1). As is unambiguous in the context of athletic imagery and in 1 Cor 15:10, it seems that these expressions of fear of failure are a negative reflection of Paul's unconsciously continuing to rely on himself and compete as a Christian.[17]

c. *Mimesis* of Paul   Paul frequently presents himself as a model to be imitated. In 1 Thess 1:6 he says that the Thessalonians have become imitators of him, and in 1 Cor 4:16 he urges the Corinthians to imitate him.[18] He says to the Galatians "become as I am" (4:12), to the Corinthians "I wish that all were

---

13. On the theme of identification with Christ see Richard Rubenstein, *My Brother Paul* (New York: Harper and Row, 1972), pp. 23-33.

14. 1 Cor 9:24-27; Gal 2:2; Phil 2:16; 3:14.

15. Victor C. Pfitzner, *Paul and the Agon Motif: Traditional Athletic Imagery in the Pauline Literature*, Novum Testamentum Supplements 16 (Leiden: Brill, 1967), especially pp. 194-95.

16. Pfitzner, *Paul and the Agon Motif*, pp. 16-18; cf. Rom 9:16.

17. Cf. Rudolf Bultmann's observation that "the hidden side of 'boasting' and 'putting confidence in the flesh' is the fear which the man who is concerned for himself has" (*Theology of the NT*, vol. 1, p. 243).

18. Cf. also 1 Cor 11:1; Phil 3:17; and 2 Thess 3:7.

as I myself am" (1 Cor 7:7) and to the Philippians "what you have . . . heard and seen in me, do" (4:9).

Paul's presentation of himself as a model seems to proceed from, and reflect, his sense of himself as a person of notable achievement. It also seems to presuppose that this achievement will, or should, be recognized by others.[19] Paul was at least partly conscious of this, and insofar as he was, he validated it by means of identification with Christ. Thus in 1 Thess 1:6 he says "you became imitators of us and of the Lord," and in 1 Cor 11:1 he says "be imitators of me, as I am of Christ."

d. Disdain   A negative counterpart to Paul's presentation of himself as a model is his occasional expression of disdain for his peers. The clearest example is in Gal 2:1-10 where he repeatedly calls the leaders of the Jerusalem church *hoi dokountes* [the influential] (vv. 2, 6, 9). This term is used both positively and negatively or ironically.[20] That Paul uses it ironically here is clear from v. 6 where he says that what the *dokountes* were does not matter to him because God shows no partiality. Paul does not deny the position of the *dokountes,* but at the same time does not consider it to be important. Therefore it seems very likely that he uses the term *dokountes* to indicate a disparity between appearance and reality: the leaders of the Jerusalem church appear to be something, and are insofar as they are recognized as such, but in reality their worth depends not on what they appear to be, but on what they are in the judgment of God.[21] Paul's emphatic disdain for the apparent importance of these leaders seems to reflect Paul's sense that he is at least their equal and can assess their worth. Paul here again reveals that he compares himself with others and competes with them, and further, that at times he thinks little of them.

The same thing is reflected even more strikingly in the following story of Paul's confrontation with Cephas in Antioch (Gal 2:11-14). Paul's public calling of Cephas to account for hypocrisy rather clearly implies that Paul is his equal and that at least in this instance Paul has no great respect for him.

---

19. On this topic see Willis P. de Boer, *The Imitation of Paul: An Exegetical Study* (Amsterdam: Kampen, 1962). At the beginning of his study de Boer asks, "Can it be that Paul fell victim to the boastful pride which, as Dodd has suggested, was his characteristic temptation?" (p. xi), but he does not explicitly pursue this question. E. Best also raises the question whether or not Paul's presentation of himself as a model involves arrogance, but does not answer it conclusively (Ernest Best, *Paul and His Converts: The Sprunt Lectures 1985* [Edinburgh: T&T Clark, 1988], pp. 8, 59-72).

20. Hans Dieter Betz, *Galatians,* Hermeneia (Philadelphia: Fortress, 1979), pp. 86-87.

21. On this see D. M. Hay, "Paul's Indifference to Authority," *Journal of Biblical Literature* 88 (1969): 36-44, especially pp. 39-42.

Closely parallel to Paul's use of *dokountes* in Galatians 2 is his description of apostles as *hyperlian* [extra-special] in 2 Cor 11:5 and 12:11. The term is ironic[22] and expresses doubt about the self-evaluation of Paul's opponents and their evaluation by the Corinthians, by exaggerating it. Paul's disdain for these opponents again seems to reflect Paul's view of himself as their equal or better. Again we see that Paul sometimes thinks little of those with whom he competes.

Paul is at least partly conscious of the competitive character of this disdain and justifies it by identifying with God. In Gal 2:6 he bases his disdain for the *dokountes* on the impartiality of God, clearly implying that God's attitude is also his.

e. *Zelos* [Zeal]   As might be expected, because zeal was so large a part of what Paul after his conversion regarded as reprehensible striving for superiority, as a Christian Paul is critical of zeal, though not as critical as he is of the striving for superiority itself. This is clear from Rom 10:2 where Paul testifies that non-Christian Israel has zeal for God (or the zeal of God), but it is not enlightened (cf. Gal 4:17-18). In v. 3 he explains that this is so because they attempt to establish their own righteousness. It seems very likely that Paul would apply this same critique to his own pre-conversion zeal. But this critique seems to imply the possibility of an enlightened zeal, one which is not part of an attempt to establish one's own righteousness (cf. 1 Cor 12:31; 14:1, 39).

That Paul as a Christian was characterized by such zeal is clear from 2 Cor 11:2 where Paul tells the Corinthians that he is zealous for them with the zeal of God. Here Paul compares his competition with his rivals in Corinth for the loyalty of the Corinthians to God's competition with idols for the loyalty of Israel. In this case Paul is consciously competitive, his competition takes the form of zeal, and this zeal is validated by being understood as a participation in the zeal of God.

From all of this it seems clear that after Paul became a Christian, despite a critical attitude toward self-reliance and competition with others, Paul continued to strive to excel. In part he was unconscious of this and so, unknowingly, inconsistent. Unconsciously Paul remained the very sort of person he preached against, which is perhaps not at all surprising psychologically.[23] In-

---

22. Betz, *Der Apostel Paulus*, p. 121.

23. We might think in this connection of the Freudian concepts of reaction-formation, i.e., defense against an undesirable unconscious attitude by adopting the opposite as a conscious attitude, and projection, i.e., defense against an unacceptable unconscious wish or impulse by attributing it to someone else. See C. Brenner, *An Elementary Textbook of Psychoanalysis*, rev. ed. (Garden City, NY: Doubleday, 1974), pp. 84-88, 91-93. Jungian psychology also speaks of projection: see M. A. Mattoon, *Jungian Psychology in Perspective* (New York: Free Press, 1981), pp. 126-33.

sofar as he was aware of his continuing self-reliance and competition, Paul could accept it by identifying with God and Christ, and his striving with their action in and through him. This stood in dialectical tension with his critique of self-reliance and competition, but was not inconsistent with it and allowed the expression of the competitive element of his personality. . . .

C. Competition and Boasting in Paul's Cultural Milieu

To the 20th century Western reader it may seem that Paul's competitive, boastful character is the main item in our portrait of him which is in need of psychological explanation. However, it seems likely that such a character was typical of Paul's culture and thus that no special explanation of it is required, unless such an explanation would apply to the entire culture. B. J. Malina argues that first century Mediterranean culture was an agonistic culture, characterized by competition for honor.[24] In support of this we may observe that Paul's use of athletic imagery and his presentation of himself as a model to be imitated, two of the things which, I argued, reveal his competitive character, have abundant parallels in his day.[25] With regard to boasting, H. D. Betz argues that Paul's boasting does not violate the rules governing proper boasting which are found in Plutarch's treatise *On Inoffensive Self-Praise*.[26]

24. Bruce J. Malina, *The NT World: Insights from Cultural Anthropology* (Atlanta: John Knox, 1981), pp. 25-50. See also his discussion of the relationship between individual and society, pp. 51-60.

25. See Pfitzner, *Paul and the Agon Motif;* W. P. de Boer, *The Imitation of Paul;* B. Fiore, *The Function of Personal Example in the Socratic and Pastoral Epistles,* Analecta Biblica 105 (Rome: Biblical Institute, 1986), pp. 33-35, 176-77; and E. Best, *Paul and His Converts,* pp. 60-63. However, Best notes that in literature apart from Paul's letters, the call to imitate "is mostly made in the third person. . . ." He mentions 4 Macc 9:23 and 2 Macc 6:27-28 as exceptions to this (p. 68).

26. Hans Dieter Betz, "De laude Ipsius (Morelia 539A-547F)," in *Plutarch's Ethical Writings and Early Christian Literature,* ed. H. D. Betz, Studia ad Corpus Hellenisticum Novi Testamenti 4 (Leiden: Brill, 1978), pp. 367-93. Earlier Betz argued the same point with regard to Paul's boasting in 2 Corinthians 10–13, appealing to Quintilian, *Institutio Oratoria* 11.1.15-26 in addition to Plutarch's treatise (*Der Apostel Paulus,* pp. 75-79). Cf. also E. A. Judge, "Paul's Boasting in Relation to Contemporary Professional Practice," *Australian Biblical Review* 16 (1968): 37-50; C. Forbes, "Comparison, Self-Praise and Irony." . . . J. T. Fitzgerald has shown the extent to which even Paul's boasting in weakness conforms to the norms of his culture. See also K. Wengst's argument that in general humility was regarded negatively in Graeco-Roman culture: Klaus Wengst, *Humility: Solidarity of the Humiliated: The Transformation of an Attitude and Its Social Relevance in Graeco-Roman, Old Testament Jewish, and Early Christian Tradition,* trans. J. Bowden (Philadelphia: Fortress, 1988), pp. 4-15.

If it is true that the basic character which we have perceived in Paul is typical of his culture, then what most needs explanation is his critique of self-reliance, competition and boasting. Of course, some critique of at least the last of these is reflected in Plutarch's recognition that self-praise can be offensive. However, for him it is offensive when it detracts from, rather than enhances, one's honor; this is very different from Paul's critique.[27]

A much closer parallel to Paul's critique of boasting is provided by Jewish literature.[28] Although Wisdom literature speaks of boasting about one's accomplishments with approval (e.g., Prov 16:31; Sir 30:2), the Deuteronomic history, psalms and prophetic writings are critical of such boasting (e.g., Judg 7:2; Ps 49:7-8). Especially important is Jer 9:22-23 (LXX 9:23-24) which Paul twice paraphrases:

> Let not the wise man glory in his wisdom, let not the mighty man glory in his might, let not the rich man glory in his riches; but let him who glories glory in this, that he understands and knows me. . . .

We also find criticism of boasting about one's accomplishments in the *Testaments of the Twelve Patriarchs* (e.g., *T. Judah* 13.2) and especially in Philo, although Philo makes little use of *kauchasthai* [to boast] and its cognates. However, in *Spec. Leg.* 1.311 Philo says, referring to Deut 10:21, "Let God alone be your boast *(kauchema)* . . . and be magnified neither in wealth, nor in glory, nor dominion, nor comeliness of body, nor strength. . . ."

If Paul was aware of this attitude toward boasting in the Bible and among his contemporaries before his conversion, he at least did not regard it as incompatible with his attempt to surpass others in zeal for the law nor, quite possibly, with boasting of his success in doing so. However, as a result of his conversion Paul explicitly embraced this critical attitude toward boasting, at least as expressed in Jer 9:22-23, and did understand it as excluding boasting about fulfillment of the law, as well as about any other human accomplishment. Since Paul's conversion was the source of his critique of self-reliance, competition and boasting, a psychological explanation of this critique must be, in effect, a psychological interpretation of his conversion.

---

27. On Greek criticism of boasting see Rudolf Bultmann, *"kauchaomai,"* *Theological Dictionary of the New Testament*, vol. 3, p. 646.

28. See Bultmann, *"kauchaomai,"* pp. 646-48; B. R. Gaventa, "'Where Then Is Boasting?' Romans 3:27 and Its Contexts," *Proceedings of the Eastern Great Lakes Biblical Society* 5 (1985): 60-61, 62-64. See also K. Wengst's argument that humility was regarded positively in Jewish literature, *Humility*, pp. 16-35.

D. Psychological Analysis of Paul's Attitude
toward Competition and Boasting

One psychological framework which seems helpful for understanding Paul's conversion is E. H. Erikson's theory that youth is the time during which a person's ego identity is formed and that this occurs by means of experimentation with various identities.[29] Thus Paul's earlier identity was that of one zealous for the traditions of his fathers, an identity supported by his unconscious identification with the zeal of God. This identity allowed unhindered expression of Paul's competitive, boastful character; and with the intolerance typical of the period of identity formation,[30] Paul persecuted the Christians.

In his conversion Paul exchanged this earlier identity for another. Paul's encounter with the risen Jesus (cf. 1 Cor 9:1; 15:8) shattered his earlier identity. It convinced him that the Christians were right and thus that the direction of his life, culminating in persecution of Christians, was wrong (cf. 1 Cor 15:9; Phil 3:7-8). But in the ruins of this identity Paul found another, that of a follower and apostle of Jesus. This second identity was also supported by an identification with God, but now a conscious identification with God as revealed in Jesus. This identity did not allow the direct expression of Paul's competitive character, but was in conflict with it since Paul now understood himself as entirely dependent upon God. However, despite the conflict it created, his new identity suited him, perhaps because it restrained his competitive character from possible excesses (such as persecution) while allowing its controlled expression through the identification of his striving with the action of God in him.

---

29. Erik H. Erikson, *Identity and the Life Cycle* (New York: Norton, 1979), especially pp. 94-100, 118-31. For a full-scale biographical application of this theory see Erik H. Erikson, *Young Man Luther: A Study in Psychoanalysis and History* (New York: Norton, 1958). It is interesting to note that there was considerable reflection on the life-cycle in antiquity; see J. LaPorte, "The Ages of Life in Philo of Alexandria," *Society of Biblical Literature Seminar Papers,* 1986, pp. 278-90. As might be expected, ancient understanding of the life-cycle is not very similar to Erikson's theory in its details. However, Philo's description of the fourth age of life, i.e., 22-28 years, in *Heres* 298-99 somewhat resembles Erikson's understanding of the stage of identity.

30. Erikson, *Identity,* pp. 97-98.

SUGGESTIONS FOR FURTHER READING

Broome, Edwin C. "Ezekiel's Abnormal Personality." *Journal of Biblical Literature* 65 (1946): 277-92.

Cassem, Ned H. "Ezekiel's Psychotic Personality: Reservations on the Use of the Couch for Biblical Personalities." In *Word in the World,* edited by R. Clifford, 59-68. Cambridge, MA: Weston College Press, 1973.

Garber, David G., Jr. "Traumatizing Ezekiel, the Exilic Prophet." In *Psychology and the Bible: A New Way to Read the Scriptures,* edited by J. Harold Ellens and Wayne G. Rollins, vol. 2, 215-35. Westport, CT: Greenwood-Praeger, 2004.

Healer, C. *Freud and St. Paul.* Philadelphia: Dorrance and Co., 1972.

Holmes, Arthur. *The Mind of St. Paul: A Psychological Study.* New York: Macmillan, 1929.

Jobling, David. "An Adequate Psychological Approach to the Book of Ezekiel." In *Psychology and the Bible: A New Way to Read the Scriptures,* edited by J. Harold Ellens and Wayne G. Rollins, vol. 2, 203-13. Westport, CT: Greenwood-Praeger, 2004.

Rubenstein, Richard. *My Brother Paul.* New York: Harper & Row, 1972.

Schmitt, John J. "Psychoanalyzing Ezekiel." In *Psychology and the Bible: A New Way to Read the Scriptures,* edited by J. Harold Ellens and Wayne G. Rollins, vol. 2, 185-201. Westport, CT: Greenwood-Praeger, 2004.

Scroggs, Robin. *Paul for a New Day.* Philadelphia: Fortress, 1977.

CHAPTER 8

Biblical Personalities:
Moses and Jesus

Michelangelo has created, not a historical figure, but a character-type, embodying an inexhaustible inner force which tames the recalcitrant world; and he has given a form not only to the Biblical narrative of Moses, but to his own inner experiences.

Sigmund Freud in *The Moses of Michelangelo*[1]

Jesus did not himself write down either the message of his words and deeds or the interpretation of his birth and death. Jesus' vision therefore needs to be deciphered from what others said about him.

Andries van Aarde in *Fatherless in Galilee*[2]

Psychological analysis of biblical personalities can take one of three routes, each with a different objective. One of these routes, as noted in the previous chapter, takes us to the "world behind the text" — the mind and world of the author as revealed in his words — as in the case of Ezekiel and Paul. Though in the strictest sense, psychological analysis of biblical figures is ruled out by the absence of the analysand, it is permissible as a tentative method to plumb the personality of a writer whose literary record provides a sufficient base of autobiographical material. Psychological observations are regularly made on figures like Gandhi, Luther, John Adams, Thomas Jefferson, Augustine, and

---

1. Sigmund Freud, *The Moses of Michelangelo*, in *The Standard Edition of the Complete Psychological Works of Sigmund Freud*, ed. James Strachey, 24 vols. (London: Hogarth Press and the Institute of Psychoanalysis, 1914), vol. 13, p. 231.
2. Andries Van Aarde, *Fatherless in Galilee: Jesus as a Child of God* (Harrisburg: Trinity Press International, 2001), p. 205.

the acerbic early church personality Tertullian, based on the legacy of their writings, out of which a sense of personality and even pathology can emerge. Nowhere in Scripture do we come closer to listening firsthand to a human soul in his own words as when reading Paul. His letters provide an index of his mind, logic, aspirations, defenses, and personal qualities.

In this chapter we would like to demonstrate how the biblical figures of Moses and Jesus provide two further opportunities for the application of psychological insight.

In Edward Edinger's discussion of the figure of Moses in our first reading, we see how psychological insight can be employed to explore the "world in front of the text," that is, the transaction that occurs between the power of a biblical figure and a reader. Freud testifies to the impact that the Moses of Michelangelo in Rome's S. Pietro in Vincoli had on him, acknowledging that this was a secondary effect of a comparable impact Moses had exercised in the life of Michelangelo. Freud writes, "No piece of statuary has ever made a stronger impression on me than this." He goes on to tell us, "There is not the slightest doubt that it represents Moses, the law-giver of the Jews, holding the Tables of the Ten Commandments. This much is certain."[3] But he acknowledges that in our response to such archetypal figures — for Michelangelo and for himself — our own inner experience is part of the equation.[4]

We will see how Edinger employs Jungian archetypal psychology to help us understand why a figure like Moses, Jesus, Paul, David, Jonah, or Jacob can play an imposing archetypal role at conscious and unconscious levels.

Psychological inquiry into a figure such as this is less a journey into the past than a review of the celebratory words, stories, paintings, and sculpture that the memory of such a figure has generated. Psychological inquiry into the "world in front of the text" examines the transaction between text and reader, where human imagination is inspired by the tales of a legendary hero, and is fed generation after generation by rehearsing his story and amplifying it in word, song, and worship. The Moses of Scripture in the "world in front of the text" is inseparable psychologically from the Moses of the Hebrew Bible (mentioned over 600 times), the Moses of the New Testament (mentioned 80 times), the Moses of the Rabbis (rehearsed in hundreds of midrashic tales exemplifying the ideal prophet, law-giver, sage, prophet, nation-founder, deliverer, ideal judge, writer, and, above all, one who speaks with God), and the Moses of Michelangelo and of Marc Chagall. The degree to which the figure of Moses was internalized by Freud is evident in a note he sent to Carl Jung:

---

3. Freud, *Moses of Michelangelo*, p. 213.
4. Freud, *Moses of Michelangelo*, p. 222.

"We are certainly getting ahead; if I am Moses, then you are Joshua and will take possession of the promised land of psychiatry, which I shall only be able to glimpse from afar."[5]

Psychological insight into the life of Jesus offers a third application of psychology to the study of biblical figures, namely, inquiry into "the world of the text," in which we understand that the figure of Jesus is a construct of the author and his community, and that the realities of Jesus are refracted through the piety, inspiration, hopes, memories, and prayers of the worshiping community. As South African biblical scholar Andries van Aarde has observed, "Jesus did not himself write down either the message of his words and deeds or the interpretation of his birth and death. Jesus' vision therefore needs to be deciphered from what others said about him."[6]

The very existence of four Gospels rather than one in the official scriptural collection of the early church makes plain that we have a story *according to* Matthew, *according to* Mark, *according to* Luke, and *according to* John. The artist is inseparable from his subject. Our psychological goal is, as Hal Ellens has observed, to ask, "what kind of character must Jesus have been to legitimately carry the freight of the stories told about him?"[7]

The goal of a psychological journey into the "world of the text" is to bring to life as much as we know of the socio-economic, political, religious, and cultural setting of first-century Palestine as background and context for understanding the psychodynamics at work in the man Jesus as portrayed in the Gospels — his teaching, his acts, his associations, and his life story — and to sense the inner history that informs what he said and did, in the secret hope that we have come closer to the Jesus "behind the world of the text." Though our research is ineluctably mired in the vested interests of the Gospel narrators in their memory of Jesus as it was refracted through the faith-filled imagination of the early Christian community, and in our own vested interests, we can nevertheless put together a portrait of the Gospel writers' version of the man Jesus. This effort at psychohistory — an indispensable part of historical Jesus research — aims at delineating the outlines of the man in history, always wondering what it was in this original event, this real human being, that smacked of the holy and inspired those around him to holiness. These questions about the psychodynamics at work in every human situation are part of the set of tools the historian must use when trying to comprehend the

---

5. Letter to Carl Jung, January 17, 1909.

6. Van Aarde, *Fatherless in Galilee*, p. 205.

7. J. Harold Ellens and Wayne G. Rollins, eds., *Psychology and the Bible: A New Way to Read the Scriptures* (Westport, CT: Praeger, 2004), vol. 4, p. 4.

realities in any human setting. And when we've done it carefully and conscientiously we come away with the sense that we have touched on a bit of the mystery of the one whose life pattern generated the tradition about him. Or, as Albert Nolan hints, "It is not necessary to speculate about Jesus' psychology. We know that he was moved to act and speak by a profound experience of compassion. And we know that the Abba-experience was an experience of God as compassionate Father."[8]

In the second reading, John Miller's exploration into the "world of the text" provides an example of the wedding of psychological insight and biblical scholarship that adds psychobiography to one of the tools of historical Jesus research.

———————

Reading 8.1   Moses and Yahweh

EDWARD EDINGER

Edward Edinger interprets the biblical story of Moses from the standpoint of a Jungian analyst reading it for the values it awakens and confirms in the life experience of the reader. He finds in the story of Moses "the greatest individuation drama of the Western psyche." Edinger maintains that as much as Moses is remembered as liberator of his people and giver of the Law, he has also become highly valued in biblical lore and rabbinic tradition as the exemplification of the archetype of the hero.

Edinger also finds in the Moses story a treasury of symbols that play recurring roles in world literature as part of the human-divine drama: the sacred fire, the veneration of the divine name, holy ground, the significance of numbers, blood rituals, the importance of the first-born, waters of bitterness, the guidance of divine light, and the chimeric image of a promised land.

In the course of his Jungian exposition Edinger employs a number of terms

8. Albert Nolan, *Jesus Before Christianity* (London: Darton, Longman and Todd, 1976), p. 124.

———————

From Edward Edinger, "Moses and Yahweh: The Exodus," in *The Bible and the Psyche: Individuation Symbolism in the Old Testament* (Toronto: Inner City Books, 1986), pp. 45-54.

and phrases drawn from Jungian analytic practice — for example, individuation, the superior and inferior function, etc. The reader is encouraged to consult the glossary at the end of this book.

Moses and Yahweh: The Exodus

The encounter between Moses and Yahweh is one of the grandest individuation dramas of the Western psyche. Moses as the mediating agent between Yahweh and Israel brings about the redemption of his people from Egyptian bondage and leads the nation to fulfillment of its destiny.

With the aid of depth psychology this sacred story pertaining to the collective history of the Jews can now be understood as applicable to the experience of the individual. The story begins in Exodus 1:8-14:

> Then there came to power in Egypt a new king who knew nothing of Joseph. "Look," he said to his subjects, "these people, the sons of Israel, have become so numerous and strong that they are a threat to us." . . .
>
> Accordingly they put slave-drivers over the Israelites to wear them down under heavy loads. . . . But the more they were crushed, the more they increased and spread. . . . The Egyptians forced the sons of Israel into slavery, and made their lives unbearable with hard labor, work with clay and with brick, all kinds of work in the field; they forced on them every kind of labor.

This describes the psychological state of the individual who is about to be hit with the imperative of individuation. . . . This act of repression against the emerging unconscious content provokes a reaction from the unconscious — the birth of the hero.

The hero is a figure lying midway between the ego and the Self. It can perhaps best be defined as a personification of the urge to individuation. The story of Moses' birth follows closely the characteristic pattern of the myth of the birth of the hero.[1] The chief features of this myth are: (1) the birth occurs under adverse circumstances; (2) the authorities seek to kill it; (3) the infant is exposed or abandoned, often in water; (4) it is rescued, usually by lowly people, and accompanied by marvels; (5) there is a double set of parents, royal ones and lowly

---

1. See Otto Rank, *The Myth of the Birth of the Hero* (New York: Vintage Books, 1959), and Carl Gustav Jung, "Symbols of Transformation," *The Collected Works of C. G. Jung* [henceforth *CW*], trans. R. F. C. Hull, ed. Gerhard Adler et al., Bollingen Series 20 (Princeton: Princeton University Press, 1953-78), vol. 5, pars. 493ff.

ones. These features all apply to the myth of Moses' birth and refer psychologically to the vicissitudes surrounding the birth of the urge to individuation....

The canonical sources say nothing about Moses' youth and education. This gap is filled by legend, one of which is particularly pertinent. According to Philo, Moses quickly surpassed the knowledge of his teachers, "anticipating all their lessons by the excellent natural endowments of his own genius; so that everything in his case appeared to be a recollecting rather than a learning."[2] ... Applied to Moses, the process of learning by recollection means that individuation involves the discovery of one's innate wisdom and pattern of being.

The Bible picks up the story of Moses as an adult (at age forty, according to Acts 7:23) when he kills an Egyptian slave-driver. Although reared as Egyptian royalty, Moses belongs to the enslaved race of Hebrews and his allegiance manifests in this impulsive act. It is a primitive, unmediated expression of individuation energy, the initial manifestation of his "call." The murder leads Moses to his personal exodus, his flight into the wilderness where he will meet Yahweh....

Those destined for individuation often have the problem of intense energy-eruptions in youth.... The constellated Self will not endure bondage or constriction. In extremis it will resort to crime. In fact, actual criminality can be considered as perverted individuation. This aspect of Moses is recognized in legend, which asserts that he was of an "originally evil disposition ... covetous, haughty, sensual; in short, disfigured by all possible ugly traits." It was through strong will, character and severe discipline that he transformed his disposition into its opposite.[3]

After living many years in exile Moses encounters Yahweh. [See Exodus 3:1-15, the story of the burning bush on holy ground, the revelation to Moses of the divine name, YHWH, and the commissioning of Moses to bring the sons of Israel, "my people," out of Egypt.] This is a classic image of an encounter with the Self. One or more of its various features often come up in dreams. Fire is a frequent synonym for the divine ... ; it signifies affects and desirousness, intense libido-manifestations which are not integrated into the ego and hence have a transpersonal quality. According to The Gospel of Thomas Jesus said, "He who is near me is near the fire."[4] The unconsuming nature of the fire emphasizes its transpersonal nature....

An important feature of the theophany is the revelation of the divine

---

2. Nahum N. Glatzer, *The Essential Philo* (New York: Schocken, 1971), p. 195.

3. Louis Ginzberg, *Legends of the Bible* (New York: Simon and Schuster, 1956), pp. 294-95.

4. James M. Robinson, ed., *The Nag Hammadi Library* (San Francisco: Harper and Row, 1977), p. 127.

name. "YHWH" apparently derives from an archaic form of the verb "to be." It thus means "I am who I am" or "I am the One who is." Empirically, the most important characteristic of the Self, which defies precise definition, is that it exists. It has effective reality. As Jung puts it, "God is Reality itself."[5]

YHWH, the so-called tetragrammaton [the "four letters" of the divine name in Hebrew], . . . is, significantly, a quaternity. It is also a triad since one of its letters is duplicated. A similar combination of three and four occurs in the sacred emblem associated with the crucifixion of Christ in ecclesiastical art. Attached to the cross is a sign with the letters INRI (Iesus Nazarenus Rex Iudaeorum) [the Latin for *"Jesus of Nazareth King of the Jews"*; John 19:19].

Yahweh proceeds to show Moses the signs of his election. Moses casts his staff upon the ground and it becomes a serpent; he picks it up and it becomes a staff. He puts his hand in his bosom; on withdrawal it is leprous. He puts it in again and it is healed. (Exodus 4:2-7) According to legend these signs followed Moses' stubborn refusal to accept his mission and pictured threats to Moses that if he was not obedient he would become a serpent or a leper.[6] This idea has a very important psychological parallel.

Once the Self has been constellated, if its imperative is refused by the ego it can turn dangerously negative — provoking perhaps an accident or illness. . . .

The same idea is expressed in the mysterious passage of Exodus 4:24. Yahweh had directed Moses to proceed to Egypt. "On the journey, when Moses had halted for the night, Yahweh came to meet with him and tried to kill him." This passage, a perpetual enigma to the commentators, can now be understood as an illustration of the dangerously ambiguous nature of the activated Self. The relativization of the ego involves a sacrifice of the ego which is accompanied by intense anxiety. As Jung says,

> Fear of self-sacrifice lurks deep in every ego, and this fear is often only the precariously controlled demand of the unconscious forces to burst out in full strength. No one who strives for selfhood (individuation) is spared this dangerous passage.[7]

Moses' assignment is to convince Pharaoh to release the enslaved Israelites and lead them out of Egypt and into the promised land. Psychologically this means that the psyche is in bondage to the tyrannical power principle

---

5. Jung, "Answer to Job," *CW,* vol. 2, par. 631.

6. Ginzberg, *Legends of the Bible,* p. 318.

7. Jung, "Psychological Commentary on 'The Tibetan Book of the Dead,'" *CW,* vol. 11, par. 849.

symbolized by Pharaoh. A lesser authority (the power driven ego) is functioning in place of the Self (Yahweh). Once the Self is activated, individuation must proceed. If the ego does not cooperate it will be hit with increasing disturbances. Thus come about the ten plagues of Egypt. [Exodus 7:14–12:42; (1) the waters of Egypt turned into blood; (2) the plague of frogs; (3-4) mosquitoes and gadflies; (5) the cattle plague; (6) the plague of boils; (7) the plague of hail; (8) the plague of locusts; (9) the plague of darkness, and finally, (10) the death of the Egyptian first-born.] . . . "And at midnight Yahweh struck down all the first-born in the land of Egypt: the first-born of Pharaoh, heir to the throne, the first-born of the prisoner in his dungeon, and the first-born of all the cattle." (Exodus 12:25)

The Israelites are spared through the sacrifice of the paschal lamb, "without blemish," whose blood is daubed on the doorposts and lintel of each Hebrew dwelling. If this rite is performed, Yahweh promises, "The blood shall serve to mark the houses that you live in. When I see the blood I will pass over you and you shall escape the destroying plague." (Exodus 12:13)

The events of Passover night present an awesome image of an encounter with the activated Self. Yahweh stalks the streets at midnight, slaughtering every first-born creature that he meets, while the Jews huddle in their homes hoping their apotropaic rites will spare them. Yahweh must have his bloody sacrifice. Those who know Yahweh (the Israelites) can deliberately offer him a lamb and thereby be spared the greater price. The Egyptians, who don't know Yahweh, have no means of mitigating his demand. The full brunt of the divine imperative falls on them.

Passover symbolism repeats itself in a new context with the death of Christ. He takes upon himself the fate of the Egyptian first-born and of the paschal lamb. Just as the first-born son of Pharaoh must be sacrificed to achieve release of the Israelites from bondage, so Christ, the first-born son of Yahweh, must be offered up like another paschal lamb as a bloody sacrifice for man's spiritual salvation. As Jung points out, Christ's blood becomes another apotropaic amulet:

> Jesus became the tutelary image or amulet against the archetypal powers that threatened to possess everyone. The glad tidings announced: "It has happened, but it will not happen to you inasmuch as you believe in Jesus Christ, the son of God!"[8]

The underlying idea is that the first-born belongs to Yahweh. "Consecrate all the first-born to me, the first issue of every womb, among the sons of

8. Jung, "Psychology and Alchemy," *CW*, vol. 12, par. 4.

Israel. Whether man or beast, this is mine." (Exodus 13:2) This notion is not confined to ancient Israel. Frazer documents many other examples,[9] so evidently it is archetypal. What does it mean? First-born children do in fact carry a quality of specialness — in their own mind, in the minds of their parents and even in the view of society (witness the law of primogeniture). This sense of specialness may be augmented by the parental projection of the Self as divine child onto the first-born. Interpreted subjectively, the first-born refers to the ego in its once-born state, that is, unconsciously identified with the Self. With the sacrifice of the first-born ego, which is required for the birth of the Self into consciousness, the second-born state is realized.

The exodus begins with the miracle of the Red Sea crossing (Exodus 14), a rite of exit occurring at the threshold between Egyptian bondage and theophany in the wilderness. . . . What follows is forty years of desert wandering before the Promised Land is reached. This corresponds to the prolonged dealing with the unconscious — the chaos or *prima materia* — that is required following an irrevocable commitment to individuation. Forty days or years is the length of the alchemical opus[10] and forty days is the traditional time required for the Egyptian embalming process (Genesis 50:3), that is, the transition between personal, temporal existence (ego) and eternal, archetypal life (Self). Thus the forty years of wandering in the wilderness signify a *nekyia* or night journey from the ego-bound existence of Egypt to the transpersonal life of the Promised Land.

The account of the wilderness wandering provides us with a whole series of profound symbolic images pertaining to the individuation process. Immediately upon departure, agencies of divine guidance make their appearance. "Yahweh went before them, by day in the form of a pillar of cloud to show them the way, and by night in the form of a pillar of fire to give them light." (Exodus 13:21) This image is reminiscent of a passage in the I Ching:

> Only a strong man can stand up to his fate, for his inner security enables him to endure to the end. This strength shows itself in uncompromising truthfulness (with himself). It is only when we have the courage to face things exactly as they are, without any sort of self-deception or illusion, that *a light will develop out of events*, by which the path to success may be recognized.[11]

9. James G. Frazer, *The Golden Bough*, 3rd ed., 13 vols. (London: Macmillan, 1919), part 2, "The Dying God," p. 171.

10. Jung, "Mysterium Coniunctionis," *CW*, vol. 14, par. 77 and note 215.

11. *The I Ching or Book of Changes*, trans. Richard Wilhelm (Princeton: Princeton University Press, 1967), p. 25, my italics.

The light that develops out of events (both inner and outer) is only visible when the ego is in a state of emptiness, that is, in the wilderness. Through the window of a brightly lighted house at night one cannot see the stars. Turn off the light and they come into view. As Eckhart says,

> By keeping thyself empty and bare . . . and giving up thyself to this darkness and ignorance without turning back, thou mayest well win that which is all things. . . . Of this barrenness it is written in Hosea: "I will lead my friend into the desert and will speak to her in her heart." (2:14) The genuine Word of eternity is spoken only in eternity, where man is a desert and alien to himself and multiplicity.[12]

In fact, Eckhart says, God has to fill whatever emptiness he finds.

> God is bound to act, to pour himself out (into thee) as soon as ever he shall find thee ready . . . finding thee ready he is obliged to act, to overflow into thee; just as the sun must needs burst forth when the air is bright and clear, and is unable to contain itself.[13]

These passages describe the way the ego discovers the guidance of the Self. The ego must be in a humbled state of darkness and need before it can perceive the dim light of the transpersonal psyche. Cardinal Newman describes this experience in his poem "Lead, Kindly Light":

> Lead, kindly Light, amid the encircling gloom,
>   Lead Thou me on!
> The night is dark, and I am far from home —
>   Lead Thou me on![14]

. . . A major source of the "kindly light" is one's dreams, and a strong incentive to study one's dreams is to be in distress, in the grip of a painful problem. Thus the guiding light manifests in the wilderness.

The first stop in the desert was Marah (meaning bitterness) where the water was too bitter to drink and the people grumbled. (Exodus 15:23, 24) Bitterness is commonly encountered in psychotherapy. An infallible indicator of an unconscious infantile complex is the presence of bitterness and resentment. . . .

---

12. Franz Pfeiffer, ed., *Meister Eckhardt*, trans. C. de B. Evans (London: John M. Watkins, 1956), vol. 1, p. 23.

13. Pfeiffer, *Meister Eckhart*, vol. 1, p. 23.

14. W. A. Briggs and W. R. Bénet, eds., *Great Poems of the English Language* (New York: Tudor, 1944), p. 644.

In alchemy, bitterness is an aspect of the prima materia. Ripley says, "Each thing in its first matter is corrupt and bitter."[15] Bitterness belongs to the symbolism of salt. Jung writes,

> The most outstanding properties of salt are bitterness and wisdom. . . . The factor common to both, however incommensurable the two ideas may seem, is, psychologically, the function of *feeling*. Tears, sorrow, and disappointment are bitter, but wisdom is the comforter in all psychic suffering. Indeed, bitterness and wisdom form a pair of alternatives: where there is bitterness wisdom is lacking, and where wisdom is there can be no bitterness.[16]

It seems appropriate therefore that the journey to the Promised Land, which is psychologically equivalent to the Philosophers' Stone of the alchemists, should begin with bitterness. Indeed there was much bitterness on the part of the Israelites throughout their wandering because of the loss of their Egyptian comforts.

As they proceeded on their way a daily supply of food was provided by Yahweh, meat in the evening and bread in the morning, but only enough for one day. If it was saved for the following day, "it had maggots and smelt foul." (Exodus 16:20) Under the condition of divine guidance, as pertains during an individual's wandering in the wilderness, one is required to live only in the immediate present — one day at a time. . . . Jung puts it psychologically:

> The great thing is now and here, this is the eternal moment, and if you do not realize it, you have missed the best part of life, you have missed the realization that you were once the carrier of a life contained between the poles of an unimaginable future and an unimaginably remote past. Millions of years and untold millions of ancestors have worked up to this moment, and you are the fulfillment of this moment. Anything that is past is no longer reality, anything that will be is not yet reality, reality is now. To look at life as a mere preparation for things to come is as if you could not enjoy your meal while it was hot. That is the disease really of our time, everybody is chiefly concerned about the future; one admits that now things are very bad, so all the more one tries to jump out of them, and therefore they never improve. One should take each moment as the eternal moment, as if nothing were ever going to change, not anticipating a faraway future. For the future always grows out of that which is,

15. Quoted by Jung, "Mysterium Coniunctionis," *CW*, vol. 14, par. 246.
16. Quoted by Jung, "Mysterium Coniunctionis," *CW*, vol. 14, par. 330.

and it cannot be sound if it grows in a morbid soil; if we are morbid and don't feel this here and now, then we naturally will build up a sickly future. We have seen that in actual historical conditions; things are so bad at present because everybody lived in anticipation of something to come, one always expected the golden age, so things got worse and worse. Therefore in psychology, in the life of the individual, it is of the greatest importance that we never think of it as merely now, with the hope of something coming in the future. You can be sure it will never come when you think like that. You must live life in such a spirit that you make in every moment the best of the possibilities.[17]

Reading 8.2 Jesus at Thirty

John W. Miller

John Miller offers a profile of the inner world of Jesus as portrayed in the four Gospels. Miller employs the model of the "Age Thirty Transition" in Daniel Levinson's *The Seasons of a Man's Life* as a heuristic device to uncover developmental stages in the life and mission of Jesus of the Gospels. He focuses his research on the Gospel accounts of Jesus' relationships: to his mother, to his "absent" father, to his own fatherlessness, to his "brothers and sisters," to his mentor, John the Baptist, to women, and to the "temptation of grandiosity" reflected in the well-known legend of Jesus' temptation in the wilderness.

Developmental psychology . . . offers the historian another way of looking at whatever facts are available for whatever insights can be garnered from viewing them in this light. Thus, even the most fragmentary data (name, place and date of birth, names of parents and siblings, vocation, time of marriage) may be approached from a psychohistorical angle for the very same reason that a historian might examine it with the help of insights from linguistics, archaeology, economics, religion, or sociology. . . .

17. C. G. Jung, "Interpretation of Visions," mimeographed notes of seminar, Zurich, 1930-34, vol. 6, pp. 185f.

From John W. Miller, *Jesus at Thirty: A Psychological and Historical Portrait* (Minneapolis: Augsburg/Fortress, 1997), pp. 2, 7, 11, 13-16, 19-21, 24, 27-29, 90-95.

Just as it is no longer possible, in our time, to read the Gospels without an increasingly acute awareness of the historicity and humanity of Jesus, it is likewise no longer possible to read them without attention to the personal developmental dynamics of the one who meets us there.

Proof of this trend, were any needed, is the surfacing, in recent books about Jesus, of a host of questions and suggestions virtually ignored by previous generations. "Was Jesus married?" William Phipps has asked in two carefully researched works.[1] "If not, why not?" other authors query.[2] Still others allude to his "egocentricity" and wonder about the impact his exceptional self-identity might have had on his contemporaries.[3] Another hypothesizes that Jesus' alienation from his family might have been the psychological fact behind his decision to leave his home in Nazareth and begin his mission.[4] . . .

In taking a fresh psychohistorical look at the Jesus of history, there is little question about where to begin. If psychology since Freud has taught us anything, it is the way early experiences in the immediate family shape our emotional outlook. If we hope to get a firmer hold on the idiosyncrasies of the adult Jesus' inner world, it is to those texts that reflect his experience of father, mother, brothers, and sisters that we must turn. . . .

Psychology has taught us that if we wish to lay hold of the emotional configuration of a given individual's life, we must pay especially close attention to any data at all that might give evidence of unique familial dynamics, even if, at first glance, such data would appear to be of little or no interest to a biography in the traditional sense. And there does happen to be in the Gospels at least one sometimes neglected item of this nature: the account in Mark 3:19b-21 of a rather shocking action on the part of Jesus' family shortly after the beginning of his public mission. . . .

> Then he [Jesus] went home [to Capernaum]; and the crowd came together again, so that they [Jesus and his disciples] could not even eat. And when those close to him [his immediate family] heard it, they went out [from Nazareth] to seize him, for they said, "He is beside himself." . . .

1. William Phipps, *The Sexuality of Jesus* (New York: Harper & Row, 1973); William Phipps, *Was Jesus Married?* (New York: Harper & Row, 1971).

2. Symptomatic of growing interest in Jesus' celibacy is Gerald Sloyan, *Jesus in Focus: A Life in Its Setting* (Mystic, CT: Twenty-third Publications, 1983), pp. 129-32. See earlier discussion of this issue in John Hayes, *From Son of God to Super Star: Twentieth Century Interpretations of Jesus* (Nashville: Abingdon, 1976), pp. 223-34.

3. E. P. Sanders, *Jesus and Judaism* (Philadelphia: Fortress, 1985), p. 271; Martin Hengel, *The Charismatic Leader and His Followers* (New York: Crossroad, 1981), p. 64.

4. David Flusser, *Jesus* (New York: Herder & Herder, 1969), p. 22.

At the very least what this passage suggests is that, for whatever reasons, an estrangement had opened up between Jesus and his family at this juncture of his life — an estrangement so deep that communication had completely broken down between them. . . . The pathos of this unexpected development is summed up by a single sentence in John's Gospel: "He came to his own home, and his own people received him not" (John 1:11). There too it is explicitly stated that Jesus' own brothers were among those who "did not believe in him" (John 7:5).

The depth of this estrangement is also revealed in the episode described in Mark 3:31-35 (Matt. 12:46-50//Luke 8:19-21), where Jesus' mother and brothers are portrayed in the very act of visiting Capernaum, ostensibly to implement the plan referred to in Mark 3:19b-21 ("they went out to seize him, for they said, 'He is beside himself'"). When, however, they arrived at the place where Jesus was teaching, a crowd surrounded him. All that was possible was to send him a message: "Your mother and your brothers are outside, asking for you" (Mark 3:32). When Jesus heard of it, Mark informs us, his response was a surprising one. "Respect for his mother," comments Joseph Klausner, "(a prominent trait among the Jews, ranked in the Ten Commandments on the same level as respect for the father) required that he should go to her at once."[5] Instead, he said: "Who are my mother and my brothers?" And then "looking around on those who sat about him," he exclaimed, "Here are my mother and my brothers! Whoever does the will of God is my brother, and sister, and mother."

Although these passages do not tell us much, they do highlight the tensions that seem to have characterized the relations of Jesus and his family during this phase of his life. . . . For the sake of a spiritual family, it seems, this now, fully adult Jesus, will not give an inch to his biological family — no direct word of response to their request to see him, not even the slightest gesture of reconciliation. Pondering this scene one thinks of the story of how Gautama Buddha, one day at about the same age in life, abruptly turned his back on his parental home (and in that instance, on wife and child as well) to seek, and then teach, a new way to a growing circle of disciples.

. . . Even if it is true that the statement in Luke 14:26 about "hating father and mother and wife and children and brothers and sisters" (if one wishes to be a disciple) is hyperbole, it is again the same intra familial conflict that surfaces. . . . "A man's foes will be those of his own household" (Matt. 10:36). . . .

---

5. Joseph Klausner, *Jesus of Nazareth: His Life, Times, and Teaching* (New York: Macmillan, 1926), p. 280.

The Turning Point

The canonical sources for the life of Jesus leave us in no doubt as to where to look for the answer to the question concerning what may have precipitated the break between Jesus and his family. They point with one accord to his encounter with one of the "great men" of his generation, John the Baptist. It is this encounter, these Gospels tell us, that marked the transition from Jesus' "hidden years" to his public ministry. In fact, it is almost as though with this event Jesus came fully alive for the first time. . . . It is first through his meeting with John the Baptist that he entered upon that way of life that so shocked his family and was eventually to disquiet the world.

It all happened, we are told, in the days when this John was preaching repentance and baptizing at the Jordan with crowds streaming to him from all Judea. It was then that Jesus also left his home to join them and was himself baptized (Mark 1:9-11). But even more important, this was the occasion, our earliest sources tell us, when Jesus had an experience that they intimate was decisive for all that was to follow.

That Jesus was in fact baptized by John the Baptist is historically unquestionable, for the memory of this event hinted at a subordination of Jesus to John and a need on Jesus' part for repentance and forgiveness that was wholly at variance with the developing Christology of the early church. "Such a scandalizing piece of information cannot have been invented."[6]

[Miller considers the historicity of the "vision."] "The case is hardly proved," writes James Dunn, "but we may say with some confidence that . . . *Jesus' baptism by John was probably the occasion for an experience of God which had epochal significance for Jesus.* . . ."[7]

The Psychological Matrix

The Gospels themselves only too clearly indicate that what happened to Jesus at this time of his life did not occur in a vacuum. There were personal antecedents to his baptismal vision, they intimate, some of which lie chronologically close at hand, others of which can be deduced from what we are told elsewhere in the Gospels about Jesus' life generally prior to and after this event. In trying to understand an experience of this nature, it can also be

6. Joachim Jeremias, *New Testament Theology, Part I, The Proclamation of Jesus* (London: SCM, 1971), p. 45.

7. James Dunn, *Jesus and the Spirit* (London: SCM, 1975), p. 65.

helpful to draw upon comparable experiences in the lives of others as well as the established results of religious and developmental psychology. . . .

Since the beginning of this century, on the basis of thousands of case histories, students of religious experience have observed that growth into personal and religious maturity generally follows one of two paths (with many variations, of course). There are those who come to religious faith gradually, moving from one stage in life to another with few or no emotionally disruptive moments. William James was a pioneer in studies of this kind. In his classic work, *The Varieties of Religious Experience,* he characterized persons of this type as the "once-born," and noted that their adult experience of God and of life corresponds to the more optimistic "healthy-minded" religion (as he termed it) usually to be found in the more liberal groups of a given period.[8]

. . . There is a second group, however, for whom the pathway to religious and personal maturity is more difficult. Those in this group typically go through a period of prolonged inner distress, lasting sometimes into adulthood. James called them "sick souls," not meaning thereby to disparage them but only to indicate what they themselves reported of their emotionally chaotic inner world during this time of their lives. . . .[9]

. . . For this group to find peace with God and others, a conversion-type experience was required, an emotional reorientation of such magnitude that it could be likened to a "second birth." Prior to this conversion it was as though these persons had hardly begun to live. They were agitated, conflicted, despairing. During the conversion experience itself, they reported encountering God in personal, tangible ways. From it they emerged surrendered, full of joy and a compelling sense of mission. . . .

. . . The facts considered thus far seem to favor the hypothesis that Jesus belongs to the ranks of those who are compelled to live through a prolonged identity crisis lasting well into adulthood, and who resolve this crisis through a "second birth," as James, Sorokin, and others have described it. . . .

Also to be kept in mind are texts . . . that intimate that this crisis, in Jesus' case, might well have orbited around disturbances between himself, his mother, and his siblings. From a psychological point of view this would not be surprising, since psychohistorical research (as already noted) has progressively illuminated the developmental importance of precisely this primary familial matrix. . . . In this light John the Baptist's possible role emerges as a surrogate parent to Jesus in his search for spiritual and vocational integrity.

8. William James, *The Varieties of Religious Experience* (London: Collier-Macmillan, 1902 [1961]), pp. 78-113.

9. James, *Varieties,* pp. 114-42.

John W. Miller

"Who do men say that I am?"

In the light of all that has been learned about him in our inquiry so far, how shall we characterize Jesus in this final momentous chapter of his life? What manner of man was he, and what, essentially, was he trying to accomplish? . . .

He is ideologically, vocationally, and emotionally close to John the Baptist, but after John's arrest and the transfer of his mission to Galilee, he seems to be increasingly his own man. . . .

This latter observation may in fact have been true in a more profound sense than is generally recognized and may afford us an important clue to the enigma we are talking about. Common to identity formation in . . . young adulthood (and the Age Thirty Transition) is the role of a mentor or guide with whom an emotional bond is formed. Gradually, however (sometimes rather quickly), the intensity of this bond diminishes as the individual reinvests his newly won self-understanding with insights and gifts of his own. Wilhelm Fliess, a Berlin physician, played this role for Freud, as we know from their lively, intimate correspondence.[10] Freud in turn served in a similar fashion in Erikson's identity formation.[11] Both men, after intense involvement with these "mentors," as we might call them, moved on to become distinguished leaders in their own right.

In a similar fashion, we might imagine, Jesus too, after identifying with John, increasingly differentiated himself in the months following John's arrest. He was free now to go his own way, think his own thoughts, do his own deeds. His return to his native Galilee may be viewed as a first step in this process. It is indeed, then, no stereotype that confronts us in the records of this period, but an increasingly individualized Jesus with his own unique sense of calling and vision.

But what calling, more specifically, and what vision? Granted his uniqueness and the difficulty of capturing his identity in any of the traditional categories, how shall we characterize the Jesus we encounter in the records of this moment of his life?

That Jesus himself on one occasion self-consciously raised a question of this nature is, to say the least, striking, and merits our attention first of all. "Who do men say that I am?" he is reported to have asked his disciples at Caesarea Philippi, shortly before he began that fateful last journey to Jerusa-

---

10. See Paul Roazen, *Freud and His Followers* (New York: New American Library, 1971), pp. 88-96.

11. Erik Erikson, "Identity Crisis in Autobiographical Perspective," in *Life History and the Historical Moment: Diverse Presentations,* ed. Erikson (New York: W. W. Norton, 1975), p. 29.

lem. . . . And then he asked; "But who do you say that I am?" (Mark 8:27-
29). . . . Peter's ecstatic "You are the Christ!" was greeted by him not with an
approving: "Blessed are you . . ." (as in Matt. 16:17) but with a stern warning to
"tell no one" (Mark 8:30) and then a sharp, emotional rejoinder (when Peter
persisted in his messianic projection): "Get behind me, Satan! For you are not
on the side of God, but of men" (Mark 8:33). It would appear, therefore, that
he asked his disciples who they thought he was, not (as traditionally thought)
to elicit a messianic confession of faith on their part, but just the opposite. He
wanted his disciples' incipient messianic idealizations brought to light so that
they could be dealt with openly and quashed. It follows that a continuing feature of Jesus' self-identity at this culminating stage of his life was a highly
emotional abhorrence and rejection of the prevailing grandiose messianic
stereotype, precisely as at the time of his temptations. . . .

If "Messiah" ["Christ"] as imagined by his disciples and John signified,
so to speak, the negative, dark side of Jesus' identity, the side he wished to reject and suppress, how, in a more positive sense, *did* he think of himself?

. . . Jesus felt himself at this moment of his life to be the prophetic medi-
ator of an embracing "revelation" of God as gracious father. When, therefore,
elsewhere in his teachings we encounter repeated references to God's radiant
fatherly love for good and bad alike (Matt. 5:45), for the birds of the air and
the flowers of the field (Matt. 6:26-32//Luke 12:24-28), for the lost (Luke 15:20-
24) and those who need "rest" for their souls (Matt. 11:29f.), then, it should be
clearer to us, in this light, that these convictions were more than ideas — but
deeply felt existential certainties. Above everything else, they seemingly are
what filled his consciousness at this climactic stage of his career.

It is understandable, therefore, that hard evidence that he appropriated
to himself any titles or dignities of a more fixed or stereotypical nature (as
once thought) is proving to be increasingly elusive. Precisely because God's
goodness was so real to him, human adulation was suspect ("Why do you call
me good? No one is good but God alone"; Mark 10:18) and honorific titles ab-
horrent ("But you are not to be called rabbi, for you have one teacher. . . . And
call no man your father on earth, for you have one Father. Neither be called
masters, for you have one master"; Matt. 23:8-10). . . .

There are, however, two additional facets of Jesus' activity at this stage
of his life that merit some attention if his "Age Thirty" identity is to be understood as fully as it might be. Often, we are told, when uncertain about what to
do next in his mission, he would withdraw into solitude for prayer (Mark 1:35;
Luke 6:12, 46; 14:32-43),[12] and when challenged by the religious elite to give an

---

12. See Joachim Jeremias, *The Prayers of Jesus* (Naperville, IL: Allenson, 1967), p. 78.

account of himself concerning that most crucial aspect of his mission, his association with sinners (Luke 15:1f.), he replied not with citations from Scripture or tradition, but with down-to-earth stories about people and events drawn from the daily life of Palestine. Both his manner of praying and his parables, I suggest, testify, to a highly individual and personal process of working out the specifics of his identity and mission. . . . From them we learn that his "role models" were not predominantly the great men of history (whether scriptural or secular) but a shepherd searching for a lost sheep (Luke 15:4-7), a father rejoicing at the return of a lost son (Luke 15:11-32), a vineyard owner paying out a day's wage to all his workers regardless of how long they had worked (Matt. 20:1-16), a despised Samaritan stopping and stooping (after others had passed by) to assist a man wounded by robbers (Luke 10:29-37), a great king not ruling in the usual sense, but forgiving the hopelessly large debt of one of his underlings (Matt. 18:23-35).

If at the Jordan, as earlier suggested, Jesus found his "father" again, and a renewed sense of sonship, then now during his "age thirty" mission to the "lost sheep of the house of Israel," he found himself as well. And it was an identity not unlike that of the Father he now served. "Be merciful," he once said to his disciples, "even as your Father is merciful" (Luke 6:36). Just such an *Imitatio Dei* — the embodiment of God's generative care and graciousness in the nitty-gritty of daily life — was, it seems, the reality that more than anything else engaged him at this climactic stage of his life.

SUGGESTIONS FOR FURTHER READING

Psychological Studies of Moses

Freud, Sigmund. *The Moses of Michelangelo*. In *The Standard Edition of the Complete Psychological Works of Sigmund Freud*, edited by James Strachey, vol. 13, 211ff. London: Hogarth Press and the Institute of Psychoanalysis, 1953-1974 (1914a).

Freud, Sigmund. "The Moses of Michelangelo, Postscript." In *The Standard Edition of the Complete Psychological Works of Sigmund Freud*, edited by James Strachey, 237ff. London: Hogarth Press and the Institute of Psychoanalysis, 1953-74.

Paul, Robert A. *Moses and Civilization: Freud and the Judeo-Christian Master Narrative*. New Haven: Yale University Press, 1996.

Sanford, John A. *The Man Who Wrestled with God: Light from the Old Testament on the Psychology of Individuation*. New York: Paulist Press, 1981.

Zeligs, Dorothy. *Moses: A Psychodynamic Study*. New York: Human Sciences Press, 1986.

Psychological Studies of Jesus

Anderson, Paul N. "Jesus and Transformation." In *Psychology and the Bible: A New Way to Read the Scriptures*, edited by J. Harold Ellens and Wayne G. Rollins, vol. 4, 305-28. Westport, CT: Praeger Publishers, 2004.

Capps, Donald. "Beyond Schweitzer and the Psychiatrists: Jesus as Fictive Personality." In *Psychology and the Bible: A New Way to Read the Scriptures*, edited by J. Harold Ellens and Wayne G. Rollins, vol. 4, 89-124. Westport, CT: Praeger Publishers, 2004.

—————. "Erik Erikson's Psychological Portrait of Jesus: Jesus as Numinous Presence." In *Psychology and the Bible: A New Way to Read the Scriptures*, edited by J. Harold Ellens and Wayne G. Rollins, vol. 4, 163-208. Westport, CT: Praeger Publishers, 2004.

—————. "Jay Haley's Psychological Portrait of Jesus: A Power Tactician." In *Psychology and the Bible: A New Way to Read the Scriptures*, edited by J. Harold Ellens and Wayne G. Rollins, vol. 4, 125-62. Westport, CT: Praeger Publishers, 2004.

—————. *Jesus: A Psychological Biography*. St. Louis: Chalice Press, 2000.

Howes, Elizabeth B. *Jesus' Answer to God*. San Francisco: Guild for Psychological Studies, 1984.

Van Aarde, Andries. *Fatherless in Galilee: Jesus as a Child of God*. Harrisburg: Trinity Press International, 2001.

Wink, Walter. "The Original Impulse of Jesus." In *Psychology and the Bible: A New Way to Read the Scriptures*, edited by J. Harold Ellens and Wayne G. Rollins, vol. 4, 209-22. Westport, CT: Praeger Publishers, 2004.

CHAPTER 9

Dynamics of Biblical Texts:
Hebrew Scriptures

[The story of Adam and Eve] is not pure myth because the unknown person or persons . . . who included this story in the Genesis narrative had a conscious intention in mind when he used it. Therefore to do justice to the story we must keep in mind not only its symbolic structure, but also the redactor's intention.

John Sanford[1]

So, is Jonah a "theological" pamphlet or a "psychological" symbolic tale?

André and Pierre-Emmanuel Lacocque[2]

Jung once remarked that the so-called "psychological" novel was less interesting to him than the novel that did not consciously seek to be psychological. In texts that did not intend to be "psychological," the traces of deep psychological processes could be found, undistorted by the consciousness of the author.[3]

So it is with the Bible — it is not a psychological document; indeed, to name it such is wildly anachronistic. As we have seen, the personalities and the stories of the biblical text present themselves easily for psychological interpretation. Still, some psychological critics probe even more deeply into the

1. John A. Sanford, *The Man Who Wrestled with God: Light from the Old Testament on the Psychology of Individuation* (New York: Paulist, 1987), p. 116.

2. André Lacocque and Pierre-Emmanuel Lacocque, *The Jonah Complex* (Atlanta: John Knox, 1981), p. xiv.

3. C. G. Jung, *The Spirit in Man, Art, and Literature*, in *The Collected Works of C. G. Jung*, trans. R. F. C. Hull, ed. Gerhard Adler et al., Bollingen Series 20 (Princeton: Princeton University Press, 1953-78), vol. 15, p. 88.

texts to find traces of psychological factors that move behind the narrative — factors that are most likely unrecognized even by the writers. We have considered the world behind the text as reflecting the history, culture, personality, and psyche of the writer. Even more deeply, as artifacts of human intention and reflections of human experience, biblical texts also demonstrate traces of deep psychological dynamics common to human beings.

This form of criticism is most often linked to depth psychology. Depth psychology is that field of psychological theory which is particularly attentive to unconscious dimensions of the human psyche. Since the unconscious is, by definition, unknown, they seek clues to its structures and influence by observing how it is manifested in such phenomena as slips of the tongue (the proverbial "Freudian slip"), dreams, symbols, fantasies, and myth. From this perspective, psychological critics approach biblical stories as one form of mythical expression, sharing common features with the myths, stories, and symbols of different cultures and times.

The two most well known depth psychologists are Sigmund Freud and Carl Jung, whom we met in Chapter 3. Both made extensive use of mythical material; both saw traces of psychological structures and forces within the stories, symbols, and myths of human tradition.

This way of reading has had a profound impact not only on biblical criticism but also on literary interpretation overall. Paul Ricoeur has suggested that since Freud alerted us to the fact that the surface meaning of things may mask deeper motives and meanings, it is essential to exercise a "hermeneutic of suspicion" when approaching any text.[4]

Some critics raise a significant challenge to depth psychological interpretations. Since the unconscious is, by its very nature, inaccessible to immediate consciousness, how are we to know that the patterns and structures described in depth psychological analysis are actually present? As we have noted, interpretation of a text (or a symbol, or a myth) does not offer the opportunity for confirmation by a living, present analysand. If the unconscious has many mechanisms for concealing and disguising its true nature, how are we to know that what we see is not simply one more level of disguise?

Thus, some critics dismiss this kind of interpretation outright, claiming that its practitioners are "psychologizing" — merely projecting their own expectations or prejudices onto the text, finding only what they expect to find. On the other hand, those who use the methods argue from their own experience of working with individuals, texts, and myths that there are profound

---

4. Paul Ricoeur, *Freud and Philosophy: An Essay on Interpretation* (New Haven: Yale University Press, 1970), p. 33.

continuities among them, and that bringing unconscious dynamics to consciousness deepens and energizes interpretation.

In the selections that follow, we examine psychodynamics in three kinds of texts: in the plot and interactions of a narrative text (Adam and Eve), in the characterization of an individual (Jonah), and in a section of biblical law (the Ten Commandments).

Reading 9.1 The Story of Adam and Eve

JOHN A. SANFORD

John Sanford, a Jungian analyst and Episcopal priest, wrote extensively on psychological dynamics in biblical texts. His interpretation of the story of the "Fall" (Genesis 2–3) demonstrates how psychological perspectives can (and should) be used in conjunction with other methods. The biblical text does not contain only unconscious psychological factors; it also reflects the author's conscious decision to select and retell certain stories, and, in the process, to make a theological point. Fuller understanding of the meaning of the text calls for attention to several dimensions of meaning. Here, Sanford contrasts this integrated perspective (the "Wisdom interpretation") with a purely psychological reading (the "Gnostic/Psychological interpretation").

According to this viewpoint, the story of Adam and Eve partakes of the genre of myth and so must be approached symbolically. But it is not pure myth because the unknown person or persons (whom we will henceforth call the redactor) who included this story in the Genesis narrative had a conscious intention in mind when he used it. Therefore to do justice to the story we must keep in mind not only its symbolic structure, but also the redactor's intention.

A myth is the product of the unconscious mind; for this reason its full

---

From John A. Sanford, *The Man Who Wrestled with God: Light from the Old Testament on the Psychology of Individuation* (New York: Paulist, 1987), pp. 116-22.

meaning goes beyond the present state of awareness not only of those who read the myth but of those who tell the myth. When the symbolism of the myth is understood, however, meanings that were hidden become conscious. However, the story of the first man and first woman is not pure myth because the conscious intent of the redactor was to include this story in what he intended to be a historical document that traced the origins and early history of the human race from Adam and Eve through Abraham and Joseph to Moses. In fact, the story of Adam and Eve is only one of a number of stories in the first eleven chapters of Genesis which explain the history behind various circumstances and traditions that existed in the present time of the redactor. Thus the mythical/symbolic element and the intentional/historical element are interwoven in the story of the Garden of Eden and both must be taken into account.

It is in this light that we are to understand the presence of the snake in the garden. The Gnostic/psychological view, as we have seen, sees the snake as a symbol of the impulse to consciousness and individuation. The traditional Christian viewpoint sees the snake as a personification of the devil tempting humankind to sin by urging disobedience to God.[1] The wisdom interpretation tries to see the snake the way the author of the story saw it, and concludes that the snake personifies not the urge to simple disobedience as such, but the temptation to indulge in abominable practices current at that time that were regarded as inherently evil and therefore antithetical to God. These unlawful practices offered to the people of Israel a kind of knowledge that was attained through evil methods, and the serpent was associated with them. For instance we read in Deuteronomy 18:9-12: "When you come into the land Yahweh your God gives you, you must not fall into the habit of imitating the detestable practices of the natives. There must never be anyone among you who makes his son or daughter pass through fire, who practices divination, who is soothsayer, augur or sorcerer, who uses charms, consults ghosts or spirits, or calls up the dead. For the man who does these things is detestable to Yahweh your God."

The reason these practices were to be abhorred is that most of them involved the usurping of divine rights and prerogatives in order to carry out human egocentric purposes. Sorcery, for instance, involved the utilization of divine spiritual power for the evil purpose of achieving a power over people that only God should possess. Divination purported to be a method of learning the future for personal profit, but knowledge of the future was seen as the

---

1. Other references to the serpent as a personification of the principle of evil include Wis 2:24 and Rev 20:2.

prerogative of God. Summoning up the spirits of the dead was perceived to be a disturbance of the divinely ordained separation of the land of the living from the abode of the dead, for the purpose of gaining knowledge from a source other than God. One of the Hebrew words for such acts is "menahesh," a word related to the Hebrew word "nahash," which is the word for serpent in the Garden of Eden story. Thus the serpent can be seen as a symbol for the desire to attain knowledge through illicit means and for evil purposes. We will look at the effects of such illicit knowledge shortly.

However, the serpent is not a universally negative symbol in the Bible. In fact, God's power can also be symbolized as the serpent. Thus when the people of Israel were bitten by serpents in the wilderness they were healed by the brass serpent that Moses held up on a staff before them (Num 21:9). The author of the Fourth Gospel likens Christ himself to this healing serpent (Jn 3:13-14). In Exodus 7:8-13 we see the serpent used both to personify the evil urge to illicit power and knowledge, and God's legitimate power. In this story Moses and Aaron confront Pharaoh and a contest develops between them and the sorcerers of Egypt. God tells Aaron to cast his staff before Pharaoh; he does and it turns into a serpent. Then the sorcerers and magicians of Egypt throw their staffs down and they also turn into serpents. But the serpent of Aaron swallows the serpents of the Egyptians. This story points out that there is a true method of power and knowledge, and an evil method. The point of the Garden of Eden story is that humankind chose the illicit method of attaining knowledge.

But is not any knowledge good no matter how it is attained? The Gnostic/psychological approach with its emphasis on knowing and becoming conscious seems to emphasize that all knowledge, no matter how one arrives at it, is desirable. The wisdom interpretation says there is a difference between knowledge rightfully gained and wrongfully gained, and this difference is represented in the story by the two trees: the tree of life and the tree of the knowledge of good and evil.

It is a significant point that the author of our tale does not find it necessary to inform his readers about these two trees. Evidently he had reason to assume that those reading the story would know the moral difference between the tree of life, and the tree of the knowledge of good and evil.

It is a prevalent theme of the Wisdom literature and Deuteronomic tradition of the Old Testament that life is to be found in obeying the commandments of God and paying heed to his teaching or Torah.[2] In several places this teaching that gives life is referred to as the tree of life. Thus Proverbs 3:18 says

2. See Dt 30:15-20; Prov 4:4, 10, 13.

of God's wisdom that "she is a tree of life to those who hold her fast.[3] It is also worth noting that in the first centuries of Christianity the Cross of Christ was consistently referred to as "the tree" because it bestowed life on the faithful.

With regard to the tree of the knowledge of good and evil, the Gnostic/psychological view, as we have seen, regards the eating of this fruit by Adam and Eve as an act of becoming conscious; it is said to represent the beginning of humanity's painful step into moral and psychological awareness and away from unconscious containment in purely natural existence. However, this conclusion fails to take into consideration two facts. First, the text does not say that eating of the fruit of the tree of the knowledge of good and evil will enable Adam and Eve to know good from evil, but to know good and evil. Good from evil is a disjunctive and implies moral development; good and evil is a collective and implies a participation in evil. It denotes, in other words, an attitude that "anything goes," consequently a lack of moral discrimination. It is interesting in this connection that in 2 Corinthians 11:3, when Paul refers to the serpent who seduced Eve, he uses to describe the serpent the Greek adjective *panourgos* which means literally, "ready to do anything" (although it is usually translated "crafty" or "cunning").

Second, it overlooks the fact that the Jewish way of knowing in the Old Testament was through concrete experience. God was known because he made himself known through his acts. For the Gnostic, God was known through metaphysical speculation or mystical contemplation. For the Greeks, God could be known through deductive reason and direct intuition, hence one could acquire abstract or conceptual knowledge of God. For them knower and known could stand apart from each other, the one the subject, the other the object of the act of knowing. Not so for the Jews of the Old Testament era, for whom knowledge was gained by direct experience of their saving actions: "Say this, then, to the sons of Israel, 'I am Yahweh. I will free you of the burdens which the Egyptians lay on you. I will release you from slavery to them. . . . I will adopt you as my own people, and I will be your God. Then you shall know that it is I, Yahweh your God, who has freed you from the Egyptians' burdens.'"[4]

This usage of the word "know" is found in English too. For instance, if a man has intercourse with a woman it is said that he "knew" her. A virgin is said to have "not yet known a man." In such usage it is clear that intimate experience of a member of the opposite sex imparts its own kind of knowledge.

The Hebrew word in the Genesis story translated "know" is the word

---

3. Cf. Prov 11:30; 13:12; 15:4.
4. Ex 6:6-7; cf. Ps 77; Jos 4:24; Ex 7:4-5, 17-18.

yada which denotes exactly this kind of knowing through experience. To eat of the fruit of the tree of the knowledge of good and evil, therefore, amounts to doing evil in order to know it. This implies that it is the human prerogative to assume for itself what can be done in life and what cannot be done. This is a hubris of the ego that leads it to ignore the boundaries God established between that which is allowable and that which is not allowable.

The Gnostic/psychological view might argue that all things are allowable if they lead to the desirable goal of knowledge, for knowledge enlightens and saves, while ignorance retards. It can be pointed out in defense of this view that people do need experiences in order to arrive at awareness and understanding. People who try to lead perfectly safe lives do not have enough experiences and so do not develop properly. The whole life is a life in which something must be risked. This may be why Martin Luther once declared that a little sin is good for the soul. It certainly is the reason Jesus spoke up in defense of the woman with the bad reputation who washed his feet with her tears and dried them with her hair. He said of her to the righteous Pharisee Simon, "It is the man who is forgiven little who shows little love."[5]

But this approach can be taken too far, and this is what the Garden of Eden story is saying. Certain experiences in life are forbidden to us because they are evil. To indulge in them may lead to a certain kind of knowledge about that experience, but it will preclude real and inclusive knowledge because these experiences will darken the soul. Partaking of evil morally defiles us and destroys our faculties for true knowledge. Such knowledge cannot therefore illuminate us or lead to individuation. For this reason some things in life are forbidden; to indulge in them would exchange the knowledge of God for the knowledge that corrupts us from within.

The Nazi SS trooper who gasses innocent people to death in concentration camps does not arrive at knowledge through his experience. To the contrary, his moral faculties become so blunted and darkened that he is unable to arrive at anything that could be called the knowledge of God. He becomes incapable of the knowledge of God. This theme has been explored by novelist Dostoevsky in his book *Crime and Punishment.* Dostoevsky's protagonist Raskolnikov murders a helpless old woman in order to know what it is like to do such a thing. He finds that out, but also finds that his soul is tormented and that he has sown the seeds of his own destruction. . . .

Thus the wisdom interpretation says that when Adam and Eve ate of the fruit of the tree of the knowledge of good and evil they experienced evil and thus became corrupted by it. For this reason, after they ate of the fruit we do

---

5. Lk 7:47.

not read that they had a great illumination but experienced shame and guilt. This is why God would not allow them also to eat of the fruit of the tree of life, for in their corrupted condition they were not fit to partake of it. It is true that God himself does know good and evil, for he says, "See, the man has become like one of us,[6] with his knowledge of good and evil" (Gen 3:22). But what is allowable to God is not always allowable to humankind. There are boundaries to the human ego that must be observed lest in striving to take over the divine prerogatives we go to our destruction.

The effects of indulging in the evil that the Garden of Eden story warns us against are clearly malevolent. We do not arrive at knowledge but become darkened in our minds and incapable of true knowledge. We become "like God" only insofar as we have trespassed into forbidden areas that are the prerogative of God. Thus we do not make a relationship with God but lose one. And our originally divine nature becomes corrupted, as is made clear in Wisdom 2:23-24:

> Yet God did make man imperishable,
> he made him in the image of his own nature;
> it was the devil's envy that brought death into the world,
> as those who are his partners will discover.

Nevertheless, God did place both trees in the garden, and also allowed the serpent to be in the garden. God's commandment is that Adam and Eve should not eat of the fruit of the tree of the knowledge of good and evil, but the serpent's tempting voice offers them different counsel. The serpent can be understood as the "devil" in the sense of the ever present possibility that we may choose evil. The serpent is thus part of the archetype of choice, since choice is only possible when there are two poles from which to choose. Although the story does not say so, we may assume that God allowed the serpent to exist in the garden in order that choice might also exist. Thus God wants us to have the moral and spiritual growth that accompanies and makes possible individuation.

---

6. "Us": that is, the *elohim* or sons of God.

André Lacocque

Reading 9.2   The Story of Jonah

ANDRÉ LACOCQUE

Biblical scholar André Lacocque explores the figure of Jonah as representative of the challenge that each person faces in order to become who he or she really is. Jonah is not to be taken as an historical personage, nor, really, as a prophet. His story concerns both a fundamental human conflict and a chance for transformation. It is also a kind of self-critical reflection — a call to compassion and universal concern written in a time of heightened hostility to strangers.

Psychologically speaking, the projection on others of the onus for evil and unhappiness is remarkably universal. The individual and collective contempt for others or heterophobia is a terrible plague. Its multifaceted grimace conveys hatred, ultra-nationalism, racism, profiling, humiliation, murder, ethnic cleansing, and camps of extermination.

In Israel's biblical history, the apex of foreigner ostracism was reached in the time of the Persian-appointed governors of Judea, Ezra and Nehemiah (cf. Ezra 10; Neh. 13). Chances are that books such as Ruth and Jonah were written against a policy based on race purity. In fact, Jonah 2 shows lowly sailors behaving much better than the Jewish prophet (and better than the Jerusalemites in the time of Jeremiah; cf. Jer. 1:16, 2:10), and Jonah 4 sets Ninevites as exemplars of the prophets' ideal image of penance fasting, lamenting, avoiding sin, and amending their ways. Transposed in psychological parlance, conversion for the prophets means opening oneself to being disoriented and reoriented. No other move of the psyche is more taxing; it is a rebirth.

Jonah knows it; at least he intuits it (cf. Jon. 4:2). That is why he is, par excellence, the reluctant prophet. His first and characteristic move is to steal away. It is a visceral attitude of his own, which he never entirely transcends (Jon. 1, 4). Now, to the extent that Jonah represents humanity at large, the biblical story conveys a lesson about the human condition in general. The quest for the fundamental human drive is the very basis of modern psychology. Sigmund Freud believed that the human's deepest longings are controlled by his/her libido, and particularly by a drive to incest, whereas Carl Jung saw

From André Lacocque, "A Psychological Approach to the Book of Jonah," in *Psychology and the Bible: A New Way to Read the Scriptures*, ed. J. Harold Ellens and Wayne G. Rollins (Westport, CT: Greenwood-Praeger, 2004), vol. 2, pp. 85-90.

such desires as purely symbolic, for the inner wish is to regress to an anxiety state reminiscent of the womb-stage, "a paradisiacal state of unconsciousness," in the words of Jolande Jacobi. . . . On that score, the biblical description of Jonah is more Jungian than Freudian, but the paradigm of Jonah takes us in another direction.

True, the prophet's sleep in the ship's hold (Jon. 1) symbolizes a regression to the womb-unconscious. But the whole story shows that Jonah's unconscious is filled with the repressed consciousness of responsibility. His unconscious is a repressed consciousness; it is a denial. He knows but does not want to know. He sleeps to avoid introspection, like others who muffle the "voice" with drugs, deafening music, "workaholism," or TV addiction.

What Jonah dreads most is to become Jonah, for to become Jonah means to be committed to other(s). Facing oneself implies paradoxically facing the "Ninevites" out there. Only where there is a "thou" is there an "I." Complacent self-absorption would be still another escape from responsibility and the fulfillment of one's calling. If there is a teaching that pervades the whole of biblical literature, it is this one: only love (commitment to other[s]) is the ultimate "that does not die." Saint Paul gave the Corinthians a definition of love in these terms, "Love . . . bears all things, believes all things, hopes all things, endures all things" (1 Cor. 13:7); Saint John defined God along the same lines, "God is love" (1 John 4:8). It may be, with Freud, that the elected other is never someone besides one's mother/father, but true love transcends incest into covenant.

As far as Jonah is concerned, his "others" are so remote from incestuous lure that they belong to a foreign and "strange people" (cf. Isa. 33:19; Ezek. 3:5-6), a threatening nation about to destroy Jonah's people sometime in the near future. The Ninevites are at the antipode of Jonah's preferences; what is demanded of him is a far cry from the fulfillment of his natural desires.[1] His only recompense for accomplishing his mission is displeasure and anger (Jon. 4:1). The same can be said of all the prophets in Israel's history. They all held self-indulgence and whatever it gains as "a loss," regarding them "as rubbish," as Paul says (Phil. 3:7-8). Their self-accomplishment meant something entirely different from the satisfaction of their inner desires. In the church's language, their self-effacement is called "saintliness," that is, care for the total stranger, the disenfranchised, the leper, the pariah (cf. Matt. 25). Ruth the

---

1. In philosophical language, the book of Jonah dissociates metaphysics from ontology and reconstructs it as an expression of *ethics*. Hebrew thinking does not distinguish essence from existence. The human being *is* what he or she experiences. Even God's being is to be understood in terms of efficiency *(wirken)* and relationship *(mit-werden)*.

Moabite then becomes the forebear of King David, of the messianic lineage, and those who are visiting the prisoner in his/her dungeon discover to their surprise the face of Christ.

Surprise? Jonah balks at the integration of the experience when he witnesses the redemption of the Ninevites. It may look like obtuseness on his part. Anti-Semites triumphantly denounce the Jewish stiff-neckedness. But once again, Jonah's reaction is simply human. In the first century C.E., Jesus said, "they will not be convinced, even if someone rises from the dead" (Luke 16:31). Processing the experience is part of the reorientation. "Go and sin no more," said the Nazarene, but there is no guarantee that his admonition will be heeded. Only a few deserve to have their name changed, like Jacob, for instance, to reflect their transformed personality. As for Jonah, seeing the Ninevites "rising from the dead" was not enough. The "old" Jonah needed one more experience, the one of the *qiqayon,* the tree growing in one day and withering in one night (Jon. 4), and even this one remains for him an open question: the tale ends with a question mark (Jon. 4:9-11).

What a strange scene is this bush, growing for the sake of Jonah's comfort in the scorching sun and removed from its shielding function the next morning. What is Jonah to do with this? God tells him that the tree represents Nineveh, which was created for God's pleasure, as it were, and turning to be a grave divine concern. Concern and compassion: Jonah, no doubt, felt no pity for the *qiqayon* but strictly for himself; God, however, experiencing the downturn of his pleasure into displeasure, is concerned for Nineveh. Jonah is invited to share his God's truth and thus to renounce his own anger (cf. Jon. 4:1, 9). This, I believe, is the core of the narrative.

Jonah is called to participate in the divine action; he is to be co-creator with God. First, Jonah becomes his mouthpiece, that is, his prophet. Second, the message he utters is in obedience to the expressed order of God but the words are his own. At no point is it said that Jonah should come with the ominous five words of his oracle in Nineveh (Jon. 3:3-4); these are his interpretation of the commandment, and only God knows whether his hermeneutic is right.[2] Third, Jonah is not to leave the scene of Mesopotamia before the outcome of his proclamation (cf. Jon. 4:5), for he is much more than just a dispassionate mailbox. The outcome belongs integrally to his prophetic function. What God will do to the Ninevites affects him so deeply that, in a fit of rage, he desires to die (Jon. 4:8-9).

---

2. On this . . . see Lacocque & Lacocque, *The Jonah Complex,* see also Pierre-Emmanuel Lacocque, "Fear of Engulfment and the Problem of Identity," *Journal of Religion and Health* 23 (3): 218-28.

This third point introduces a fourth one: Jonah must feel sympathy with God and for God. There is in the all-important Chapter 4 of the tale a striking shift from judgment to compassion. Jonah has proclaimed the justice of God to the Ninevites. In his oracle, there is not one word of charity. He has delivered a message of implacability, as if God would delight in wrath and in overthrowing Nineveh. The partner of God must now learn to commiserate with the condemned, that is, simultaneously to commiserate with the judging God. For human tragedy is first and foremost divine tragedy. Nineveh was not created to be overthrown, nor the *qiqayon* to die in one night. Death is always the failure of creation; Jonah is to shed tears on "a great city, in which there are more than a hundred and twenty thousand persons" (Jon. 4:11). Conversely, he must rejoice when such tragedy is avoided and the pleasure of God in his creation is restored. Human repentance *(t'shubah)* is also divine consolation *(nehamah)*. That is why Jonah's refusal to pity Nineveh is also a refusal to comfort the Creator (4:10-11). Co-creation is commiseration. Compassion is the highest call.

At first Jonah is angry at God, a very common human reaction when things do not turn according to one's desires. . . . The anger of Jonah is far from absurd. Taken seriously, it raises the problem of who is right, God or Jonah? Isn't sparing Nineveh a way to destroy God's own people and protect his enemies? The response belongs more to theology than to psychology. From the latter's point of view, however, Jonah's displeasure after his resounding accomplishment in bringing the Ninevites to their knees may appear surprising. But psychology knows of a so-called fear of success, a phenomenon more common than generally believed. Fear of success is an aspect of the narcissistic complex of inferiority and is particularly exemplified among members of the teaching and helping professions. Jonah would foot the bill, although we have shown elsewhere that the psychological aspect of Jonah's ire does not exhaust by far the prophet's rationale.[3] It remains that balking at goal attainment is part of the picture here.

In retrospect it appears that Jonah not only shrank his message to a skeletal five words but his tone must have been dull to say the least. In fact, he expected and hoped to fail in his mission, if it is granted that the very delivery of the divine indictment had the purpose of providing a last chance to the condemned Ninevites. Jonah did not himself believe in the potency of the oracle. Lack of conviction, of course, is still another escape from commitment. Role playing is self-hiding. Deception of others is also self-deception. However, the acting or the message may be convincing in itself. The Ninevites go

---

3. Lacocque & Lacocque, *The Jonah Complex.*

through a true conversion, and so do also the nuns of Port-Royal after the sermon by a monk to which he himself gave no credence. An actress may excel in playing the ingenue while being a kleptomaniac in real life.

Jonah is no kleptomaniac, but all the same he robs the Ninevites of respect and honor. Were he a psychologist, he would be a quack. Granted that psychological quacks abound today on television, and they are at times successful with their sham therapies, but the devastation in others and in themselves remains untold. Cover-up is added to crookedness. True, such a judgment as regards Jonah would be way too unfair, but obviously he needs to be reoriented. That is why the story does not end with the Ninevites' repentance but shifts again to the person of the prophet. Jonah's shipmates are healed, and the Ninevites are cured, but the healer himself is in need of his own medicine. The lesson is clear: psychological analysis is no one-way street. Ministering is also soul-searching the soul of the analyst. Interpreting a text is ultimately being interpreted by the text. Jonah's oracle to Nineveh is subtly addressed as well to himself, "still forty days and X will be destroyed!" As for the *qiqayon* shielding Jonah, it took only one night to wither away. How long would it take to strip Jonah? The death of the prophet/analyst is very much present as a possibility in the narrative (cf. Jon. 2 and 4:3, 8, 9). Clearly, prophecy/analysis is a deadly serious business.

The image of humanity set up by the figure of Jonah is complex. Contrary to a certain modern psychological trend, here the focus is on human relations. Jonah emerges from anonymity and meaninglessness when realizing that he is called to reach out to others. There is something that Jonah must and can do, and it could even change the course of history. This is certainly true as far as the destiny of the Ninevites is concerned and, consequently, as regards Israel's destiny.

Reading 9.3   The Ten Commandments

EDWARD EDINGER

"Individuation" was C. G. Jung's term for the process of development of the person into the individual he or she was intended to be. In myths and stories, the patterns of individuation are most often unfolded in the actions and attitudes of characters responding to challenges and hardship. In this passage, though, Jungian analyst Edward Edinger identifies key themes of individuation in a non-narrative, non-mythical text: the Ten Commandments. As guides to proper behavior, the commandments point to the kind of actions that will enable individuation. We examine just the first five commandments.

What do the ten commandments mean psychologically?

1. *You shall have no gods except me.* This is the origin of monotheism and of supreme importance psychologically. It announces the fact that the Self is a unity and not a multiplicity.[1] This is the basis of the responsibility and integrity of the individual, for only an integer is capable of integrity. Responsible consciousness can be carried only by a centered personality which is an indivisible (individual) unity. Psychopathology offers us many examples of psychic dissociation in which a unified center is missing, notably chronic alcoholism and drug addiction.

2. *You shall not make yourself a carved image or any likeness of anything in heaven above or on earth beneath or in the waters under the earth; you shall not bow down to them or serve them.* Two ideas are intermixed here: the making of images (imagination) and idolatry. For ancient man the making of an image must have had such a powerful effect on the unconscious that the image immediately became an idol, evoking projection of divine or magical powers. Psychologically, idolatry means the worship of one archetypal aspect or power of the unconscious at the expense of the whole. The ego almost always develops out of an initial state of idolatry. One psychic function is granted preeminence and the value of the whole is carried by that one function, which, in effect, becomes an idol. As Jung says, "Mephistopheles is the diabolical aspect of every psychic function that has broken loose from the hi-

---

1. Empirically the Self is both unity and multiplicity, or better, unified multiplicity.

From Edward Edinger, "Theophany in the Wilderness," *The Bible and the Psyche: Individuation Symbolism in the Old Testament* (Toronto: Inner City Books, 1986), pp. 60-63.

erarchy of the total psyche and now enjoys independence and absolute power."[2] This commandment forbids idolatry, that is, the worship of a part for the whole.

In addition to idolatry, the commandment also forbids image-making. This means that imagination itself is interdicted and no spontaneous congress with the unconscious is allowed. Thus was erected a psychic incest taboo. Evidently the danger of succumbing to the regressive pull of the unconscious is so great at that stage of ego development that fantasy and all the powers of the imagination must be suppressed. As part of nature the imagination was linked with the fertility rites and the religion of the Great Mother which the spiritual religion of Yahweh was replacing. Modern individuals, in an effort to unite the opposites which Yahwehism separated, must have a different attitude to imagination and to image-making. Just as they strive to reconcile the masculine and feminine principles which Yahweh sundered, so they seek to combine the unitary principle of the spirit with the multiple facets of the creative imagination as exemplified by ancient polytheism.

3. *You shall not utter the name of Yahweh your God to misuse it, for Yahweh will not leave unpunished the man who utters his name to misuse it.* This apparently refers to the false swearing of an oath in which one invokes God's name to guarantee the truth of a statement. Zedekiah is a terrible example of violation of this commandment (2 Chronicles 36:13). Psychologically, one can understand an oath invoking the name of God to refer to the claim that one is in harmony with the Self, the presumptuous assumption that one is operating out of wholeness. This is a dangerous disregard for the reality of the shadow and of the "other" in the unconscious. Christ revises this commandment in Matthew 5:33-37.

> You have learnt how it was said to our ancestors: You must not break your oath, but must fulfil your oaths to the Lord. But I say this to you: do not swear at all. . . . All you need say is "Yes" if you mean yes, "No" if you mean no; anything more than this comes from the evil one.

4. *Observe the sabbath day and keep it holy, as Yahweh your God has commanded you. For six days you shall labor and do all your work, but the seventh day is a sabbath for Yahweh your God. . . . For in six days Yahweh made the heavens and the earth and the sea and all that these hold, but on the seventh day he rested; that is why Yahweh has blessed the sabbath day and made it sacred.*

2. C. G. Jung, *Psychology and Alchemy,* in *The Collected Works of C. G. Jung,* trans. R. F. C. Hull, ed. Gerhard Adler et al., Bollingen Series 20 (Princeton: Princeton University Press, 1953-78), vol. 12, p. 69.

The seven-day week, having no astronomical basis, is a purely arbitrary invention. In other words it is a projection of a psychic image. Ancient Rome had an eight-day cycle, but the seven-day week became established throughout the empire about the beginning of our era, perhaps influenced by the seven-day week of the Jews. The wavering between seven and eight is analogous to that between three and four and is characteristic of individuation symbolism.[3] Perhaps it is significant that our era opted for the dynamic number seven rather than the static number eight. The seven-day week became the temporal embodiment of the seven planetary deities, each having a sacred day: Sunday (Sun), Monday (Moon), Tuesday (Mars), Wednesday (Mercury), Thursday (Jupiter), Friday (Venus), Saturday (Saturn). The fact that the Jewish sabbath fell on Saturday led to the idea of certain Gnostics that Yahweh was synonymous with Saturn.

In ancient Israel willful sabbath-breaking was a capital offense (Numbers 15:32-36). The day itself was a container for the sacred essence of Yahweh, a temporal version of the ark of the covenant. This institution established decisively the prerogatives of the sacred, transpersonal dimension of the psyche, over and against secular pursuits. The word "sabbath" means to cease or to rest. According to the usual interpretation, the sabbath was meant as a blessing to man. However, Jastrow has demonstrated that

> the Hebrew Sabbath was originally a day of propitiation like the Babylonian *šabatum* (*American Journal of Theology,* II, 312-52). [Jastrow] argues that the restrictive measures in the Hebrew laws for the observance of the Sabbath arose from the original conception of the Sabbath as an unfavorable day, a day in which the anger of [Yahweh] might flash forth against men.[4]

Although orthodox commentators object to this observation, the practice of executing those who declined the blessing of the sabbath does lend itself to the idea that the anger of Yahweh did "flash forth against men" on that day.

Christ took a more lenient attitude toward the sabbath, claiming that "the sabbath was made for man, not man for the sabbath" (Mark 2:27); and that on the sabbath, "My Father goes on working and so do I" (John 5:17). The latter is a shocking remark to be made in ancient Israel and the Pharisees were properly shocked. Such a statement can only be made by one who has an individual relation to the Self. For such a person the numinous content of the

---

3. See C. G. Jung, "A Psychological Approach to the Dogma of the Trinity," in *Psychology and Religion,* in *The Collected Works of C. G. Jung,* vol. 11, pp. 164-65.

4. James Orr, ed., *International Standard Bible Encyclopaedia,* vol. 4 (Grand Rapids: Eerdmans, 1980), p. 2630.

sabbath has been internalized. What is a crime in a collective setting is permissible to the individual, *providing he has sufficient consciousness.* According to an uncanonical source, Christ, seeing a man working on the sabbath, said to him: "Man, if indeed thou knowest what thou doest, thou art blessed: but if thou knowest not, thou art cursed, and a transgressor of the law."[5] Jung says about this saying, "It might well be the motto for a new morality."[6]

5. *Honor your father and your mother, as Yahweh your God has commanded you, so that you may have long life and may prosper in the land that Yahweh your God gives to you.* Understood psychologically, this commandment enjoins respect for the archetypal images of father and mother wherever they may manifest. They connect us with our roots and origin and remind the ego that it is only a twig on the tree of life. Yahweh indicates that his power stands behind these images and connection with them is connection with life and prosperity. Dependent neurotics may misuse this passage to justify regressive dependence on their personal parents.

SUGGESTIONS FOR FURTHER READING

Kille, D. Andrew. *Psychological Biblical Criticism.* Edited by Gene M. Tucker, Guides to Biblical Scholarship, Old Testament Series. Minneapolis: Fortress Press, 2001.

———. "Jacob: A Study in Individuation." In *Psychology and the Bible: A New Way to Read the Scriptures,* edited by J. Harold Ellens and Wayne G. Rollins, vol. 2, 65-82. Westport, CT: Praeger, 2004.

L'Heureux, Conrad E. *In and out of Paradise: The Book of Genesis from Adam and Eve to the Tower of Babel.* New York: Paulist, 1983.

Lacocque, André, and Pierre-Emmanuel Lacocque. *The Jonah Complex.* Atlanta: John Knox, 1981.

———. *Jonah: A Psycho-Religious Approach to the Prophet.* Columbia: University of South Carolina Press, 1990.

Sanford, John A. *King Saul, the Tragic Hero: A Study in Individuation.* New York: Paulist, 1985.

5. M. R. James, *The Apocryphal New Testament* (London: Oxford University Press, 1960), p. 33.

6. Jung, "A Psychological Approach to the Dogma of the Trinity," p. 197.

CHAPTER 10

Dynamics of Biblical Texts:
New Testament

But divine inspiration necessarily comes through a human heart and a mortal mind, through personal prejudice and communal interpretation, through fear, dislike, and hate as well as through faith, hope, and charity.

John Dominic Crossan[1]

Even the larger questions of language are psychological. . . . It is regrettable that so little has been done and is being done to match the study of expression with a study of mind and experience. Here is perhaps a relatively neglected area of New Testament research.

Henry J. Cadbury[2]

In the previous chapter we noted that every piece of writing in the Bible contains traces of historical, cultural, literary, and psychological "fingerprints." These traces can consist of unintended hints of the author's geographic location, favorite words, pet peeves, dominant concerns, affective echoes of recent traumatic events, literary conventions, or possibly even a subliminal index of "friends" and "enemies." The author will also leave traces of his or her unconscious life, whether drives, passions or prejudices, dislikes, hidden fears, inner conflicts, neurotic obsessions, or powerful intuitive images of the future.

Uncovering these traces is one of the special tasks of the biblical critic.

1. John Dominic Crossan, "Who Killed Jesus? Crossan Responds to Brown," *Explorations* 10, no. 1 (1996): 2-4.
2. Henry Cadbury, "Current Issues in New Testament Studies," *Harvard Divinity School Bulletin* 19 (1953): 54.

Traditionally, the *historical critic* looks for clues to the cultural-historic context. The *literary critic* looks for stylistic habits, vocabulary, organizational scheme, and hints of sources. The *psychological critic* attends to the habits of the human psyche on display in the text.

For what sort of things is the psychological critic "on the alert" when inspecting the psychological dynamics of biblical texts? He or she is bent on observing the habits of the human psyche manifest in the text — either in the author's agenda, or among the characters within the stories told. These habits might, for example, include "defense mechanisms" that we all know about and often use — for example, denial (Adam and Eve in the garden), intellectualization (the Johannine Pilate in conversation with Jesus), projection (Peter's acclamation of Jesus as a victorious Messiah), rationalization (Eve's passing the buck to the serpent) — along with patterns of obsessive compulsion (Paul's persecution of the Way in his earlier career). Biblical narratives can also demonstrate the larger psychic patterns formulated by Freud and Jung — for example, individuation (as with Jacob), homeostasis (Proverbs), neurosis (King Saul), psychosis (the Gerasene demoniac), extraversion (Paul), introversion (Saul, the earlier Paul), and regression (Esau).

Though neither of them was a professional biblical scholar, Freud and Jung engaged in psychological criticism of biblical texts. Freud drew attention to the *obsessive-compulsive motives* in the formulation of ritual law, the inevitable *projection* involved in all God-images, and the *repression* implicit in socio-sexual taboos. In his one major essay on a biblical topic, *Answer to Job,* Jung offered psychological commentary on the development of the God-concept from Job to early Christian concepts of the God-man, along with observations on unconscious elements in the imagery of violence in the Apocalypse.[3]

More recently, John Gager introduced the concept of *cognitive dissonance* to describe the dilemma of early Christians in dealing with the failure of Christ to return in their own lifetime, as was expected.[4] Gerd Theissen illumined the psychological dynamics in Jesus' conversation with the Syro-Phoenician woman (in Mark 7:24-30) by introducing *social-psychological analysis* of Jewish-Gentile relations in first-century Tyre and Galilee.[5] Brooke

3. Carl Gustav Jung, *Answer to Job,* in *The Collected Works of C. G. Jung,* trans. R. F. C. Hull, ed. Gerhard Adler et al., Bollingen Series 20 (Princeton: Princeton University Press, 1953-78), vol. 11, pp. 355-470.

4. John Gager, *Kingdom and Community: The Social World of Early Christianity* (Englewood Cliffs, NJ: Prentice-Hall, 1975).

5. Gerd Theissen, "Lokal- und Sozialkolorit in der Geschichte von der syrophönikischen Frau (Mk 7:24-30)," *ZNTW* 75, nos. 3-4 (1984): 202-25.

Hopkins employed *object relations theories* to provide insight into the psychological "power" of the resurrection narratives.[6]

In the end, a psychological critical approach brings us in touch with the perennial traits of the human psyche on display in the biblical authors, in the constructed characters with which they've populated their stories, and in us the readers. To engage in psychological biblical criticism therefore brings us into fuller relation with the humanity (and the sublimity) of the text and with ourselves.

The readings in this chapter demonstrate inquiry into three types of psychological issues: family relations, archetypal symbolism, and conversion. The first reading concerns the dynamics between Jesus and his mother in the story of the wedding at Cana; the second, the psychological origin and effect of the Christ-Antichrist symbolism in Revelation; and the third, the psychological dynamics at work in Paul's conversion from an ethic of law to an ethic of the Spirit.

Reading 10.1 The Wedding at Cana

FRANÇOISE DOLTO AND GÉRARD SÉVÉRIN

Françoise Dolto, a Roman Catholic laywoman and psychoanalyst affiliated with the Freudian School in Paris, has collaborated with her psychoanalytic colleague, Gérard Séverin, in dialogue on Gospel sayings and stories about Jesus. The dialogues were originally presented on radio in French, with Séverin interviewing and Dolto offering psychological commentary.

Despite the church's earlier resistance to the application of psychoanalytic insight to Scripture and faith, Dolto and Séverin came to see the Gospel stories as virtual "psychodramas" that illustrate behavioral traits long familiar to psychoanalysts. As they put it earlier in their book, "These texts illustrate and shed light on the laws of the unconscious discovered in the last century" (p. 19).

---

6. Brooke Hopkins, "Jesus and Object-Use: A Winnicottian Account of the Resurrection Myth," *International Review of Psycho-Analysis* 16 (1989): 93-100.

From Françoise Dolto and Gérard Séverin, *The Jesus of Psychoanalysis: A Freudian Interpretation of the Gospel*, trans. Helen R. Lane (New York: Doubleday, 1979), pp. 57-62.

The authors' concern is with the psychological truthfulness of the stories, not with their historicity. Their interest in the story of the wedding at Cana (John 2:1-11) is the psychodynamic relationship between Mary and Jesus within the story of the wedding at Cana — and possibly in real life. Their conclusion? That the wedding at Cana is a birth story.

Let us examine this first miracle now, this first "sign" that Jesus makes. He works this miracle at the behest of his mother. Something important happens between this son and his mother! "My hour has not come yet," he says, and yet in the end this hour arrives. What is happening here?

What happens is a birth!

A wedding feast risks ending too soon: there is no more wine. Mary says to Jesus, "They have no wine." And what does Jesus answer her?: "My hour has not come yet."

Whereupon Mary does not say: "Very well, then. His hour has not yet come." On the contrary she says to the servants: "Do whatever he tells you," as though she had not heard Jesus' words.

But what has she understood from what he says, to give signs of such assurance?

She has understood that by expressing himself in these words, Jesus is resisting being born to his public life because he is feeling anxiety.

In fact, Jesus is a man, and man experiences anxiety when faced with important acts wherein his destiny and his responsibility are at stake. Later, in the Garden of Gethsemane, he will weep, he will sweat blood, he will say that he is sad unto death.

In Cana, Jesus feels anxiety. Mary is less anxious than he; that is why her presentiments are correct.

Jesus is about to leave behind a life of silence, a hidden life, and embark upon a public life. This change of life is the cause of great anxiety.

For her part, Mary knows that his hour has come, in precisely the way a mother knows that her hour has come, knows that she is about to give birth.

Isn't Jesus' reply negative? Isn't saying "My hour has not come yet" a polite way of saying "No"?

Not at all. It is not a negation; it is a denial.

In fact, as you know, there is no negative in the unconscious. Hence, if Jesus answers, it is because at some level within himself he has "heard" his mother's request. If he answers by a denial, it is because he is anxious, and Mary has perceived his anxiety, which is witness to a desire.

What does she understand by his question: "Woman, why turn to me?"[1] Why does she speak with such quiet authority to the servants, despite her son's verbal negation?

She is sure of the power that this prodigious man is about to exert, a power perhaps still unknown to him until he is thus pressed by her words.

But . . . where do Mary's words come from?

That is a question I am still asking myself. . . .

Does Mary really realize the dynamic impact of her words when she states, "They have no wine"? Is this feminine intuition? A subtle or an unconscious pressure? A foreknowledge of the time that is at hand?

In fact, nothing is logical here. Mary asks for nothing and yet Jesus answers, "No." The simple words "They have no wine" become an order for the son. And what sort of a guest is this who gives orders in a house that is not hers? Who has caused her to speak in this way? Why do the servants heed her order?

Yes, from what level of her being has Mary said to her son, "They have no wine"? And to the servants, "Do what ever he tells you"? Does she not prove herself the initiator of Jesus' first steps in his public life?

Everything may seem so simple at the beginning, like everything that is really important — a banal reflection pronounced as a factual statement perhaps: 'They have no wine." And yet . . . This story presents us with questions on every hand. This is because it is fraught with meaning.

Did Mary have any precise intention? Did Mary voluntarily take the initiative? Or did Jesus, by these everyday words, hear and recognize the sign from the Holy Spirit that he was waiting for, did he identify this as a message from his Father to manifest publicly the power of his creative word?

It is at Cana that the Gospels show us Mary speaking to her son and acting for the last time from this unique and mysterious position as an initiator.

It is now by other people, by the servants of the master with all their weaknesses, that Jesus will be roused to action.

Do you believe that Mary knows the role that she plays at this wedding feast?

I really don't know. . . . I believe that she is necessary but I also believe that she is totally open and that she speaks out of sympathy: if wine is missing, won't joy be missing too? Without knowing it, in a very natural way, she is preternatural.

In the light of reason, in fact, nothing about Mary's behavior at Cana is logical . . . and yet it works!

In the end she speaks on one plane and the action takes place on another!

1. The King James Version here is "Woman, what have I to do with thee?" (Translator's note).

This entire story and this dialogue might well make us believe that we're confronting a language of the deaf!

It is a little like what happens in psychoanalytic sessions. Something like a language of the deaf does in fact exist. One says something and, thanks to this language, something else is said in reply.

I find it interesting, when one reads the Gospel as a psychoanalyst, to see how, with denials as the point of departure, one ends up with light and the Christ, who is a man, passes by way of this psychological labyrinth where "no" means "yes" and vice versa. This is not lying, but rather a sign of anxiety within the birth process of a desire, which never occurs in a rational way.

If Jesus had not "heard" the words "They have no wine," he would not have answered and Mary would have understood that this was not the right moment for him to hear something on the subject.

Hence, Mary waits for him to be born to social life, and it is astonishing to see how something in Jesus still resists manifesting itself.

"My hour has not come yet."

"Do whatever he tells you."

You must understand that it is the strength of Mary that has given birth, phallically,[2] if you'll permit me the word, to Jesus, through an act of power.

Jesus says: "What wouldst thou have me do, woman?" I have always heard these words explained as the equivalent of "Why, woman, are you interfering in my affairs?" But as I see it, this means: "Woman, what is it that I suddenly find within myself? What is this extraordinary resonance that I hear in your words?"

It is a question. Christ asks his mother a question exactly as the fetus asks its mother a mute question at the moment when it first kicks in the womb, so that the mother says: "Ah, there, so a child is going to be born, is it?"

The same thing happens at this moment between Jesus and Mary: "Woman, why turn to me?"

Between a mother and her son, between a mother and her living fruit, which her child represents, this complicity is certainly present. And there is something that should not pass unnoticed: this is the moment when both reach a tacit agreement in order that a mutation, a birth, may take place.

Perhaps it is at this moment, at the marriage feast at Cana, that Mary becomes the Mother of God.

---

2. Rashkow explains elsewhere that in Freudian and post-Freudian terminology, "phallic" is not a biological but psychological term, referring to an entity of power that dominates the scene.

Reading 10.2 Christ and Antichrist

CHARLES T. DAVIS III

Using insights from Jungian archetypal theory, Davis identifies the myth-laden language of the Apocalypse, with saints and dragons, Christ and "Antichrists," as expressive of a battle that originates within the depths of the human psyche, often projected on any perceived enemy within range. Davis assesses the apocalyptic mind-set in early New Testament literature, its origin within the psychodynamics of the psyche, and its psycho-historical effects.

The "End of the World" story is a psychic drama that is spontaneously projected on the world. . . . The Christ-Antichrist story as an End of the World drama has endured through two millennia because it arises from the unconscious and expresses the deepest fears, desires, and needs of our hearts. This vision is deeply embedded in our tradition and is often difficult to detect. Like Proteus, the Christ-Antichrist story shifts its forms. In this respect, the story functions like a repressed neurotic symptom that needs to be brought to consciousness by critical analysis. . . .

The Christ-Antichrist Story

The term "Antichrist" is found only in I John 2:18, 22 and 4:3 and II John 7, but it is traditionally associated with the Beast of the Apocalypse.

In Revelation 11:7, the Beast ascends from the mythical bottomless pit into history to kill the two prophets in Jerusalem. Revelation 12 follows with a cosmic drama. The Red Dragon, Satan, seeks in vain to devour the child of the Celestial Woman. . . . War erupts in Heaven. Satan is cast down to earth along with his angels (Rev. 12:7-9). The cosmic conflict ends. . . . The primordial, cosmic battle between good and evil shifts into the historical realm.

The Beast from the Sea with seven heads (Rev. 13:1), which are the hills of Rome and seven kings as well (Rev. 17:9), embodies the power of Satan on earth. The world comprised of those whose names are not written in the pri-

---

From Charles T. Davis III, "Revelation Seventeen: The Apocalypse as Psychic Drama," in *Psychology and the Bible: A New Way to Read the Scriptures*, ed. J. Harold Ellens and Wayne G. Rollins (Westport, CT: Praeger Publishers, 2004), vol. 3, excerpts from pp. 213-18, 220-23, 228-30.

mordial Book of Life (Rev. 13:8) worships this beast — the Roman Empire — which wages war upon the saints (Rev. 13:7). The king, . . . now appears as the second beast arising "out of the earth" (Rev. 13:11). His name is "666" (Rev. 13:18) — *Neron Caesar.* . . . The members of the false church of the Lamb are marked on their foreheads, or right hand, by the Beast (Rev. 13:16). . . . This is the Christian church that accommodates itself to Rome.

When the dramatic action shifts to the wilderness in Revelation 17:3, the Celestial Woman has been replaced by the Whore of Babylon (Rev. 17:3-6) drunk with the blood of the saints. She is seated upon the Beast from the Sea — now identified symbolically as Nero (Rev. 17:8-11), the emperor who was raised from the dead in parody of Jesus.

Christ appears in Revelation 19:11 as the warrior on the white horse descending to earth leading the "armies of heaven" to war (Rev. 19:11-16). He is identical with the child who would rule with an iron rod (Rev. 17:15). . . . Satan who only recently was cast from heaven to earth is bound in the mythical pit for a thousand years (Rev. 20:2-3) while the martyr church sealed by God rules the earth with Christ. Satan is then released to lead his armies against Jerusalem. Fire from heaven consumes his army, and he is cast into the lake of fire (Rev. 20:9-10).

The Christ-Antichrist Story as a Challenge to Critical Scholarship

There is an understandable temptation to dismiss this story as a neurotic vision. We must, however, reject Freud's contention that religion (and art) is *only* a garbage dump for repressed desires and hostilities. Paul Ricoeur observes in *A Philosophical Interpretation of Freud* that "man is capable of neurosis as he is capable of religion, and vice versa" as he responds to the "triple suffering dealt the individual by nature, his body, and other men."[1] Certainly, Christian communities have used this story to focus the desires of the neurotic and to direct repressed hatreds, sadistic tendencies, and violent impulses toward the enemies of their religious group.[2] . . .

Since "the Antichrist legend can be seen as a projection, or perhaps better as a mirror, for conceptions and fears about ultimate human evil,"[3] our

1. Paul Ricoeur, *A Philosophical Interpretation of Freud,* trans. D. Savage (New Haven: Yale University Press, 1970), p. 533.

2. Bernard McGinn, *Antichrist: Two Thousand Years of the Human Fascination with Evil* (Dunmore, PA: Torch, 1994), p. 3; Ricoeur, *Philosophical Interpretation,* p. 532.

3. McGinn, *Antichrist,* p. 2.

critical consciousness must purge the story of the End of its archaic literal or descriptive (historical) projections.[4] We may then explore its archetypal symbols and the trajectory of hope that arises from its orientation to future human possibilities.

If unchallenged . . . the Christ-Antichrist story invites an eisegesis that justifies violence against both Christians and non-Christians. . . . When an American General Officer characterizes the 'war' in Afghanistan and Iraq as a battle against Satan, he is implicitly speaking from two millennia of Christian apocalyptic eisegesis and can expect to draw a large following. . . .

The Dynamics of a Psychic Drama

A myth is a psychic drama driven by an archetypal plot that arises spontaneously from the unconscious. . . . From a literary perspective, Bernard McGinn in *Antichrist: Two Thousand Years of the Human Fascination with Evil* characterizes apocalyptic material as "future" or "apocalyptic legends" that present history in terms of "mythic language and symbols."[5] Apocalyptic writers are interpreting history through psychic projections that reveal the unconscious life of the soul. . . . Schuyler Brown . . . observes in *Text and Psyche* that "whatever the author's conscious intention may have been, a religious text arises out of a world of archetypal imagery," and it speaks to the reader as it powerfully engages "his or her unconscious feelings."[6]

Carl G. Jung defines archetypes as structuring influences arising from the unconscious "which, independently of tradition, guarantee in every single individual a similarity and even a sameness of experience, and also of the way it is represented imaginatively."[7] In more pedestrian terms, an archetypal plot is a spontaneous template which normally functions below the level of consciousness. Consider the sports cheer: "Two bits, four bits, six bits a dollar/Everyone for _____ stand up and holler." One need only fill in the blank with one's team name for this 'boilerplate' to work. The Christ-Antichrist story is a psychic boilerplate that can be projected as a cultural drama in which the Antichrist is pitted in battle against Christ, or his representative. As social conditions change, the Antichrist is identified with the person or movement that

4. Ricoeur, *Philosophical Interpretation*, p. 542.

5. McGinn, *Antichrist*, p. 19.

6. Schuyler Brown, *Text and Psyche: Experiencing Scripture Today* (New York: Continuum, 1998), p. 26.

7. Carl Jung, *The Archetypes and the Collective Unconscious*, trans. R. F. C. Hull (Princeton: Princeton University Press, 1959), p. 58.

is perceived as the Christian enemy: Nero, the Jews, Muhammad, Islam, the Pope, heretics, Luther, America — to name some major figures. . . .

Carol Pearson states in *Six Archetypes We Live By: The Hero Within* that an archetype "carries with it a way of seeing the world" that we project with the result that "the external world tends to oblige us by reinforcing our beliefs about it."[8] Archetypal plots are dangerous because they are self-validating. To the uncritical mind, the map of reality defined by the archetype simply appears as 'the way things really are.' There is no awareness of the psychic projection of the archetypal plot upon the world. Analysis changes the situation by naming the plots and thus withdrawing the projection. Pearson warns that when we do not name the archetypes, "we are hostages to them and can do nothing else but live out their plots to the end. When we name them, we have a choice about our response."[9]

. . . Upon careful examination, archetypes can be found lurking under our cultural stereotypes, like "Antichrist." "Stereotypes are laundered, domesticated versions of the *archetypes* from which they derive their power."[10]

The term "Antichrist" is a stereotype in contemporary culture. McGinn notes that Protestant appeals to the Antichrist story, on the one hand, deteriorated "into a monotonous insistence on the pope Antichrist motif" from the seventeenth century to the present. On the other, the term was "directed against so many foes, both real and imagined, that it lost much of its invective power" with the result that the Antichrist plot suffered a severe decline and exists largely in "repetitious forms."[11]

The Christ-Antichrist stereotypes are not without power. Newport cautions us that "the eighty or so charred bodies at Waco are an unwelcome and sobering reminder of the fact that when placed in the hands of certain readers, certain texts can and do become volatile and potentially explosive."[12] Newport's study reveals that David Koresh was not an eccentric, or a demented individual, but the exponent of a Seventh Day Adventist tradition that can be traced back to William Miller's failed prediction that Jesus would return on October 22, 1844.

According to Newport the Seventh Day Adventists inherited the stereotypical equation of the Roman Catholic Church with the Antichrist, but they

8. Carol Pearson, *Six Archetypes We Live By: The Hero Within* (San Francisco: HarperSanFrancisco, 1989), p. xxi.

9. Pearson, *Six Archetypes,* p. xx.

10. Pearson, *Six Archetypes,* p. xix.

11. McGinn, *Antichrist,* p. 7.

12. K. G. C. Newport, *Apocalypse and Millennium: Studies in Biblical Eisegesis* (New York: Cambridge University Press, 2000), pp. 199-200.

"added a new dimension" by arguing that the second beast of Revelation 13, the False Lamb, "was none other than the United States of America."[13] At Waco, true believers understood themselves to be doing battle with Satan and his Beast, the USA. Such is the power of a stereotype. Archetypal plots can surface to take over our lives at any time. Denying their existence only increases their corrosive influence by allowing it to remain unconscious.

. . . This mechanism is already evident in I John. The world is divided in two communities: the children of God and the children of Satan (I Jn 3:9-10). The antichrists, following the Antichrist who is already in the world, have left the Johannine community to join the children of the Devil (I Jn 2:18-19). These former brothers, who dared to disagree with the community, are envisioned as the enemies of the Son of God who was sent to destroy the works of the Devil (I Jn 3:8).

The Johannine community evidences a deeply felt psychic need to abolish the old time with its worn out institutions and to embrace the hope of a New Creation. Unfortunately, this real psychic need, that can appear in any community, most often goes unacknowledged and is projected onto historical events and persons, as in this case where the antichrists are former members of the community. The psychic need to abolish and recreate the world can only be satisfied by an inward journey that leads to a transformation of the symbols by means of which we construct our map of reality.

The Assimilation of Jesus and Nero to an Archetypal Plot

. . . Mircea Eliade notes in *Cosmos and History: The Myth of the Eternal Return* that an historical figure endures in the popular memory for no more than two or three centuries without being assimilated to the heroic archetype.[14] Persons capable of imitation by later generations lose their historical particularity, as they become universal, timeless, images available for story telling. Celtic Arthur won long forgotten battles; King Arthur, the archetypal Christian king, has moved the souls of millions for a millennium.

Nero, the Emperor, and Jesus, the Peasant, represent the extreme poles of the social continuum. They had no significant historical relationship. Their association in the Apocalypse is the result of their being appropriated by the collective memory as the opposing images of the human tyrant and the

---

13. Newport, *Apocalypse and Millennium*, p. 198.

14. Mircea Eliade, *Cosmos and History: The Myth of the Eternal Return*, trans. W. R. Trask (New York: Pantheon, 1965), p. 43.

true human king. Throughout Christian literature, they stand like Siamese twins: Nero — the Antichrist, the very embodiment of ego, Satan, and cosmic evil; Christ — the embodiment of the Logos and Light, Self, and the god-man of the End Time.

As the symbols of the primordial struggle are re-oriented to the End and are embodied in a quasi-historical drama, their focus shifts from the cosmic perspective to the inner, psychic perspective. . . . McGinn identifies Origen as the first to seek the meaning of the Antichrist in the inner life of individuals.[15] The projection is most fully withdrawn by Augustine who argued that the Apocalypse is "a message about the perennial struggle between good and evil in the souls of men."[16] Augustine's principle is "go not outside, return into thyself: Truth dwells in the inward man."[17] In effect, Augustine recognizes that the Christ-Antichrist story is a psychic drama.

The introspective interpretation of the Christ-Antichrist story exercised a strong influence in the West through the twelfth century.[18] It is this line of interpretation that needs to be revived today as criticism withdraws projection by stripping away the literal-historical aspects of the story.

Jesus and Nero as Polarities in the Image of the Self

The Self archetype coincides with the God archetype. As Jesus was assimilated to the Christ, the hero and the god-man, he became an archetypal image of the Self for Christian culture. In *Symbols of Transformation*, Jung writes:

> In the Christ-figure the opposites which are united in the archetypes are polarized into the "light" son of God on the one hand and the devil on the other. . . . Christ and the dragon of the Antichrist lie very close together so far as their historical development and cosmic significance are concerned.[19]

The result of the cultural projection of the Self archetype upon Jesus is a split in the cultural image of the Self/God. All the good is projected on God's

---

15. McGinn, *Antichrist,* pp. 64-65.

16. Bernard McGinn, *Visions of the End: Apocalyptic Traditions in the Middle Ages* (New York: Columbia University Press, 1979), p. 26.

17. Carl Jung, *Psychology and Religion: West and East,* trans. R. F. C. Hull (Princeton: Princeton University Press, 1958), p. 107, translated from *Liber de Vera Religione,* XXIX. 72.

18. McGinn, *Antichrist,* p. 79.

19. Carl Jung, *Symbols of Transformation,* translated by R. F. C. Hull (Princeton: Princeton University Press, 1956), p. 368.

Christ; all the bad on Satan's agent, the Antichrist. This split prevents human/divine wholeness and encourages the projection of human evil upon our enemies as the Shadow archetype — the repudiated and thus unconscious aspects of our own life. The expulsion of Satan from Heaven (Revelation 12) splits the God archetype as well. All that is evil in Heaven is projected first upon the earth (Rev. 12) and then upon the underworld (Rev. 19). The Perfect God with his Perfect Son are counterbalanced by the Evil Satan and the Nero Antichrist. So long as the God/Self archetype is split by projection, Christian Man will be dogged by his Pagan Shadow, Christ by the Antichrist, God by Satan, Heaven by Earth and Underearth. The Christ cannot exist without the Antichrist once this split in the Self archetype is made. McGuinn makes a similar point from a theological perspective when he observes that "the early Church's rapidly evolving Christology seems to have stimulated the development of an obverse 'Antichristology,' that is, a more detailed and inflated account of the career and person of the final enemy."[20] The myth of the Dragon-King fight projected through prophecy into a future historical event was an ideal narrative container for this new psychic orientation.

The ancient leader, who is assimilated by his culture to the God-man hero archetype, is always vulnerable to an ego inflation that deceives him into claiming the powers of divinity for himself, as emperor worship demonstrates. This ego inflation lays the groundwork for the emperor to be portrayed negatively as the monster who as "the giant of self-achieved independence is the world's messenger of disaster, even though, in his mind, he may entertain himself with humane intentions."[21] The true hero, by contrast, is one who has achieved the submission of his role to the higher powers of the inner world. Hero and Dragon/Antichrist are the two roles that leaders may play in the psychic drama as aspects of the Self. . . .

In Revelation 13 and 17, the Nero of popular culture is assimilated to the image of the Antichrist, the enemy of Jesus, the Jewish Messiah. John paints the image of two Christian communities in bold colors. One dominated by Rome; the other by Christ. In short, the existence of the Christian community itself, like Jesus and Nero, has been assimilated to the Hero-Dragon archetypal plot. Life is understood quasi-historically, as a battle between a false, Roman-sanctioned Christianity deriving from Satan and a true Christian community of martyrs led by the Son of God. This image of the Christian

---

20. McGinn, *Visions of the End*, p. 17.

21. Joseph Campbell, *The Hero with a Thousand Faces* (Princeton: Princeton University Press, 1973), p. 15.

community as the embodiment of the Hero slaying the Dragon is an abiding legacy of the Apocalypse. It has provided a firm foundation for Christian eschatological and apocalyptic activity from Patmos to Waco.

Conclusion

. . . The Christ-Antichrist story specifically should alert us to an inner warfare — within individuals and/or society — between the good self and the bad self. . . .

The Christ-Antichrist archetypal plot is toxic when it is projected as a political boilerplate upon one's enemies. . . . The projection must be withdrawn and faced. Repressing the plot is counterproductive. Whether it is allowed an underground existence through theology, movies, story telling or tolerated as a stereotype, it continues to be toxic. Augustine correctly interpreted the story as a psychic drama that unfolds in the human heart.

Reading 10.3   The Theology of Paul

ROBIN SCROGGS

In the 1970s and 1980s, a body of psychological commentary on Paul emerged that has yet to be superseded. In this excerpt from an article in 1982, Robin Scroggs touches on some of the themes he developed more fully elsewhere. In "The Heuristic Value of a Psychoanalytic Model in the Interpretation of Pauline Theology" (1978),[1] Scroggs offered a compelling application of the thought of post-Freudians Herbert Marcuse and Norman O. Brown to an understanding of the psychodynamics of Paul's conversion from an ethic of law to an ethic of spirit. In *Paul for a New Day* (1977),[2] written for a more popular audience, Scroggs developed his insights at length.

In addition, the reader will want to follow up on Scroggs's opening allusion

1. Robin Scroggs, "The Heuristic Value of a Psychoanalytic Model in the Interpretation of Pauline Theology," in *The Text and the Times* (Minneapolis: Fortress, 1993), pp. 125-50.
2. Robin Scroggs, *Paul for a New Day* (Philadelphia: Fortress Press, 1977).

From Robin Scroggs, "Psychology as a Tool to Interpret the Text: Emerging Trends in Biblical Thought," *Christian Century*, March 24, 1982, pp. 337-38.

to Richard Rubenstein's *My Brother Paul* (1972).[3] Rubenstein offers post-Freudian reflections on his experience with the psychic reality of "the law" from his Jewish youth and that of his Jewish "brother," Paul.

Beyond that, no survey of psychological perspectives on Paul's life is complete without reference to the masterwork by Gerd Theissen, *Psychological Aspects of Pauline Theology* (1987),[4] which refracts five sets of Pauline texts through the psychological lens of three psychological approaches: learning theory, psychodynamic theory (Freud and Jung), and cognitive psychology. We have already seen how Theissen applies learning theory to Pauline theology in Chapter 4, and we will return to him in Chapter 12.

The reader is also reminded of the reading in Chapter 7 by Terrance Callan on the polar roles of boasting and humility in Paul's personality and development.

Of all published studies in recent years, perhaps the most provocative remains that of Richard Rubenstein in *My Brother Paul* (Harper & Row, 1972). This author applies Freud, as interpreted by Norman O. Brown, to the study of Paul's theology. Whether Rubenstein is ultimately right or wrong seems to me not the issue, but rather whether he has provided some new avenues for interpretation. Freud saw Paul as an agent in the "return of the repressed," and Rubenstein pushes further in this direction. The apostle understood the Pharisaic "system" as an attempt to justify oneself before the Father. But this means, in psychoanalytic terms, that persons must be righteous before the Father who threatens otherwise to kill. At the heart of Paul's theology is, therefore, an attempt to find a way to escape from death.

Paul resolves the dilemma by interpreting Christ as the elder brother who has paid the price of the Father's anger and with whom the believer can identify, in part through the sacraments. Through this participation the believer is safe from infanticide. Salvation is participation in the Last Adam and ultimately a return to the primal scene, the garden of Eden. It is the end of repression and the reality principle, a return to primary narcissism and the womb.

Almost two thousand years before the depth psychology that his religious imagination helped to make possible, Paul of Tarsus gave expression to mankind's yearning for a new and flawless beginning that could finally

---

3. Richard Rubenstein, *My Brother Paul* (New York: Harper & Row, 1972).

4. Gerd Theissen, *Psychological Aspects of Pauline Theology,* trans. John P. Galvin (Philadelphia: Fortress, 1987).

end the cycle of anxiety, repression, desire, and craving — the inevitable concomitants of the human pilgrimage. Paul made of that yearning a force for the spiritual unification of the majority of men in the western world. [*My Brother Paul,* p. 173]

Finally I would like to share with the reader my own concern for a possible Freudian perspective applied to Paul's theology. I am also decisively informed by Norman O. Brown, yet I end in a place somewhat different from Rubenstein's, primarily because I see Paul's theology of justification by grace to be the central focus of what the apostle has to say, whereas Rubenstein works more with the symbols of Paul's so-called "Christ mysticism."

Paul has spoken to me for a long time, and I have been able to understand him through his own language-system. For many people in the modern world this has not been possible, even though they have been searching for just the message of liberation I have heard Paul teaching. For them Paul is an ideological mystagogue, who mouths strange, long-lost symbols and outdated myths. For these people Paul simply cannot be heard. Perhaps if one can see the close analogy between a psychoanalytic interpretation of society and Paul's theology of culture, a new way toward an understanding of the message of the apostle may emerge.

This is a massive task I have not yet completed and have only hinted at in my book *Paul for a New Day. . . .* I can only hint here as well. Paul's thought is oriented toward an interpretation of the two civilizations of death and sin, and life and grace. The world of death is the world of the performance principle (justification by works); it is the world of repression dominated by the superego. God's act of justification by grace enables persons to switch worlds, to leave that culture of death and to enter a world always intended by God for people (the new creation), founded on the total and entirely free gift from God (justification by grace). This transformation does not involve "trying harder," which would be a return to the performance principle; rather it is the giving up of effort, the acceptance of life as total gift. Expressed in Freudian terms, it is the way back behind the processes of sexual organization, not toward the womb but rather toward a transformed narcissism culminating in joyful and loving unification with others. For Brown (as distinct from Freud), such a movement is possible once persons have integrated death with life, because repression can then come to an end. For Paul the movement is, of course, based on the transcendent act of God. But the description of the two worlds and their fundamental dynamics is strikingly analogous.

This does not mean that Paul's theology is reduced to psychoanalytic realities. It does mean — and I would insist on this — that divine transformative acts can be described in psychoanalytic terms as well as theological ones. If this terminology makes it possible for some modern persons better to understand Paul, why not? God needs, in this secular and troubled generation, all the help she can get.

And here, in conclusion, is my own apology for the use of psychology in the study of the biblical text. What we are interpreting in religious discourse is never the discourse itself, but those acts of divine power which lie behind and which, indeed, create that discourse. Any language, including the explicitly theological, is thus penultimate. Theological language is never the "queen of the sciences" nor is it the only language useful in describing the acts of God. Since psychological language aims at revealing the depths of human transformation, and since this is the goal of theological language as well, there is no reason the two cannot walk together in the search for truth.

SUGGESTIONS FOR FURTHER READING

Bash, Anthony. "A Psychodynamic Approach to the Interpretation of 2 Corinthians 10–13." *Journal for the Study of the New Testament* 83 (2001): 51-67.

Blessing, Kamila. "Differentiation in the Family of Faith: The Prodigal Son and Galatians 1–2." In *Psychology and the Bible: A New Way to Read the Scriptures,* edited by J. Harold Ellens and Wayne G. Rollins, vol. 3, 165-92. Westport, CT: Praeger Publishers, 2004.

Gager, John. *Kingdom and Community: The Social World of Early Christianity.* Englewood Cliffs, NJ: Prentice-Hall, 1975.

Hopkins, Brooke. "Jesus and Object-Use: A Winnicottian Account of the Resurrection Myth." *International Review of Psycho-Analysis* 16 (1989): 93-100.

Jung, Carl Gustav. *Answer to Job.* In *The Collected Works of C. G. Jung,* edited by Gerhard Adler et al., vol. 11, 355-470. Princeton: Princeton University Press, 1953-78.

Mitternacht, Dieter. "Theissen's Integration of Psychology and New Testament Studies: Learning Theory, Psychodynamics, and Cognitive Psychology." In *Psychology and the Bible: A New Way to Read the Scriptures,* edited by J. Harold Ellens and Wayne G. Rollins, vol. 1, 101-18. Westport, CT: Praeger Publishers, 2004.

Rubenstein, Richard. *My Brother Paul.* New York: Harper & Row, 1972.

Sanford, John A. *Mystical Christianity: A Psychological Commentary on the Gospel of John.* New York: Crossroad, 1993.

Scroggs, Robin. "The Heuristic Value of a Psychoanalytic Model in the Interpretation of Pauline Theology." *Zygon* 13 (1978): 136-57.

————. *Paul for a New Day.* Philadelphia: Fortress Press, 1977.

Theissen, Gerd. *Psychological Aspects of Pauline Theology.* Translated by John P. Galvin. Philadelphia: Fortress, 1987.

Wuellner, Wilhelm H., and Robert C. Leslie. *The Surprising Gospel: Intriguing Psychological Insights from the New Testament.* Nashville: Abingdon, 1984.

CHAPTER 11

Biblical Religious Experience:
Dreams, Prophecy, and Healing

We cannot here characterize or perhaps even name all the old problems that are beginning to glow with a new light. . . . Sacrifice, poverty, obedience, chastity, asceticism, renunciation and its motives and forms, creeds, dogma and doctrine, worship including sacraments, rites, ritual and ceremonies, priests and saints, the psycho-pedagogic aspect of miracles, especially those of healing, as related to mental states, the nature, value and limitations of personality, the feminine aspects and functions of religion and Mariolatry, the Sabbath as a philosophical institution and the uses of rest from fatigue of body and soul, the relation of religion to art and aesthetics, the place and form of symbols, vows and oaths, the psychology of sects, the relations of religious feeling and belief to morals and conduct: — all these and many more topics have anthropological sides which theology has too often failed adequately to recognize which are quite distinct from, and to some extent, independent of, historical criticism or textual exegesis.

G. Stanley Hall[1]

As the quote above suggests, G. Stanley Hall, the pioneer American psychologist, understood the psychological richness evidenced in the variety of religious experience and phenomena. It is here that psychological biblical criticism especially overlaps the field of the psychology of religion. For in the text of the Bible are to be found descriptions of religious experience ranging from guilt to conversion, from dreaming and ecstatic visions to ritual practices. Even more, these manifestations continue to unfold in communities of inter-

---

1. G. Stanley Hall, "Editorial," *The American Journal of Religious Psychology and Education* 1, no. 1 (1904): 3.

preters, whose behavior, attitudes, and worldviews continue to evolve in response to the Bible and their changing situations.

Examination of religious experience in the Bible involves connecting the world behind the text — the historical experience of men and women in other times and other places — to our own, the world in front of the text. Implicit in all biblical interpretation is the assumption that there is some continuity, some commonality and consistency in human life. Without that connection, it would be futile for us to attempt to interpret ancient texts meaningfully. We dare to read the Bible believing that, while there may be significant differences between the ancient world and our own, those differences are not insurmountable. Something of what we know of ourselves today can help to illuminate the world of the Bible. Insights from the biblical world can help us to understand ourselves better. If this is not so, then not only psychological criticism but all of biblical criticism is endangered.

In this chapter and the next, we will look briefly at only a small sample of studies of religious experience and practice in the Bible. In this chapter, we will consider dreaming, prophecy, healing, and self-identity. In the next we will turn to experiences of the demonic and exorcism, glossolalia (speaking in tongues), and conversion. As Hall so aptly commented, we cannot hope to categorize or even name all of what could be explored from psychological perspectives.

Reading 11.1   Dreams and Visions in the Bible

JOHN A. SANFORD

Dreams and visions play a significant role in the Bible — from the dreams of Jacob and Joseph in Genesis to the apocalyptic vision of John recounted in the Book of Revelation. However, dreams were commonly disregarded in Western culture until Freud himself reawakened an interest in dreams as the "royal road to the uncon-

---

In John A. Sanford, *Dreams: God's Forgotten Language* (San Francisco: Harper & Row, 1989), pp. 77-79, 93-96.

scious." John Sanford argues for a renewed attention to dreams as an important connection with the spirit, breaking through our ordinary consciousness. Note how he considers dreams, visions, and encounters with angelic messengers to be different manifestations of the same reality.

Dreams and Visions in the Bible

To deal completely with the subject of the dreams and visions in the Bible would require a book in itself. For not only are there the passages referring specifically to dreams, but there are also passages referring to visions, appearances of angels, trances, and "being in the spirit," all of which are described in such a way that the distinction between them is not sharply drawn; the Bible regards dreams, visions, certain trances, appearances of angels, and experiences of the spirit in much the same way.

In regarding dreams and visions as similar in source, construction, and significance the Bible is on solid scientific ground. All of us know from our firsthand experience what a dream is. Psychologically we call a dream an experience a person might have during sleep, that is, during a naturally unconscious state. A dream is in fact a "story" that "happens" to us during sleep, of which we are a part or at least a spectator. A vision can be understood as a "dream" we have while semiconscious or awake. If the unconscious breaks through into our consciousness during our waking state with a dreamlike image or action then we are experiencing a vision.

It is sometimes supposed today that to have a dream is permissible enough, but to have a vision is a sign of insanity or mental derangement of some kind. This, however, is not the case. It is not the vision that is a sign of mental derangement, but the point of view from which the ego regards the vision. In insanity the vision is accepted as literal, external reality, and consciousness does not distinguish between the external and the internal world. In the normal ego, however, the vision is recognized for its subjective, internal nature. It is not the vision that is a sign of sickness, nor the unconscious that is "insane"; but the ego that is sick or has lost its bearings; and the fact that the insane are more prone to visions than more stable individuals is simply due to the vulnerability of their weakened and shattered egostructure to invasions from the unconscious.

When, therefore, the Book of Numbers (12:6) says: "And he said, 'Hear my words: If there is a prophet among you, I the Lord make myself known to him in a vision, I speak with him in a dream,'" thus equating clearly the common origin and significance of dreams and visions, it is resting upon very good psychological foundations. But the Bible likewise often equates the appearance of an angel with a dream or a vision. Take, for instance, the following passages from the Gospel of Matthew: As Joseph considers putting Mary away quietly after discovering her pregnancy we read that "the angel of the Lord appeared to him in a dream," bidding him to retain Mary as his wife and telling him her child is of the Holy Spirit (Matthew 1:20). Later the Wise Men, having found and worshiped the child Jesus, are "warned in a dream not to return to Herod" (Matthew 2:12). Immediately after, Joseph again is visited by an angel of the Lord in a dream, bidding him flee to Egypt for safety (Matthew 2:13). And after a sojourn in Egypt he is bidden once more by an angel in a dream to return to the land of Israel (Matthew 2:19). In still another dream the angel bids him to return not to Judea, but to Galilee (Matthew 2:22). We thus find in the first two chapters of Matthew no less than five dreams, and we further establish that every decision in this action-packed section is based upon a revelation made by God through a dream. Further, four of these specifically cite the appearance of an angel, so that the Bible clearly equates the revelations given by angels and the revelations by dreams and visions.

Matthew is not the only one who equates angels and dreams. We find, for instance, in Luke 1:22 that Zechariah's experience with the angel Gabriel is a vision, and that the angels who appeared to the women after the Resurrection were regarded as a vision (Luke 24:23). To cite only one example from the abundant material in Acts, the Centurion Cornelius has an experience in which an angel comes to him in a vision (Acts 10:3). And from the Book of Revelation (9:17) we learn that the entire revelation given to John by an angel is a vision, a fact borne out by the visionary quality of the book as a whole.

Even experiences "of the spirit" are frequently regarded by the biblical writers as similar in kind to experiences of visions and dreams. The similarity between having a vision or dream and being "in the spirit" is abundantly shown, for instance, in the Book of Ezekiel. . . . Again and again in Ezekiel we read verses such as these: "He put forth the form of a hand, and took me by a lock of my head; and the Spirit lifted me up between earth and heaven, and brought me in visions of God to Jerusalem . . ." (8:3; also 11:24 and 40:2). Ezekiel, however, is by no means the only book where experiences of the Spirit are equated with visionary experiences. St. Paul himself goes on to describe "visions and revelations of the Lord" (2 Corinthians 12:1ff.), and the Book of Joel is quoted in the Book of Acts (2:17) in this significant verse: "And in the last days it shall be, God declares, that I will pour out my Spirit upon all flesh, and your sons and your daughters shall prophesy, and your young men shall see visions, and your old men shall dream dreams. . . ." We have then a very fine line indeed between visions, dreams, the appearance of angels, and an outpouring of the Spirit of God.

Following a survey of passages dealing with dreams, visions, and angelic messengers in the Bible, Sanford summarizes how the Bible deals with dream materials.

Let us stop here for a moment and summarize what we have found in the Bible about dreams. We have noted some seventy passages referring to dreams and visions. On the basis of this abundant material we must conclude the following:

1. Dreams and visions were regarded in both the Old and New Testaments as revelations from God. Those skilled in their interpretation, such as Daniel or Joseph, were revered; those who understood the revelations God had given them, such as Abraham or Solomon, became great and wise; those who were overcome by their inner experience, such as St. Paul or Ezekiel, became great missionaries and prophets.

2. Viewed from this perspective the entire Bible is the story of God's breakthrough into the human conscious mind via the unconscious.

3. Many other religious experiences, such as Jacob's wrestling with the adversary, or Moses' encounter with the burning bush, were of a visionary kind.

4. The early church regarded dreams the same way as the Bible: as revelations from God.

The people of the Bible did not first sit down to intellectualize about God. God broke through into them with a personal experience. He "convinced" them, as he did St. Paul, to use the word which literally in the Latin derivation means "to overcome." Only after their experience did they sit down and think about God, to give structure to and expand the meaning of their experience. First the great dreams were revelations from God. Only later were there priests and a church to give form to the experience and to build it into ritual and dogma.

But today many of us have decided we do not want to "contaminate" our contemplation of the divine by allowing anything as nebulous and unsettling as the unconscious to intrude. We have decided that we may find God through rational thinking, or a "group experience," or education, or formal worship — everywhere except in our own soul, which is in fact the fountainhead of religious experience. The result is that we Christians are afraid today of that very soul from which our heritage springs; we want creeds, not religious experiences, and dogma, not inspiration. Above all, we refuse to accept the nonrational unconscious, because it threatens the tyranny of rationality that has gripped us today.

We think of all sorts of excuses, of course: Dealing with the unconscious, we say, is only for the mentally ill; dreams are only for the psychiatrist; revelation stopped with the New Testament, so why endanger our dogma with further revelations through dreams? In this we differ greatly from the early church Fathers, most of whom also declared the dream to be the Voice of God and the spiritual world. But our objections are rationalizations. The truth is, as the Epistle to the Hebrews says (10:31), "It is a fearful thing to fall into the hands of the living God." We much prefer the security of our rationality to the awesome experience of dealing with a living voice.

We could of course dispense with our dreams if we wanted to, were it not for two difficulties. We could say that this belief in dreams that we see in the Bible and in the early church Fathers is outmoded, a superstition; that it is forgivable to people of ancient days but not for us enlightened Christians, just as we no longer have to accept Adam and Eve as literally the first man and the first woman. Or, granting the validity of the dreams of the Bible, we could state that this was well and good but only for those times. There are only two difficulties in the way. First is the pressing need we have today. For all of our highly sophisticated consciousness, the human mind is sick. We need a healing, a meaning, a balance, and a revelation for our minds that our rational consciousness cannot provide us. Our very urgent inner need demands that we turn again to God for revelation, if only to reveal to us as individuals what he had already revealed in the Bible, in order that we might understand it.

And second, we Christians discover that this neglected part of our religious life has been recognized as valuable by others in this world. Just because the churches have decided to pay no attention to their unconscious does not mean that God will stop trying to speak to us. So it is that scientific psychology and medicine, in search of a way to help us find healing and wholeness, have discovered what the Bible knew all along but Christians had forgotten: that dreams and their interpretation can heal the sick soul. Carl Jung, more perceptive and receptive than his contemporaries, discovered that the dreams of people today are not only dreams about themselves, but also about God; that at the basis of our dreams there is a religious process.

Are we not like the little boy who is afraid in his room at night and calls his mother? His mother reassures him not to be afraid, since God is there in the room with him. As the mother returns downstairs, she hears the boy say anxiously: "All right, God, it's okay for you to be here; just don't move or I'll be scared to death!" We also reassure ourselves that everything must be all right, for God is here with us, and we graciously give our consent to his presence. But we add secretly: "Just don't come to us in anything as personal as a dream or an experience which really involves our personality or we will be frightened to death!"

The presence of God is a disturbing presence, especially when his voice is as close to us as our nightly dreams. We cannot deny the closeness of his presence, for we also dream dreams as did the men and women of the Bible. But we must look at dreams not only from the point of view of inspired intuition, as did Daniel, for instance, but also from the objective viewpoint of modern science.

Reading 11.2 The Psychology of the Prophets

Max Weber

Prophets and prophetic experience have drawn a lot of psychological attention. Unfortunately, much of it has been expressed in efforts to diagnose the prophets, to presume that their unusual behavior expresses some profound pathology. In Chapter 7, we saw an example of an effort to understand the personality of the prophet Ezekiel. Max Weber here is not concerned with the quirks of individual prophets; rather, he asks what is common about the prophetic experience. He suggests that in Hebrew prophecy there is a reflective, non-ecstatic, and individualized dimension that distinguishes it both from the classical Greek forms and from later prophetic activity in the Christian church.

This is not the place to classify and interpret, as far as that is possible, the various physiological, psychological, and possibly pathological states of the prophets. Attempts made thus far, especially with respect to Ezekiel, are not convincing. It affords, furthermore, no decisive interest for us. In Israel, as throughout antiquity, psychopathic states were valued as holy. Contact with madmen was taboo still in rabbinical times. The royal overseers appointed over the prophets (Jer. 29:24f.) were called "overseers of madmen and prophets." And tradition reports that even Jehu's officer, at the sight of the prophet's

From Max Weber, "Judaism: The Psychology of the Prophets," in *The Symbolic Instrument in Early Times*, vol. 1 of *Propaganda and Communication in World History*, ed. H. D. Lesswell, D. Lerner, and H. Speier (Honolulu: University of Hawaii Press, 1967), pp. 320-26.

disciple offering the ointment to the king to have asked "Wherefore came this mad fellow to thee?" But our concern here is with something very different.

Of interest, in the first place, is the emotional character of prophetic ecstasy per se, which differentiates it from all forms of Indian apathetic ecstasy. The preeminently auditive nature of classical prophecy, in contrast to the essentially visual apathetic ecstasy of the ancient "seers," was purely historically conditioned by the contrast between the Southern Yahwistic conception of Yahwe's revelation and the conception of the North. The corporeal "voice" of God appears in place of the old corporeal epiphany, which the North, with its different representation of God, theoretically rejected and which did not agree with the psychic quality of Northern piety, which had sublimated orgiasticism into apathetic ecstasy. With the increasing recognition of the auditive character of the inspiration as the sole badge of authenticity was correlated the intensification of the political excitement of the listeners. This corresponded to the emotional character of prophecy.

A further important characteristic is that the prophets interpreted the meaning of their own extraordinary states, visions, compulsive speeches, and acts. Despite their obviously great psychological differences their interpretations always took the same direction. The act of interpretation per se, however close it seems to us today, could by no means be taken for granted. A prerequisite was that the ecstatic states were not valued for themselves, as personal and sacred possessions, but an entirely different meaning was ascribed to them, that of a mission. This is still more obvious in the homogeneity of interpretations, a point which deserves more detailed elucidation.

Only at times did the prophets speak out of direct ecstasy (Is. 21:3, 4; Jer. 4:19f.). Usually they speak about their ecstatic experiences. The typical oracle begins with "Yahwe said unto me. . . ." There are diverse shades. Ezekiel, on the one hand, squeezes whole treatises out of some of his visions although he was an apparently quite pathological and ecstatic character. On the other hand, there are numerous short verses of pre-Exile prophets which were thrust into the addressee's face in supreme passion and apparently in a state of esctasy. The most ecstatic and timely pronouncements were forthcoming without the prophet being asked[1] but solely inspired and pressured by Yahwe. The prophet was then carried away in the face of an especially dangerous situation of the country or under an especially shattering impression of sin.

In contrast we find among the classical prophets those relatively rare cases in which the prophet had been previously asked to prophesy. He seems

---

1. Ezekiel, however, was once seized by ecstasy in the presence of the elders who consulted him (Ezek. 8:1).

but rarely to have answered at once. Like Mohammed he brooded in prayer over the case; Jeremiah once did so for ten days until the ecstatic seizure occurred (Jer. 42). Even then, as a rule, the visionary or auditory experience was not at once broadcast among the tarrying listeners, for such experience was often obscure and ambiguous.

The prophet then pondered in prayer about the meaning; only when he possessed the meaning would he speak out. Some of the prophets used the form of divine speech — Yahwe spoke through them directly in the first person — other prophets used the form of reporting about Yahwe's words. Human speech predominated with Isaiah and Micah, divine speech with Amos, Hosea, Jeremiah, and Ezekiel. Finally, all prophets were given to the interpretation of events including those of their workaday life, as significant manifestations of Yahwe (cf. especially Jer. 32).

Characteristic of the typical dicta of the pre-Exile prophets in general is that they have been spoken or, as is once said of Isaiah (5:1), chanted, in tremendous emotion. To be sure, one may find occasional verses which were perhaps left deliberately ambiguous, as was the well-known *kroisos* [Croesus] oracle of the Delphian Apollo[2] and individual intellectual elaborations such as those of Ezekiel. But this was not the rule. Moreover, it is probably justifiably held that one may discern the conscious adherence to certain stylistic rules of prophetic poetry. For instance, usually the name of the person thought of is not mentioned unless it is to be cursed.

These rules did not alter the timely and emotional nature of prophecy. The conception of deity, though, delimited the content of experience. The corporeality of Yahwe's voice for the prophets meant that the prophet on the one hand felt decidedly "full of God" and on the other that the traditional nature of Yahwe's majesty precluded a true "embodiment" of God in the creature. Therefore, the euphemisms for the corporeally inaccessible were chosen.[3]

All Hellenic oracular dicta known to us were delivered on request. In their tempered and "perfect" form they do not remotely attain the emotional forcefulness of the spontaneous prophetic verses of Amos, Nahum, Isaiah, Zephaniah, and Jeremiah. In the partly fragmentary tradition, the great

2. [This refers to a story related by Herodotus, in which king Croesus asks the oracle at Delphi if he should attack the Persians. The oracle replies, "Croesus will destroy a great empire." Encouraged, Croesus attacked, but was defeated and captured when the Persians invaded his lands. The empire in the oracle was his own. — Editors' note.]

3. Sellin, *Der alttestamentliche Prophetismus* (Leipzig, 1912), p. 227, rightly observes that the form in which the divine word reaches the prophet as a rule is not stated in detail. What was decisive was that the prophet had given an interpretation of his intentions which was evident and therewith conclusive to him.

power of rhythm is yet surpassed by the glow of visionary images which are always concrete, telling, striking, concise, exhaustive, often of unheard of majesty and fecundity; in this regard they belong to the most grandiose productions of world poetry. They only lose in articulateness when the great acts of the invisible God on behalf of Israel had to be fashioned out of a vague vision of fantastic but indeterminate images of the future.

Whence did this emotion come if the truly ecstatic and pathological excitement was already dated and had faded out, as was often the case? The emotion simply did not flow from the pathos of these very psychopathological states, but from the vehement certainty of successfully having grasped the meaning of what the prophet had experienced. The prophet, unlike ordinary pathologically ecstatic men, had no vision, dreamed no dreams, and heard no mysterious voices. Rather he attained clarity and assurance through a corporeal divine voice of what Yahwe had meant by these daydreams, or the vision, or the ecstatic excitement, and what Yahwe had commanded him to say in communicable words.

The tremendous pathos of prophetic speech in many cases was, as it were, a post-ecstatic excitement of in turn semi-ecstatic nature which resulted from the certainty of truly having stood "in Yahwe's council," as the prophets put it — have said what Yahwe had told them or to have served as a mouthpiece, through which Yahwe literally spoke. The typical prophet apparently found himself in a constant state of tension and of oppressive brooding in which even the most banal things of everyday life could become frightening puzzles, since they might somehow be significant.

Ecstatic visions were not required to place the prophets in this state of tension. When the tension dissolved into a flash of meaningful interpretation, coming about in the hearing of the divine voice, the prophetic word burst forth. Pythia and the interpretive priestly poet were not separated here. The Israelite prophet united both in his person. This explains his tremendous élan.

Two further circumstances are important. First, these psychic states of the prophet were not connected — as, for example, was the ecstasy of Pythia — with the use of traditional ecstasy means of the Nebiim [the biblical "sons of the prophets"], nor, generally, with any external mass stimulation, hence, an ecstatic community. We find nothing of the kind among the classical prophets of our collection of scriptures. They did not seek ecstasy. It came to them. Besides, not one of them is reported to have been received into a guild of prophets through the laying on of hands or some such ceremony or to have belonged to any sort of specialized community. Always, rather, the prophet's calling came directly from Yahwe, and the classical prophets among them told us of their visionary or auditory "call." None of them used any intoxicants, the use of which they cursed on every occasion, as idolatry. Similarly, we hear nothing of fasting as a means of ecstasy evocation among the pre-Exile prophets, though tradition once recounts of Moses (Ex. 34:28) fasting. Thus, emotional ecstasy does not appear among them in the form of the early Christian community (and its possible antecedents).

In the apostolic age the spirit did not come upon the solitary individual, but upon the faithful assembly or upon one or several of its participants. This, at least, was the rule and the form of experience which the community evaluated as typical. The "spirit was poured out" to the community when the Gospel was preached. Speaking in tongues and other gifts of the spirit, including, also, prophecy, emerged in the midst of the assembly and not in a solitary chamber. All these things obviously resulted from mass influence, or better, of mass gathering and were evidently bound up with such, at least, as normal precondition.[4] The culture-historically so extremely important esteem for the religious community as depository of the spirit in early Christendom had, indeed, this basis. The very community, the gathering of the brethren was especially productive of these sacred psychic states.

This was totally different for the ancient prophets. Precisely in solitude did the prophetic spirit come. And often the spirit first drove the prophet into solitude, into the fields or desert, as happened, still, to John and Jesus. But when the prophet was chased by his vision into the street among the multitude, this resulted only from his interpretative construction of his experience. Be it noted that this public appearance of the prophet was not motivated by the fact that the prophet could experience holiness only in public under the influence of mass suggestion like the early Christians. The prophets did not think of themselves as members of a supporting spiritual community. On the contrary. Misunderstood and hated by the mass of their listeners they never felt themselves to be supported and protected by them as like-minded sympathizers as did the apostles of the early Christian community. Hence, the prophets spoke at no time of their listeners or addressees as their "brethren." The Christian apostles always did so.

. . . The sacred states of the prophets were in this sense truly personal[5] and were thus experienced by them and their audiences, and not as the prod-

4. This holds for all "speaking with tongues" and also for the "prophecy" which then addressed itself to the present. Similarly it reappeared among the Anabaptists and Quakers of the sixteenth and seventeenth centuries; today it occurs most characteristically in the American Negro churches (also of the Negro bourgeoisie, for example, in Washington, where I witnessed it).

5. Consideration must always be given the fact that all contrasts are linked by transitions and that similar phenomena are to be found also with the Christians. Among them, too, individuals are the psychic "centers of infection."

uct of an emotional mass influence. No sort of external influence, but his personal God-sent condition placed the prophet in his ecstatic state. And during the very epoch of the prophets the tradition and high esteem of ecstasy per se as holy, clearly receded into the background. After all, both prophecy and counterprophecy confronted one another in the street. Both equally claimed ecstatic legitimation and cursed one another. Where is Yahwe's truth? everybody had to ask. The conclusion was, one cannot know the true prophet by ecstasy alone. Therewith the substantive significance of ecstasy declined, at least with respect to its manner of communication. Only exceptionally and only as a means to an end is it mentioned which emotional states the prophet has experienced in his ecstasy. For, in contrast to Indian counterparts, this did not count. Ecstasy did not guarantee genuineness. Only the hearing of the corporeal voice of Yahwe, the invisible God, assured the prophet that he was Yahwe's tool. Hence, the tremendous emphasis upon this point.

This, the hearing of the voice of Yahwe, is the prophet's self-legitimation, not the nature of his holy states. Hence, the prophet abstained from gathering a community about him which might have engaged in mass ecstasy or mass-conditioned ecstasy or ecstatic revivals as a path to salvation. Nothing whatever is known of this with regard to classical Yahwe-prophecy. The nature of its message contradicted it. Unlike the possession of pneuma in the early Christian sources, the prophet's attainment of a state of ecstasy or his ability to hear Yahwe's voice is nowhere said to be a prerequisite also for his audience. Prophetic charisma rather was a unique burdensome office — often experienced as torment. Unlike early Christian prophets, the Yahwe prophets never aimed at allowing the spirit to come over the audience.

Reading 11.3   Healing

WILHELM WUELLNER AND ROBERT LESLIE

In *The Surprising Gospel,* Wilhelm Wuellner, a biblical scholar, and Robert Leslie, a pastoral counselor, deal with a variety of New Testament experiences, including waiting, confronting, rejoicing, enabling, and listening. Their perspectives are informed by the psychological theories of Viktor Frankl, C. G. Jung, Fritz Kunkel,

From Wilhelm Wuellner and Robert Leslie, *The Surprising Gospel: Intriguing Psychological Insights from the New Testament* (Nashville: Abingdon, 1984), pp. 49-53.

Harry Stack Sullivan, and Virginia Satir, along with the conviction that we as readers find ourselves in the biblical story as well.

The focus of this section is healing, based on the story of the healing of the paralytic in Matthew 9:1-8. Wuellner and Leslie suggest that, by focusing on the man's total being and not just on his physical disability, Jesus was able to address the real problem in the man's whole emotional life.

Believing as a Prerequisite for Healing

The healing of the paralytic took place in an atmosphere of faith.[1] Matthew does not specify who the people were who carried the paralyzed man, but Jesus points to their faith as being crucial.[2]

The importance of an atmosphere of faith cannot be overstressed. Jerome Frank, in his book *Persuasion and Healing*,[3] notes how crucial the atmosphere of faith is for any healing. Referring to the healing miracles of Lourdes, he points out how the French peasant who seeks healing at Lourdes goes with the backing of his entire village so that faith in the anticipated healing is a highly significant factor. In a communal atmosphere of faith, there is a readiness for healing.[4]

1. For other faith references in Matthew, see 9:22, 29; 15:28; 17:20 (like mustard seed); 21:21 (never doubting); 23:23 (justice, mercy, faith as "the weightier matters of the law"). See also the use of the verb to believe. On "Faith, Faithfulness in the New Testament," see John Reumann's article in *The Interpreter's Dictionary of the Bible*, Supplementary Volume (Nashville: Abingdon, 1976), pp. 332-35, especially p. 333 on Matthew.

2. In Jesus' own city, Capernaum (4:13, 8:5, 11:23, 17:24; cf. his own country 13:57), "they" bring him someone crippled (weakened or paralyzed, literally "dissolved" — *para-luo*; 4:24, 8:6, and here). On paralysis as "one of the diseases of the New Testament," see R. K. Harrison, *The Interpreter's Dictionary of the Bible*, vol. 1 (New York: Abingdon, 1962), pp. 851-52. See below, n. 4. There is "faith" in Israel (see 8:10, "not even in Israel have I found such faith"). On the five different aspects of faith which "general Christian usage" has in common with Old Testament and Jewish traditions, see Rudolf Bultmann, *"pisteuein," Theological Dictionary of the New Testament*, vol. 6 (Grand Rapids: Eerdmans, 1968), pp. 205-8 (and 215-17).

3. Jerome Frank, *Persuasion and Healing* (Baltimore: Johns Hopkins University Press, 1973), chap. 3. On "the cloud of witnesses," i.e., the supportive social, communal setting for therapy to occur, see anthropologist Ailon Shiloh's "paradigm [for interpreting] the dynamics of faith healing," in his book *Faith Healing: The Religious Experience as a Therapeutic Process* (Springfield, IL: Thomas, 1981), pp. 51-68.

4. The text with its emphasis on healing and on resistance is part of a larger unit (4:18–13:58) which has the same two foci: the healing ministry of Jesus and the growing opposition. The whole larger unit ends on the opposition note: due to the unbelief, there is no more healing in the therapist's own home and country (13:58). See Jack Dean Kingsbury, *Matthew*, Proclamation Commentaries, ed. Gerhard Krodel (Philadelphia: Fortress Press, 1977), pp. 21-29. On "the cul-

Wilhelm Wuellner and Robert Leslie

Freeing for Health through Forgiveness

A second element in healing is the emphasis on the spirit as the healing agent for the body. Instead of dealing with the physical problem, Jesus looks to a deeper concern. Instead of seeing the paralytic as one primarily crippled in his legs, Jesus saw him as one crippled in his spirit. Before being concerned about his physical well-being, Jesus was interested in his spiritual well-being.

It is in this same sense that Jesus proclaims God's forgiveness of the paralytic's sins. In the time of Jesus, it was believed that sin and illness were related, and Jesus was a part of the culture of his day.[5] However, there is no evidence that Jesus believed that sin was the only cause of illness. It is clear that Jesus' attitude toward sin anticipates the findings of contemporary psychotherapy in noting the close connection among emotional, spiritual, and physical well-being.

One of the fascinating fields of medical study lately is the exploration of how emotional states are related to the onset of cancer. One study uncovered data demonstrating that in 95 percent of cancer cases studied, there was an unresolved loss in the period immediately prior to the onset of the illness.[6] The emotional turmoil associated with the loss (usually the death of a loved one) created a climate within the physical organism that made the organism susceptible to the growth of the cancer cells that are always present but normally stay under control.

Pastoral counselors Newman Cryer and John Vayhinger tell of the case study of a woman who was troubled with recurrent migraine headaches that made her life miserable. When she sought professional help for the headaches, it became apparent that she harbored deep resentment against her in-laws because of their intrusion into her relationship with her husband. When, in personal counseling, she reached the point where she could understand her in-laws as well-meaning even if ill-advised, and could forgive them for their unintentional interference, her migraine headaches dramatically disappeared. By forgiving her in-laws, she restored herself to health![7]

---

tural factors that account for [both the revival or decline of interest in the supernatural in therapy]," see Theodore Ziolkowski, *Disenchanted Images: A Literary Iconology* (Princeton: Princeton University Press, 1977), pp. 227-57; see also Klaus Seybold and Ulrich B. Mueller, *Sickness and Healing*, Biblical Encounter Series (Nashville: Abingdon Press, 1981), pp. 9-13.

5. On disease as punishment for sin, see Harrison's essay cited above, n. 2.

6. Lawrence LeShan, *You Can Fight for Your Life: Emotional Factors in the Causation of Cancer* (New York: Jove/Harcourt Brace Jovanovich, 1978), p. 69.

7. Newman S. Cryer, Jr., and John Monroe Vayhinger, *Casebook in Pastoral Counseling* (Nashville: Abingdon Press, 1962), pp. 44-47.

Challenging Growth

It is common knowledge that some kind of challenge is needed to effect change in a person's condition. What is less well understood is that for challenge to be effective, it needs to be preceded by some indication of support. One writer defines the therapeutic task as combining the hand extended in support with the finger pointed in challenge.[8]

In dealing with the paralytic, Jesus began with words of support, with encouragement. The term "my son" is used as an endearment. Leslie Weatherhead suggests that the "my son" might be rendered as "laddie" since the Greek word means "child."[9] In these words Jesus reaches out with words that might be used within the intimacy of a family. When the "take heart" (note also 9:22 and 14:27) is added to the "my son," the impact is that of a loving parent undergirding a child in need. The words help reduce apprehension and fear and thus make a challenge more possible.

A careful reading of the New Testament records of encounters that Jesus had with individuals demonstrates how typically Jesus initiated contact with some kind of affirming support. He understood that change is difficult, that resistance to change is easily created, and that a pre-condition for change is some demonstration of acceptance. Any marriage counselor is familiar with the attitude expressed by the housewife whose husband was critical of her housekeeping. "How can I help him to understand," she pleaded, "that I cannot find the strength to pick things up until I am sure that he loves me whether I pick things up or not?"

Acceptance by itself, however, is seldom enough. A challenge is often needed to produce results. With the paralytic, the words of support are followed by a challenge in three forms. He is challenged first of all to get up and walk, to leave the passive role of helplessness and to involve himself actively in his own recovery. Lawrence LeShan expresses this attitude in the title of his book: *You Can Fight For Your Life.* Psychiatrist Viktor Frankl puts the challenge in a somewhat similar book title: *Say "Yes" to Life in Spite of Everything.*[10] Nor-

8. John C. Whitehorn in foreword to Jerome Frank, *Persuasion and Healing* (Baltimore: Johns Hopkins Press, 1961), p. vii.

9. Leslie Weatherhead, *It Happened in Palestine* (New York: Abingdon Press, 1936), writes: "The same Greek word was often used by Saint Paul as a term of endearment. He used it of Timothy. See II Tim. 1:2. Cf. also Philemon 10. Note the same word in III John 4" (p. 93). See also J. T. Holland, who writes of Jesus: "By addressing people by their first names or other endearing terms, he indicated the affection and sense of dignity by which he regarded them." "Jesus, a Model for Ministry," *Journal of Pastoral Care* 36 (December 1982): 262.

10. Viktor E. Frankl, *Trotzdem Ja zum Leben sagen* (Wien: Franz Deuticke, 1947).

man Cousins has written a best-selling book, *Anatomy of an Illness,*[11] in which he describes his own self-healing after he decided to call forth the natural defense mechanisms of his own body. He appeals to physicians and patients to take an active role in learning to manage the forces of both body and mind that work toward healing.

The second challenge to the paralytic is to take in hand the very crutches which up to this point had defined his life, to pick up his bed and thus demonstrate that the bed no longer controls him.

The third challenge is to face his home, the very social, religious matrix which had in part sustained and perhaps even generated the paralysis. The recognition of the involvement of the paralytic's family in his condition is at the heart of the current approach in counseling known as family therapy. One of the ablest of family counselors (or therapists) is Virginia Satir. . . . She popularized the concept of "identified patient" by noting that although one person in a family is often identified as the sick one, it is the total family that is involved in creating and continuing problems.

For example, if a boy is found stealing cars, he is likely to be considered a juvenile delinquent. But if further investigation turns up the fact that the only time he steals a car is when his parents threaten to divorce, it then becomes apparent that the problem is not so much in the boy alone as it is in the whole web of relationships in the family.

For the paralytic to be sent home is for him to relate to his family and friends in a new way.

Resisting Unorthodox Change

Change of any kind is never easy, and change of an unexpected sort is even harder. In the story of the paralytic, "certain of the scribes"[12] objected to unorthodox change, to a change which did not fit their system. It was not that they objected to growth; they simply wanted the change expressed in growth to follow certain prescribed patterns. The "blasphemy"[13] to which

11. Norman Cousins, *Anatomy of an Illness as Perceived by the Patient: Reflections on Healing and Regeneration* (New York: W. W. Norton & Co., 1979).

12. This combination of two "forms," miracle and controversy, is unusual. It stresses how difficult change is. Cf. Walter Wink, who notes the scribe in each of us, i.e., that feature "endemic to all religions wherever blame or moral standards are established." *The Bible in Human Transformation: A New Paradigm for Biblical Study* (Philadelphia: Fortress Press, 1973), p. 55, n. 43. Wink also invites readers to identify how they, too, are paralyzed, pp. 56ff. On "scribes," see Matthew Black, *The Interpreter's Dictionary of the Bible,* vol. 4, pp. 246-48.

13. Blasphemy: first mentioned here; also 26:65 and 27:39; and blasphemy of the Spirit in

the scribes objected was the challenge to their particular way of ordering life.

There is a good bit of the scribe in most of us. Whenever there is a challenge to grow in new and unexpected ways, there is resistance. Growth is hard, and anyone trying to be an agent of growth will experience resistance. The resistance expressed in this story is typical of the kind of resistance that Jesus met whenever he surprised people by not fitting into the status quo.

In the story of the paralytic, the challenge issued by Jesus is not only to the sick man and the scribes; it is also to the onlookers as well. As Matthew puts it, the crowds were "afraid."[14] They sensed that Jesus was calling for a change not just in the paralytic but in the whole social order as well. They resisted change. They did not want to be disturbed in their own way of life and so were afraid.

The kind of change Jesus was calling for had been referred to earlier in the passage known to us as the Lord's Prayer. The significant words are:

> And forgive us our debts,
> As we also have forgiven our debtors. (6:12)

Jesus was reminding the people that they could forgive people who had wronged them, and that this was God's way. "They were afraid," but they also "glorified God, who had given such authority" to them (9:8, see also 18:18).

It is Fritz Kunkel who calls our attention to the "ground-shaping innovation" of this story: "Jesus is not simply a miracle-working rabbi. . . . Does he dare to forgive sins? Is he stronger than the laws of our old religion? . . . Will he destroy all our former convictions, all tradition, all reasonable ways of life?"[15]

Kunkel goes on to point out that "skepticism and paralysis belong together," and that we simultaneously are both "the paralyzed man and the

---

12:31. In 15:19, "slander" is one of the things which comes out of the heart. The high priest's charge of blasphemy in 26:65 is in response to Jesus' quoting of Dan. 7:13 (seeing the Son of man sitting . . . and coming . . .). See Simon J. DeVries, "Blasphemy," *The Interpreter's Dictionary of the Bible,* vol. 1, p. 445.

Such "evil thoughts" are discerned by Jesus twice in Matthew: here and in 12:25. On "what is easier," see 19:24 ("easier for a camel to go through the eye of a needle").

14. There are twenty-one references to fear in Matthew. "Fear" may sometimes appear as a constitutive element of faith.

15. Fritz Kunkel, *Creation Continues: A Psychological Interpretation of the Gospel of Matthew* (Waco, TX: Word, 1973), p. 128.

skeptic scribe."[16] The story of the paralytic is no longer just the story of an unknown man with paralyzed legs. It is our story.

―――――――

SUGGESTIONS FOR FURTHER READING

On Dreams

Kelsey, Morton. *God, Dreams, and Revelation: A Christian Interpretation of Dreams.* Minneapolis: Augsburg, 1991.

Lewin, Isaac. "The Psychological Theory of Dreams in the Bible." *Journal of Psychology and Judaism* 7, no. 2 (1983): 73-88.

Walsh, John A. "The Dream of Joseph: A Jungian Interpretation." *Journal of Psychology and Theology* 11 (1983): 20-27.

Watt, Ian. "Joseph's Dreams." In *Jung and the Interpretation of the Bible,* edited by D. L. Miller, 55-70. New York: Continuum, 1995.

On Prophecy

Buss, Martin J. "Role and Selfhood in Hebrew Prophecy." In *Psychology and the Bible: A New Way to Read the Scriptures,* edited by J. Harold Ellens and Wayne G. Rollins, vol. 2, 277-94. Westport, CT: Praeger, 2004.

Carroll, Robert P. "Prophecy and Dissonance: A Theoretical Approach to the Prophetic Tradition." *Zeitschrift für die alttestamentliche Wissenschaft* 92, no. 1 (1980): 108-19.

Edinger, Edward. *Ego and Self: The Old Testament Prophets from Isaiah to Malachi.* Toronto: Inner City Books, 2000.

Kaplan, Jacob H. *Psychology of Prophecy: A Study of the Prophetic Mind as Manifested by the Ancient Hebrew Prophets.* Philadelphia: J. H. Greenstone, 1908.

Klein, Walter C. *The Psychological Pattern of Old Testament Prophecy.* Evanston: Seabury-Western Theological Seminary, 1956.

Merkur, Daniel. "Prophetic Initiation in Israel and Judah." In *The Psychoanalytic Study of Society,* edited by L. B. Boyer and S. A. Grolnick, 37-67. Hillsdale, NJ: Analytic Press, 1988.

Povah, John W. *The New Psychology and the Hebrew Prophets.* New York: Longmans, Green & Co., 1925.

16. Kunkel, *Creation Continues,* p. 129.

Widengren, Geo. *Literary and Psychological Aspects of the Hebrew Prophets.* Uppsala: A.-B. Lundequistska Bokhandeln, 1948.

Wiener, Aharon. *The Prophet Elijah in the Development of Judaism: A Depth Psychological Study.* London: Routledge and Kegan Paul, 1978.

On Healing

Davies, Stevan L. *Jesus the Healer: Possession, Trance and the Origins of Christianity.* New York: Continuum, 1995.

———. "Whom Jesus Healed and How." *The Fourth R* 6, no. 2 (1993): 1-11.

Kelsey, Morton. *Healing and Christianity.* Minneapolis: Augsburg Fortress, 1995.

Sanford, John A. *Healing and Wholeness.* New York: Paulist Press, 1977.

———. *Healing Body and Soul: The Meaning of Illness in the New Testament and Psychotherapy.* Louisville: Westminster/John Knox Press, 1992.

CHAPTER 12

Biblical Religious Experience:
The Demonic and Exorcism,
Glossolalia, and Conversion

*Religious experience . . . in the end resists analysis and rational explana-
tion. . . . We are obliged to ask whether or not in addition to the supernatural factors which alone impressed the early Christians, there were other
factors involved in this enthusiasm, factors which may be much more
readily understood by us. We must ask about the human and historical antecedents of this inspiration, and its psychological conditionings.*

Johannes Weiss[1]

*Numerous examples could be cited showing the necessity of a collaborative
effort on the part of exegetes and psychologists: to ascertain the meaning of
cultic ritual, of sacrifice, of bans, to explain the use of imagery in biblical
language, the metaphorical significance of miracle stories, the wellsprings
of apocalyptic visual and auditory experiences.*

Pontifical Biblical Commission[2]

*Divine transformative acts can be described in psychoanalytic terms as
well as theological ones.*

Robin Scroggs[3]

---

1. Cited in Werner Georg Kümmel, *The New Testament: The History of the Investigation of
Its Problems*, trans. S. McLean Gilmour and Howard C. Kee (Nashville: Abingdon, 1972), p. 280.

2. Pontifical Biblical Commission, "The Interpretation of the Bible in the Church," *Catholic International* 5, no. 3 (1994): 122.

3. Robin Scroggs, "Psychology as a Tool to Interpret the Text: Emerging Trends in Biblical
Thought," *Christian Century*, March 24, 1982, p. 338.

As early as 1950, Frederick C. Grant, an eminent biblical scholar in the United States, included a sentence in his *Introduction to New Testament Thought* that probably went unnoticed by most readers. He spoke of the need for "the student of the New Testament . . . [to] understand religious psychology, especially the various types of religious experience to be met within the Jewish and Hellenistic world of the first two centuries."[4]

Most likely the model Grant had in mind was the 1902 classic in American psychology, William James's *The Varieties of Religious Experience,* a book that was reprinted thirty-eight times in the first thirty-three years following its publication. It has probably done more to cultivate popular interest in psychology among undergraduates than any other book. James's objective was to look at religious experience and religious phenomena through the lens of psychology. Armed with clinical anecdotes, historical records, and stories from classical literature, James took his readers on a voyage into the mysteries of the religion of the healthy-minded and the sick soul, of conversion, mysticism, saintliness, asceticism, sacrifice, confession, and prayer.

It is to this subject of religious experience that we have turned in the present and previous chapter, providing examples from the three major areas of research in the field: conventional religious experience, religious practice, and paranormal religious experience.

Conventional religious experience would include the phenomena of prophetic inspiration, dreams, apocalyptic visions, glossolalia, and the common religious states and processes in the lives of individuals, for example, temptation and salvation, sin and forgiveness, repentance and regeneration.

The area of *religious practice* would include cultic rites like baptism, circumcision, foot washing, eucharist, and sacrifice, along with religious holidays, prayer, and cultic law.

The third area, *paranormal religious experience,* includes miracle stories, faith healing, demon possession, exorcism, clairvoyance, faith healing, telepathy, and telekinesis.

The readings in this chapter provide examples of psychological reflection on three types of biblical religious experience: the experience of the demonic and exorcism, the experience of glossolalia or "speaking in tongues," and the experience of conversion, focusing on biblical references to Paul's conversion.

---

4. Frederick C. Grant, *An Introduction to New Testament Thought* (New York: Abingdon, 1950), p. 26.

Robert Leslie

Reading 12.1 The Gerasene Demoniac

ROBERT LESLIE

Next to Freud and Jung, Viktor Frankl is one of the best known psychotherapists in the West; Robert Leslie is one of his prime interpreters in the United States. Frankl's existential psychotherapy or "logotherapy" (healing through "meaning" or *logos*) is applied to an understanding of the phenomenon of demon possession and exorcism in the dramatic tale of the Gadarene demoniac in Mark 5:1-20. The work of the logotherapist centers on aiding the patient to find personal meaning no matter how dire the circumstances, a feat that Frankl himself achieved as a prisoner in a Nazi death camp from 1942 to 1945, as recounted in his classic *Man's Search for Meaning*. Frankl wrote that meaning is forged in three ways: creative meaning, achieved by doing something new; experiential meaning, finding the meaning in one's surroundings; and attitudinal meaning, assuming a new attitude toward one's condition. Leslie finds the latter mode at work in the transaction between the demoniac and Jesus.

Although the story of the encounter of Jesus with the Gerasene demoniac is clothed in the thought patterns of a pre-scientific age, the predicament of one who feels himself possessed by a power outside of himself is well known in our own day. The biblical term "demon-possessed" is useful as a graphic description of the sense of helplessness that some know so well. Moreover, the joining of the story of the Gerasene demoniac with folklore about the destruction of a herd of swine is easily understood when we consider the folklore which gathers even today around mental illness.

The task to which Jesus addressed himself with the demoniac was the restoration of the man's sense of human dignity. The rediscovery of the dignity of man is one of the major achievements of our times. It is to the credit of existentialist thinkers like Frankl that, without discounting the contributions made by the psychological approach that studied man as an instinct-directed animal, the real essence of man is to be found in those very characteristics which distinguish him from the animal. An animal, as Frankl says in agreement with Max Scheler, has an environment, but man has a

From Robert Leslie, "The Gerasene Demoniac," in *Jesus and Logotherapy: The Ministry of Jesus as Interpreted Through the Psychotherapy of Viktor Frankl* [reprinted as *Jesus as Counselor* (Nashville: Abingdon Press, Festival Book, 1982)] (Nashville: Abingdon, 1965), pp. 102-11.

world.[1] It is man with a conscience, man making free decisions, man accepting personal responsibility, who is dealt with in the most adequate kind of psychotherapy. It is man in the biblical image, made "only a little lower than the angels, crowned with glory and honor" (Ps. 8:5, KJV).

It is when man is robbed of his dignity that he becomes ill. . . . Consider the delinquent whose sense of dignity has been so offended by an unresponsive society that he seeks recognition in antisocial ways, turning his anger against his fellowmen. Or consider that illness that is neither organic nor social but rather psychic, the illness of psychosis. Here, again, the dignity of a human being has been injured, his sense of personal adequacy has been undermined, his freedom to be unique has been curtailed. Now his anger is not turned outward toward his world but is turned in against himself. Angry at himself, at war with himself, he feels only the conflict of the unresolved forces struggling within his make up and loses sight of the essential unity that dignity implies. The only name which seems to make sense to him is "Legion: for we are many" (Mark 5:9b).

When mental illness is conceived of as a loss of human dignity, then the indicated approach becomes clearer.[2] . . . I have often watched the transformation in mental patients from what appeared to be angry assaultiveness to eager receptivity when the apparent anger was understood as fear and approached accordingly. When it was demonstrated clearly that the fear was unnecessary, the angry attack was replaced by requests for help. Often the best therapeutic agent was the tiny student nurse who, obviously, could do the patient no harm. But even more often the change took place in the presence of a therapeutically oriented person whose whole manner indicated an acceptance of the patient and reflected an appraisal of dignity and worth for him. So it must have been with the demoniac of the Gerasenes whose wild ravings were completely subdued in the patient and understanding (and hence fearless) approach of Jesus.

The change that can take place in a psychotic person in the presence of a truly therapeutic person is vividly illustrated by Carroll Wise as he tells of watching the psychiatrist Harry Stack Sullivan at work. Sullivan was visiting Worcester State Hospital when a schizophrenic patient was being presented to the staff. The doctor making the presentation was unable to get any commu-

1. Cf. Frankl's "Ten Theses about the Person," in *Logos und Existenz* (Wien: Amandus-Verlag, 1951), chapter two. For a summary in English of these ten theses, see Donald Tweedie, *Logotherapy and the Christian Faith* (Grand Rapids: Baker Book House, 1961), pp. 69-71.

2. Cf. Ernest E. Bruder who notes how Jesus in this incident with the Gerasene demoniac was the one "who . . . paid him the dignity of treating him like a person." Ernest E. Bruder, "Learning from Deeply Troubled People," *Pastoral Psychology* 11 (November 1960): 34-35.

nication from the patient. With a shrug of futility he turned to Sullivan with an unspoken offer for the visiting doctor to try his hand. Wise describes what followed:

> Sullivan's first move was to edge his chair just a little closer to that of the patient and to lean forward so that he could look directly at the patient in a very friendly, warm manner. To the amazement of all, the patient responded to every question and comment that was made by Dr. Sullivan. For half an hour or more they conversed together, seemingly oblivious to the fact that there was any one else in the room.[3]

. . . I recall vividly a young girl of eighteen who, as a patient in a mental hospital, was as unhappy as a person can be. Approaching her one day as the hospital chaplain I tried to initiate conversation, but she rejected me with the angry words: "Go away! I don't want to talk with you!" And to make herself very clear, she turned her chair so that it faced the wall. My first impulse was to leave, but then, remembering that she was sick, I turned my chair, too, sat beside her facing the blank wall, and began to talk. Half an hour later when I rose to go she reached for my arm, clutched my coat sleeve and pleaded: "Don't go away. Don't leave me alone." The earlier angry outburst was prompted by her fear that she was unacceptable, that no one would want to talk with her. Here, in a mild form, is the same kind of resistance to potential help that the demoniac demonstrated when he cried out: "What have you to do with me? Do not torment me."

The story of the Gerasene demoniac has the ring of authenticity about it. When Jesus asked: "What is your name?" he was really asking the kind of a question that a modern therapist would ask. Leslie Weatherhead translates the question as follows: "'What is thy name?' is the equivalent of the question a modern therapist would ask: 'How did it all begin? What power is it that has dominion over you?'"[4] It may very well be that Jesus, who had sought refuge from the crowds by going to the wilderness of the Gerasenes, spent most of the night exploring with this pitiful man the story of his life in the pattern of contemporary psychotherapy. Weatherhead, for example, believes that the demoniac may have been helped to bring forth long repressed emotions, perhaps related to atrocities committed by Roman legionnaires.[5] Like some ser-

---

3. Carroll A. Wise reviewing Sullivan's *Psychiatric Interview* in *Pastoral Psychology* 5 (November 1954): 57.

4. Leslie D. Weatherhead, *Psychology, Religion and Healing* (Nashville: Abingdon, 1951), p. 55.

5. Leslie D. Weatherhead, *It Happened in Palestine* (Nashville: Abingdon, 1936), p. 117.

vicemen suffering in our own time from battle trauma, a violent emotional catharsis sometimes results in a complete cure.

Whether the causal factors of the illness were ever really uncovered or not, the final scene showing the "demoniac" restored to normalcy, sitting talking with Jesus, suggests the renewal of communication, the breakthrough from isolation to interpersonal relationships. . . .

It was important to him that Jesus was not afraid of him. The people were, both when he was sick and later when he had been restored to health. In their fear they had banished him outside of the city; and even when he was well they were uncertain about him and hesitant to accept him. Fearful of the impulses that raged unchecked within himself, he could not be helped by those who also feared him, but only by one who stood outside of the fear. . . . Sensing the unchecked anger that was driving the man, Jesus could confront him calmly with a direct approach: "You are angry, but you don't have to be ruled by anger." ("Come out of the man, you unclean spirit.")

It was as if Jesus was saying to him: "You are not accountable for your feelings, they are a part of your sickness which you cannot control. But you are responsible for your attitude toward them." This is the approach which Frankl follows. He believes that even the schizophrenic retains a residue of freedom for confronting his illness.

> Even the manifestations of psychosis conceal a real spiritual person, unassailable by mental disease. Only the possibility of communication with the outside world and of self-expression are inhibited by the disease; the nucleus of man remains indestructible. The schizophrenic, as well as the manic-depressive, has a remnant of freedom with which he can confront his illness and realize himself, not only in spite of it but because of it. . . .[6]

Indeed, in asserting that the attitude toward life is the area with which to work, even with the psychotic, Frankl is underscoring a point of view which Anton Boisen has been pressing for decades. Boisen sees acute mental disturbances, including his own,[7] as indications of an inner struggle to grasp the meaning of life in a personal way. As such, acute psychotic episodes rather than being merely indicators of unhealthy disturbances in a self-system, may be evidence of a struggle toward a rebirth, an effort at assimilating hitherto unassimilated aspects of the personality into a unified and meaningful whole. . . .

6. Viktor Frankl, *Existence and Values: Foundations of Logotherapy,* Manuscript in preparation, 1965, p. 98.

7. See Anton Boisen, *Out of the Depths* (New York: Harper & Row, 1960).

If life does not make sense, if there seems to be no meaning to personal existence, then emotional illness easily fills the void. Frankl treated a seventeen-year-old Jewish youth, a student of the Talmud, who had been through Nazi persecution followed by two and a half years in a mental hospital. Following discharge he was unable to reestablish himself in any normal pattern of life, blaming God for making him different. Frankl helped him to see his plight in a meaningful light,

> Who knows whether it was not quite good for you, for you had to be brought nearer to yourself and finally to find yourself. Weren't you more careless before in your way of life? Whereas now you have become a more earnest and thoughtful personality. Is it inconceivable that through the two and a half years of confinement God wanted to confront you with a task; perhaps your confinement was your assignment for that period of your life. . . . Your study of the Talmud will from now on be easier and yet will penetrate deeper into its wisdom. . . . For now you have been purified like gold and silver. . . . Through your tears which you wept, the clinkers were removed from your old self.[8]

Frankl's rationale for the treatment of this young student was called forth by a comment made by a visiting psychiatrist. The visitor noted that when the boy left the office he was different; he had definitely changed during the interview. . . .[9]

Helped in seeing some meaning in his suffering, the young Talmudic student was then able to pick up the threads of his life and resume a pattern that was quite normal in most respects. That is, Frankl had helped the patient to detach himself from the psychotic processes which were affecting him by mobilizing the distinctly human capacity, present even in psychosis, to take a stand against the illness. . . .[10]

It comes as no secret that conflicting claims are resolved when reference to the spiritual (noetic) dimension is made. . . .

It was not by chance that Jesus admonished the young man who had been considered a demoniac to consider his life in the light of God's mercy toward him. We have seen continually in the Gospel record how man's problems are never considered as solved except as they are viewed from a more than human perspective. The logotherapeutic approach aims at more than a

8. Recorded notes from Summer, 1960. Frankl compared the patient's hospitalization with the story of Jonah's stay in the whale.

9. Recorded interview of discussion, Summer, 1960.

10. Class lecture, April 4, 1961.

mere change of behavior patterns, it is a complete reorientation to a life of a broader spectrum. It is introducing the concept of a relationship to a larger world than the world in which scientific man normally lives. It is seeing man in the largest possible perspective.

It is not strange that the man of the Gerasenes wanted to stay with Jesus. Having found someone who had helped him to accept himself and to see himself related in a more meaningful way to life, he wanted to hold onto this new interpreter of life.

But Jesus would have none of it. The real test of life, he knew so well, was in the resumption of daily tasks, at home among old friends. But even here the pattern of life was changed, for now the man was no longer preoccupied with his own troubles but was commissioned to tell of the changes that God had made in his life. His orientation was now no longer on himself but on his relationship with God. No wonder that men marveled at the transformation.

Reading 12.2   Glossolalia — Language of the Unconscious?

GERD THEISSEN

Gerd Theissen offers the most comprehensive exegetical and psychological analysis to date of "speaking in tongues" in the early Christian church. For an analysis of tongues speaking in the twentieth-century charismatic and Pentecostal communities, see H. Newton Malony and A. A. Lovekin, *Glossolalia: Behavioral Science Perspectives on Speaking in Tongues* (New York: Oxford University Press, 1985).

These excerpts represent only a small portion of Theissen's extensive treatment of "glossolalia," which covers close to eighty pages in all.

As background, Theissen offers a masterful survey of phenomena analogous to biblical glossolalia, namely, "ecstatic speech" in Greco-Roman culture. This tradition ranges from Bacchanalian frenzy, to Platonic mystical speech, to the "heavenly language" of "inexpressible words" in the Apocalypse.

From Gerd Theissen, *Psychological Aspects of Pauline Theology*, trans. John P. Galvin (Philadelphia: Fortress, 1987), pp. 267-341, specifically pp. 277-78, 280-84, 288-89, 292-93, 302-4, 312-14, 322-23, 327, 330. Theissen's extensive footnotes have not been reproduced here.

Bacchanalian Frenzy

The most forceful literary depiction of Bacchanalian frenzy is found in the Bacchae of Euripides (ca 485-407 BCE). The Theban king Pentheus seeks to combat the Dionysian ecstasy that is rampaging among the women in his country. It has already made inroads at the royal court. . . . There can be no doubt that the Bacchanalian frenzy is a breakthrough of unconscious drive dynamics. Or, more precisely, the Dionysian cult is the ritualization of unconscious drives and is as such also a socially recognized way of channeling them. . . .

The ecstatic phenomena in the Corinthian community cannot be derived genetically from the cult of Dionysus. But the two religious manifestations have comparable functions from the viewpoint of social psychology. . . . Both Bacchanalian ecstasy and the pneumatic doings in Corinth were manifestations of a collective ecstasy. "If, therefore, the whole church assembles and all speak in tongues, and outsiders or unbelievers enter, will they not say that you are mad?" (1 Cor. 14:23). Admittedly, Paul is only depicting a hypothetical case. In fact, all did not speak in tongues (1 Cor. 14:30). But there must have been tendencies in the direction of an uncontrolled collective ecstasy (14:27). . . . And Paul is well aware of this. . . .

Platonic Inspiration

If Paul prefers individual forms of ecstasy to collective frenzy, he stands near the tradition of the Platonic doctrine of inspiration. Plato once distinguished four types of divine madness (as distinguished from pathological madness): the prophetic madness that Apollo confers; the cultic madness of Dionysus; the poetic madness of the Muses; and the erotic madness produced by Eros and Aphrodite. . . .

. . . It is constantly said that prophets, poets, and philosophers do not know what they say in the state of inspiration. Is this theme of ignorance an indication that inspiration surfaces from the unconscious? . . .

The ignorance of the poets is brought into connection with the ecstatic state of inspiration. Socrates (Apology 22B-C) comes to realize "that what they composed they composed not by wisdom, but by nature and because they were inspired, like the prophets and givers of oracles; for these also say many fine things, but they know none of the things they say. . . ."

But Plato would not have been a philosopher had he not insisted in principle on a rational appropriation of what was experienced in ecstasy. . . .

Plato probably has in view the practice at Delphi, where prophets or poets interpreted the oracle's unintelligible statements. . . .

Apocalyptic Heavenly Language

An analogy to the linguistic phenomenon of glossolalia is first found in Jewish apocalyptic conceptions of a heavenly language which is not accessible to human beings. In the Slavonic version of Enoch (2 Enoch 19.6; cf. 2 Enoch 17), Enoch is transposed into heaven, where he hears the song of the angels, "having but one voice and singing in unison, And their song is not to be reported." Paul knows comparable traditions. He was caught up into the third heaven and there heard "inexpressible words" (2 Cor. 12:4). To him, glossolalia is the tongue of angels (1 Cor. 13:1). . . .

There are further analogies between Corinthian glossolalia and the apocalyptic heavenly language in the Testament of Job. In Corinth too the angels were known to be near in the liturgy (1 Cor. 11:10). . . . In both instances, women play a special role. In both cases paralinguistic occurrences are conceived as "angelic language." . . .

In the second section Theissen provides a thorough exegesis of I Corinthians 13 and 14. Paul's familiar opening words of chapter 13 take on new meaning when we read them in the context of a critical discussion of "tongues": "If I speak in tongues of men and of angels but have not love I am nothing."

The third section presents Theissen's threefold psychological analysis of glossolalia. Theissen runs each set of passages through the perspective of three different psychological schools: (a) learning and behavioral theory, (b) psychodynamic theory (Freud/Jung), and (c) cognitive psychological theory.

(a) Learning theory focuses on the ways in which the speaking in tongues is actually a learned form of behavior, cultivated within a subgroup in Corinth. This behavior is modeled and reinforced by practitioners of glossolalia among a selection of members in the Corinthian congregation. One benefit is that it creates social cohesion — they "speak the same language." The downside is that it can divide the congregation and nurture an arational, ego-centered exclusivism.

Glossolalia is socially learned behavior, which is acquired upon entrance to a new religious community. . . .

In 1 Corinthians 12–14, Paul wishes to restrict speaking in tongues. His central problem is not glossolalia itself but a system of social reinforcement, developing in Corinth, that attributes exaggerated value to glossolalia and thus requires this behavior more than is appropriate. . . .

Paul's chief goal is to reduce through argumentation the social reinforcement of glossolalia. To this end he pursues two strategies. First, he introduces a clear hierarchy. Prophecy is superior to glossolalia, but love surpasses all charismatic gifts. . . . Glossolalia is without constructive value in the community, however worthwhile it may be for the individual (1 Cor. 14:4, 19). It should therefore be excluded as much as possible from community life.

In the next section Theissen ventures three educated guesses on the social identity of the glossolaliacs within the Corinthian community.

First he surmises that the glossolaliac group was probably gathered around an authority figure. Paul hints of such authority figures earlier in his letter, citing the different loyalties at Corinth: "'I belong to Paul,' or 'I belong to Apollos,' or 'I belong to Cephas,' or 'I belong to Christ'" (1 Cor. 1:12).

A second probable quality of the glossolaliacs is that they are drawn from the same conservative socio-cultural strata as those who rejected mixed marriages, who refused to eat meat offered to idols, and who espoused asceticism in the Corinthian church.

A third characteristic of the group is that many may have been predominantly women. Theissen writes:

In the midst of the admonitions on speaking in tongues within the community stands the famous, and infamous, "women should keep silence in the churches" text (1 Cor. 14:33b-36). Even though it could be an interpolation, it is hardly coincidental that it stands in this place. One may surmise that glossolalia occurred more frequently in women, in other words, in a group that in all strata was socially disadvantaged but that in principle had equal rights in the early Christian communities (Gal. 3:28). It cannot be coincidence that ecstatic phenomena are attested precisely for women in early Christianity. Think of the soothsaying girl (Acts 16:16), the prophesying daughter of Philip (Acts 21:9), the prophetess Jezebel in Thyatira (Rev. 2:20), the Montanist prophetesses Priscilla and Maximilla, the prophetess Amma in Philadelphia, or the prophetesses of the Gnostic Marcus. Ecstatic phenomena were also connected with women elsewhere in antiquity. Bacchanalian frenzy first seized women. The manticism of inspiration made use of female mediums, the Pythia of Delphi, the priestesses of Dodona, or the sibyl. The apocalyptic heavenly language was spoken by the daughters of Job. Prophetic women are well attested in Corinth (1 Cor. 11:2ff.). It is therefore possible that glossolalia was widespread among the Corinthian women. . . .

Paul reacts. . . . First he establishes a clear hierarchy. Glossolalia and the groups that stand behind it are shunted to the second place, and the authority of the rationally inclined group is strengthened. . . . Second, he tends toward privatization of speaking in tongues, that is, to its exclusion from community life. But in doing so he deprives glossolalia of its basis of existence. Without social stimuli, models, and reinforcers, it is bound to wither. . . . No wonder that in the realm of Pauline Christianity we hear nothing more of an ability to speak in tongues.

(b) Psychodynamic theory focuses on another aspect of speaking in tongues, namely its unconscious roots. The unconscious aspect of glossolalia is evident from the fact that tongues speakers do not know consciously what they are saying and that they depend on another member of the community, "a prophet," to interpret. From a psychodynamic perspective these eruptions of unintelligible speech bear resemblance to a young child's attempts at coherent speech.

In what follows, three hypotheses toward explaining the individual value of speaking in tongues will be discussed on the basis of the Pauline texts. The positive value of glossolalia could lie, first, in its affording access to unconscious dimensions; second, in its allowing repressed impulses access to consciousness; and third, in its being a regressive resumption of childish forms of behavior and experience. . . .

From a linguistic perspective, the experience of glossolalia presupposes a reactivation of childhood abilities to learn speech. . . . Of the three dimensions of language — the expressive, semantic, and appellative — the semantic dimension is lost. In this, glossolalia regresses to the level of childhood sounds, which as yet signify nothing but are merely expression and appeal. Saying this is not intended to imply that glossolalia is a repetition of early childhood babbling. . . . But no doubt can exist that glossolalia is a return to more primitive forms of speech.

This regression becomes even clearer if we observe the social relationship of speaker and listener. The first babbling monologues of the child are completely egocentric. . . . Paul confirms the egocentric character of glossolalic speech in early Christianity. One who speaks in tongues edifies oneself (1 Cor. 14:4); no one hears such speakers (14:2), who speak for themselves and for God (14:28). The return to egocentric speaking is itself an indicator of psychic regression. . . . Thus a psychic state is brought about in which the subject-object relationship is not yet developed, in which the I and the environment rather merge with one another. In other words, glossolalia is connected with the a-dual experience of the world that is characteristic of early childhood, which revives in religious mysticism and can also be experienced in an intense state of being in love. . . . After his admonition on intelligible speech in the community, he proceeds, "Brethren, do not be children in your thinking; be babes in evil, but in thinking be mature" (1 Cor. 14:20). And he is surely also thinking of glossolalia in 1 Cor. 13:11: "When I was a child, I spoke like a child, I thought like a child, I reasoned like a child; when I became a man, I gave up childish ways."

(c) Cognitive analysis focuses on Paul's attempts at providing a new cognitive framework for understanding glossolalia. Paul's goal is to mitigate what will appear to outsiders as well as thinking insiders as "mindless" gibberish.

In fact, Theissen argues that such language born of the unconscious can nevertheless communicate, even through what appears to be arational discourse. Theissen shows how such language can mediate meaning through cryptosemantic and non-verbal cues as well as secondary linguistic forms, which enable the "prophets" to make more than a wild guess at what the speaker is saying, especially when the "prophet" knows the speaker personally. When translated by the "prophet," these utterances from the unconscious can be rendered in "plain speech" that provides inspiration, even spiritual direction, for the community.

The most striking characteristic of glossolalic speech is its lack of semantic content. No specific content can be ordered to the phonetic elements, although the structure of speaking in tongues, which is similar to language, suggests a content and is experienced within the glossolalic community as significant. "Mysteries" (1 Cor. 14:2) are communicated. But how? . . .

Glossolalia contains, first, cryptosemantic elements, that is, fragments of language that involuntarily evoke significant associations. Expressions like "Yezu," "Yeshua," and "Yay-so" are reminiscent of Jesus. . . . Ancient magical texts with cryptosemantic names of gods offer analogies. As far as primitive Christianity is concerned, one could think of elements from foreign languages such as "Abba" (Rom. 8:15-16; Gal. 4:6) and "Maranatha!" (1 Cor. 16:22), and possibly also of short acclamations such as "Kyrios Iesous."

Secondary means of linguistic expression like intonation, tempo, and tone are to be mentioned in the second place. We can tell from these whether someone is questioning, narrating, admonishing, or commanding. . . . Thus it could be that the different "kinds of tongues" (1 Cor. 12:10) are distinguished through such secondary linguistic means.

Third, nonverbal means of communication — posture, mimicry, and gestures — are very important. In almost every cultural region one can recognize from posture whether someone is praying or not. It is clear from 1 Corinthians 14, for example, that it was possible to distinguish in Corinth between glossolalic messages and prayers.

Nevertheless, Paul is concerned about the egocentrism that glossolalia seems to cultivate. Above all he wants to scotch the exclusivism that it engenders. Within a new cognitive framework Paul would have the Corinthians see "tongues" no longer as the primary manifestation of gifts of the Spirit, but as just one of many gifts. He would also have them perceive that tongues edify only one person, the speaker, but that speaking with words of the mind edifies the whole community. With this cognitive restructuring of the community's perception of "tongues" Paul succeeds in mitigating its spread.

. . . What Paul is seeking may be formulated psychologically as follows. He wishes to achieve a cognitive restructuring of social perception with the aid of a more general concept of the Spirit. The personal gift is to be understood as the effect of precisely that power which is at work in all members of the community.

This cognitive restructuring of social perception becomes even more clear in the image of the body of Christ. . . . The multiplicity of Christian activities have the same origin in the Spirit and the same value in the body of Christ. The Corinthian interpretation of glossolalia was determined by a theme of separation: glossolalia is the sign of the elect. . . . Paul, on the contrary, restructures the interpretation of glossolalia on the basis of a theme of social connection: it is part of a diversity held together by the Spirit and the body of Christ.

Reading 12.3   On Conversion

M. SCOTT FLETCHER

This selection from M. Scott Fletcher, a fellow and lecturer at Oxford University in 1912, represents a period of cordial and cooperative relationship between psychology and biblical studies that stretched over a hundred years from the nineteenth to the early twentieth centuries. But one year after Fletcher's book was published, Albert Schweitzer delivered his devastating critique of psychiatric approaches to the life of Jesus in *The Psychiatric Study of Jesus: Exposition and Criticism,* catalyzing a half-century of hostility between the two fields.

In Fletcher's time, however, psychology and biblical scholarship had developed a harmonious working relationship. Fletcher's work was fully endorsed by leading biblical scholars of his time. It was supervised by B. H. Streeter of Queen's College, Oxford, one of the premier source critics in New Testament studies. In his introduction to Fletcher's book, Professor H. Rashdall, of New College, Oxford, described it as "a serious effort to utilize all the resources which modern philosophy, psychology, and Criticism have put at the disposal of the theologian for understanding the true and permanent meaning of the New Testament" (p. v).

The table of contents provides a vignette of Fletcher's interest. His opening chapter is entitled "The Relation of Biblical to Modern Psychology," reflecting his goal of comparing the biblical view of the human personality with that of secular psychology, selections from which are found in Reading 1.2. Other sections are titled "The Psychological Terminology of the New Testament," "The Psychological Experiences of the New Testament" (from which the present reading is taken), and "Comparative Conceptions of Personality." Fletcher's research shows familiarity with the best of biblical and psychological scholarship of his time, with acknowledgment of his debt to William James and to Edwin Starbuck, in their research on conversion (p. 84).

In this passage on conversion, focusing on the conversion of Paul, Fletcher argues that "historical criticism fails to reveal the deepest springs of Paul's convictions and missionary activities" (p. 175) and that it is necessary to explore the inner history of conversion to understand the phenomenon of changed behavior that typified early Christian experience. Without access to the contemporary labels, Fletcher touches on the concerns of learning theory, cognitive psychology, and psychodynamic theory.

From M. Scott Fletcher, *The Psychology of the New Testament,* 2nd ed. (New York: Hodder & Stoughton, 1912), pp. 164-68, 175, and 179-81.

An examination of the psychological terminology of the books of the N.T. [New Testament] has shown a modification and development of Biblical language running through these writings. The O.T. [Old Testament] terminology largely sufficed for the writers of the Synoptics, but the [reports of the] Crucifixion and Resurrection . . . and the gift of the Spirit at Pentecost . . . marked a turning-point in the spiritual experience of believers, and an enriched psychological terminology was found necessary to express the fuller life that followed. . . .

Consequently men began to view themselves in a new light, both as to their previous condition under sin and as to their changed condition in fellowship with Christ. One of the first to experience and express the change was Saul of Tarsus, who became Paul the missionary. But the N.T. is full of these spiritual experiences.

If the psychological language of the N.T. has given us some indication as to the changes that were taking place, an examination of the experiences themselves will afford us psychological data for estimating what the human personality may attain to under Christian and spiritual conditions. The spiritual crisis which often marked the entrance of men into the Christian life demands our first attention. It is usually called Conversion. . . .

The N.T. contains two sources of information about the Conversion of Paul, viz. the Book of Acts, and the personal testimony of Paul contained in his Epistles.

Three accounts of the event are given in Acts — that which forms part of the narrative of the book itself (Acts ix.1-19), that reported to have been given by the Apostle in Jerusalem from the castle stairs (xxii.6-21), and that which he gave in his defence before Agrippa (xxvi.12-18). . . .

The Pauline Epistles contain a number of short references. . . . To the Galatians, while maintaining the authority and validity of his presentation of the Gospel, he writes, "It is not after man. For neither did I receive it from man, nor was I taught it, but it came to me through revelation of Jesus Christ (i.11, 12); and again, in referring more specifically to his conversion, he says, "It was the good pleasure of God . . . to reveal his Son in me, that I might preach among the Gentiles" (i.16). To the Corinthians he writes, "Am I not an apostle? have I not seen Jesus our Lord?" (1 Cor. ix.1); and again, when speaking of the Resurrection and of the appearance of Christ to the disciples and others, he says, "Last of all . . . he appeared to me also" (1 Cor. xv.8). . . .

It must be felt that historical criticism fails to reveal the deepest springs of Paul's convictions and missionary activities. . . .

Paul's inward state was really one of great complexity psychologically. There is every ground to suppose that his ideas, his conscience, and his sensitive nature were all alike stirred to their depths by what he heard and saw in Jerusalem of the Christians, and also that these psychical elements came into conflict with one another. It is agreed that Paul was a thinker, a man of deeply religious feeling, full of purpose and mystic experience. Such a nature could not but be thrown into a state of commotion and inward conflict by the testimonies of the Christian martyrs, by the defence and death of Stephen, and by all that had happened to Jesus, especially after Paul's own bitter experience of impotence to fulfil the righteousness of the law. In the interests of historical accuracy, some writers will allow of the existence of no previous mental disturbance, because none are recorded; writers, too, who wish to preserve the supernatural aspect of the change wrought in Paul may deprecate the mention of any such conflict. But the probabilities of the whole case lead us to suppose that there actually was a period of internecine strife going on in Paul's heart and mind, and this for a time only intensified his zeal as a persecutor. The defect of [some scholars] . . . is that they wish to find one element only that will account antecedently for the sudden change. Far more probable is it that the conversion followed on the interaction of all the elements of Paul's consciousness — intellectual, emotional, and moral. The whole man was moved. Impulses and inhibitions, reason and passion, old traditions and new truths, produced a state of such inner discord and doubt that at last he raged forth a persecutor. His only hope of relief seemed to lie in action. Fanaticism is often the expression of inward doubt. The persecutor's fury is blind because he shuts his eyes. But Saul of Tarsus carried in the depths of his mind an idea and an image — the idea of the crucified Messiah, the image of the risen, exalted Christ. Ideas and images may be suppressed, but they live and work in the sub-conscious realm of personality until some crisis or experience brings them into the light of full consciousness.

SUGGESTIONS FOR FURTHER READING

On the Demonic and Exorcism and the Psychology of Viktor Frankl

Frankl, Viktor. *Man's Search for Meaning*. Boston: Beacon Press, 1962.
Hollenbach, Paul W. "Jesus, Demoniacs, and Public Authorities: A Socio-Historical Study." *Journal of the American Academy of Religion* 99 (1981): 567-88.

Newheart, Michael Willett. *My Name Is Legion: The Story and Soul of the Gerasene Demoniac.* Interfaces. Collegeville, MN: Liturgical Press, 2004.

Tweedie, Donald. *Logotherapy and the Christian Faith.* Grand Rapids: Baker Book House, 1961.

Wuellner, Wilhelm H., and Robert C. Leslie. *The Surprising Gospel: Intriguing Psychological Insights from the New Testament.* Nashville: Abingdon, 1984.

On Glossolalia

Malony, H. Newton, and A. A. Lovekin. *Glossolalia: Behavioral Science Perspectives on Speaking in Tongues.* New York: Oxford University Press, 1985.

Meadow, Mary Jo, and Richard D. Kahoe. *Psychology of Religion: Religion in Individual Lives.* New York: Harper & Row, 1984, particularly pp. 133-35.

On Conversion

Gager, John. "Some Notes on Paul's Conversion." *New Testament Studies* 27 (1981): 697-703.

Johnson, Cedric B., and H. Newton Malony. *Christian Conversion: Biblical and Psychological Perspectives.* Rosemead Psychology Series. Grand Rapids: Zondervan, 1982.

Malony, H. Newton, and Samuel Southard, eds. *Handbook of Religious Conversion.* Birmingham, AL: Religious Education Press, Inc., 1992.

Rubenstein, Richard. "Damascus." In *My Brother Paul.* New York: Harper & Row, 1972, particularly pp. 35-53.

CHAPTER 13

Biblical Effects:
The Pathogenic and
the Therapeutic

The Holy War, which in most cases was only longed for and not waged, and the message of Deuteronomy, are loaded with violence, and those responsible for them wanted in their minds to exterminate whole peoples in the name of God. . . . The visions of violence associated with this had devastating consequences in subsequent centuries of Jewish history, and indeed right down to the present day.

Gerd Lüdemann[1]

The most effective statement of the proper and positive therapeutic use of the Bible is stated in Rom. 15:4: "For whatever was written in former days was written for our instruction, that by steadfastness and by the encouragement of the scriptures we might have hope."

Wayne Oates[2]

Down through the centuries, the Bible continues to have an ongoing impact on human behavior for both good and ill. It has inspired awesome works of art and powerful political movements; it has been used as a weapon in battles both theological and military. Its readers have been moved to acts of compassion, mercy, and forgiveness as well as to acts of destruction, cruelty, and genocide. The complex dynamics of what happens psychologically when a text, in this case the Bible, is taken as sacred Scripture, and thus given a privi-

---

1. Gerd Ludemann, *The Unholy in Holy Scripture* (Louisville: Westminster John Knox, 1997), p. 73.
2. Wayne E. Oates, *The Bible in Pastoral Care* (Philadelphia: Westminster, 1953).

leged role in "teaching, reproof, correction, and training in righteousness" (2 Tim. 3:16), have only begun to be explored.

Religious leaders and counselors have long recognized the value of the Bible in the "cure of souls" — enabling individuals to grow and mature and to develop healthy relationships with themselves and with others. But what of other attitudes and perspectives that individuals claim are based in the Bible? The Bible has historically been read as a justification for racism, for child abuse, for anti-Semitism, and more. The "afterlife" of the Bible — the history of its interpretation and its effect on human beings — proves to have both therapeutic and pathological potentials.

The undeniable fact is that we find ourselves in a grey zone when we begin to speak of "therapeutic" and "pathological" biblical effects. How are we to define them? What one person might identify as a pathological use of the Bible (for example, considering the use of corporal punishment on children as child abuse) for another is considered a Bible-based necessity (enabling children to grow up with a proper sense of discipline and self-control).

We stand here at a second-hand level of interpretation, in that we are not so much *making* an interpretation as *evaluating* an interpretation, often using criteria drawn from outside the text and/or its interpretative tradition. Some will consider this evaluative process to be an essential part of the ongoing growth of understanding and religious development; others will reject it outright as contentious and faithless. Still, over time, with shifts of cultural expectations and new perspectives on interpretation within communities, that which was once considered therapeutic, or at least justifiable, comes to be rejected as wrongheaded, if not pathological. For example, citing the Bible as a justification for human slavery, once accepted by a broad range of Christians, is now considered unacceptable.

What role does a (sacred) text play in instilling, inspiring, or enabling healthy or unhealthy perspectives and attitudes? Can we honestly refer to a text as a "toxic text"? It is clear that it is not the Bible in and of itself that stimulates behavior. Issues of therapeutic and pathological effects arise in the world in front of the text, where the words, ideas, and symbols of the text meet the psychological life of the reader, but where also the reader him- or herself is linked to others by relationships of identity, social convention, and shared cognitive frameworks. We are then justified in examining all three worlds — the ancient world behind the text, the narrative and symbolic world of the text, and the community of interpretation in front of the text — recognizing that specific attitudes or behaviors have their origin in the complex interplay of all three.

The very fact that different individuals can respond to their encounter with a sacred text in different, if not entirely opposite, ways is witness to the fact that the text itself does not control the interpretation. It is not possible to speak of a "toxic" text in the sense that the Bible can *compel* someone to destructive behavior. And it is significant that those who explore therapeutic and/or pathological effects of Scripture usually do not take the text as their starting point. Issues of biblical effects are considered as part of a broader investigation into a social issue, such as violence or racism, or counseling and therapeutic relationships. This is the case in the readings we will consider. Both texts on the pathogenic or toxic dimensions of Scripture are taken from *The Destructive Power of Religion: Violence in Judaism, Christianity, and Islam*, a collection of essays dealing with violence in religious traditions. The two texts on therapeutic effects come from the field of pastoral counseling. A third arena (not considered here) in which such issues arise involves teaching — engaging students with the Bible in ways that will lead to more integrated, healthy, and life-giving understanding. Walter Wink's *The Bible in Human Transformation* is an example, describing a group study process grounded in a model of psychological growth and human transformation.

Reading 13.1 Defining a Toxic Text

CHARLES T. DAVIS III

In his investigation of a "toxic text" from the Pauline tradition (Gal. 4:21-31), Charles Davis suggests that it is, in fact, meaningful to speak of a "toxic text." Basing his argument in principles of narrative theology, he proposes that stories can be identified as revelatory tales or toxic texts, based on whether the story serves to suppress or to support and develop one's own personal "authentic" story.

From Charles T. Davis III, "The Evolution of a Pauline Toxic Text," in *The Destructive Power of Religion*, ed. J. Harold Ellens (Westport, CT: Praeger, 2004), vol. 1, pp. 192-95.

Defining a Toxic Text

Narrative therapy emerges at the intersection of a multiplicity of domains including literary theory, psychoanalysis, anthropology, family sociology, and narrative theology. In their pioneering work *Narrative Means to Therapeutic Ends,* Michael White and David Epston build upon the work of anthropologist Gregory Bateson and the literary psychologist Jerome Bruner as they propose a narrative model for understanding the function of the family. White and Epston argue that as family members organize their lives around specific meanings that constitute a narrative, "they inadvertently contribute to the 'survival' of, as well as the 'career' of the problem."[1] Following Michel Foucault, White and Epston argue that one narrative may emerge as the dominant story claiming a universal validity with the result that it subjugates all other stories to itself. Persons who come for therapy may be understood as persons whose full experience of their own reality is being truncated by a subjugating story. Therapy seeks to challenge the dominant narrative by leading the client to externalize the story so that it may be examined with greater objectivity. Concurrently, attempts are made to uncover moments of unique outcome — moments when one did not enact the dominant story but acted positively in a novel manner. These previously unstoried moments are thereby made available for a process of reauthoring one's life story.

From White and Epston's perspective, toxic stories are subjugating stories. The subjugating process is clearly at work within the family-oriented Jewish milieu of the first century where Jewish factions were engaged in a fierce struggle to re-vision Jewish identity in the Hellenistic world. Luke T. Johnson argues in *The Writings of the New Testament* that the Jewish symbolic world was being redefined by interpretative acts among Sadducees, Pharisees, Zealots, the Covenanters of Qumran, and the apocalyptic sects like that of John the Baptist even before the appearance of the Jewish-Jesus sect founded by Peter in Jerusalem.[2] Symbols such as the "People of God," "the Temple," "the martyr," and the "resurrection" were being redefined in a variety of contexts.

There is, however, another dimension of the problem of identifying toxic texts. Alan Parry and Robert E. Doan (1994) in *Story Re-visions: Narrative Therapy in the Postmodern World* call attention to the collapse of the major metanarratives of the West: the Bible, Science as the Hope of a Better Fu-

---

1. M. White and D. Epston, *Narrative Means to Therapeutic Ends* (New York: W. W. Norton, 1990), p. 3.

2. L. T. Johnson, *The Writings of the New Testament* (Philadelphia: Fortress Press, 1986).

ture, Progress, and Democracy and the Triumph of the People.[3] They argue that "each person's stories become self-legitimizing" in the postmodern world.[4] Toxic stories emerge as dominant individuals attempt to question the validity of another's personal narrative in the name of an external story having normative value. Parry and Doan argue that in the postmodern context such attempts are nothing less than a form of interpretive terrorism perpetrated against an Other. Such attempts are

> coercive, and to the extent that such methods are used to silence or discredit a person's stories, they represent a form of terrorism. We use such a strong word advisedly, for when one person tries to silence the legitimate voice of another, this is done invariably by throwing into question that person's only resource for discerning reality, her/his own judgment. All those who are thrown into that position of self-doubt are being thrown out of their own stories and robbed of their own voices.[5]

Building upon the insights of Parry and Doan, we can classify stories as revelatory tales or as toxic texts. Revelatory tales, as defined by Belden C. Lane in *Story-telling: The Enchantment of Theology,* heal through their power to facilitate the discovery of one's authentic story. Toxic texts subjugate one's authentic voice to a dominant story by inappropriately claiming the privilege of superior validity.[6]

Parry and Doan incorporate the ethical insights of the French philosopher Emmanuel Levinas into their understanding of narrative therapy. Levinas argues that Western thought in its quest for universal truth has privileged the Same over the Other.[7] Unerringly, the West has destroyed the Other by incorporating it into the Same or by excluding it altogether. We may say, according to Levinas, that Westerners, both Christian theologians and philosophers, have a cultural bias toward the creation of subjugating interpretations that masquerades under the prestigious emblem of the search for universal truth. Levinas also argues that the ethical demand of the Other is prior to both knowledge and consciousness of self and activates them. Accordingly,

---

3. A. Parry and R. E. Doan, *Story Re-visions: Narrative Therapy in the Post-Modern World* (New York: Guilford, 1994), pp. 5-9.

4. Parry and Doan, *Story Re-visions,* p. 26.

5. Parry and Doan, *Story Re-visions,* p. 27.

6. B. C. Lane, *Story-telling: The Enchantment of Theology* [Cassette] (Minneapolis: Bethany, 1981).

7. C. Davis, *Levinas: An Introduction* (Notre Dame: University of Notre Dame Press, 1996).

the ethical is prior to myth and storytelling, and it calls them into being.[8] Parry and Doan conclude that in the postmodern world

> A personal metanarrative would play the role metanarratives have always played: calling forth responsibility toward the Other, or, in other words, addressing the ethical domain.[9]

Parry and Doan stress against relativism that the collapse of meta-narratives is not an invitation to self-indulgence. As we live in an increasingly multicultural world, "difference rather than sameness becomes the order of things and the other becomes the ethical challenge of the present."[10]

Are the insights of Parry and Doan potentially applicable to the New Testament? I am convinced on historical grounds that they are. The Hellenistic Age was, in many respects, like the postmodern era. Alexander's religious reforms sought to impose a single official, Greek religious story upon the Empire. This led to the collapse of the city-state and other local corporate religions. A new quest for a personal religious story began that brought into existence the Mystery Religions, including Christianity.[11] Given this state of affairs, it is appropriate to look for subjugating texts in the New Testament of the type that seeks to suppress the voice of the individual in the name of an older but effectively defunct national religion. The tension between Jewish religious identity and Jewish national identity reached the breaking point when the Temple was destroyed in 70. Jewish religious identity survived this epoch-making event. Two new world religions emerged at the end of the century: Orthodox Judaism founded by Rabbi Johanan ben Zakkai and Christianity.

Richard Q. Ford, in *The Parables of Jesus: Recovering the Art of Listening*, identifies an additional toxic tendency by means of which the Other is excluded. The gospel editors denigrate the subordinate characters in their stories on the assumption that "the economically superior figure represents some aspect of divine intent."[12] This assumption sets up a "black and white" pattern of exclusion and inclusion in which the superior figure is the source of all resolution while the subordinate figure is the source of all difficulty.

---

8. R. A. Cohen, "Introduction" in R. A. Cohen (ed.), *Face to face with Emmanuel Levinas* (Albany: SUNY, 1986), pp. 1-9.

9. Parry and Doan, *Story Re-visions*, p. 30.

10. Parry and Doan, *Story Re-visions*, p. 31.

11. J. Godwin, *Mystery Religions in the Ancient World* (New York: Harper, 1981); Johnson, *The Writings of the New Testament.*

12. Richard Q. Ford, *The Parables of Jesus: Recovering the Art of Listening* (Minneapolis: Fortress, 1997), p. 3.

This process of projection by means of which one person is viewed as the source of the solution is evoked by the rubric of the idealizing of the superior character. Ford urges his readers to approach the parables in anticipation of "a balanced and complex tension between two persons, with each contributing to the evident pain of their compromised interdependence."[13] In the drama that develops in a parable, neither figure should be regarded solely as constructive or as destructive.

Ford's observations apply equally to the editors of the Gospels as authors and to the modern reader. There is a tendency on both sides to idealize the superior figure and to exclude the subordinate characters as in some sense other and thereby unworthy of positive attention. Readers should resist the tendency to subjugate the stories of the biblical characters to an official, theological story or cultural metanarrative. For example, both the Apostle and the Pharisee should be viewed with a regard for their positive and negative aspects. The quest for theological unity and historical continuity easily leads to the idealization of the perceived superior characters.

Reading 13.2   "The Bible Made Me Do It":
Text, Interpretation and Violence

D. ANDREW KILLE

Is it meaningful to claim that the Bible (or any other sacred text) directly affects individual or group behavior? D. Andrew Kille suggests that in actuality there are multiple levels of individuals' interaction with the Bible, involving the experience of the writers, the text itself, and the community interpreting the text. Here, he considers how early traces of group-identity formation strategies may be transmitted in the text and find resonance with a contemporary group.

---

13. Ford, *Parables of Jesus*, p. 5.

From D. Andrew Kille, "'The Bible Made Me Do It': Text, Interpretation and Violence," in *The Destructive Power of Religion*, ed. J. Harold Ellens (Westport, CT: Praeger, 2004), vol. 1, pp. 60-62.

Group Identity Formation

Scriptures may provide a particularly potent tool for supporting aggression and hostility to others due to the significant role sacred texts play in developing group identity and setting group boundaries. Formation of a group identity is essential in the creation and sustaining of a religious community (or any other human community). W. W. Meissner identifies this process of identity formation, especially when it involves a new group's emergence from a previously existing movement, as the "cultic process." Although in some ways it may appear to be a conscious endeavor, what undergirds it is an unconscious dynamic of individual and intergroup relationships that Meissner dubs the "paranoid process." The term *paranoid* here does not indicate necessarily a pathological condition. Rather, Meissner employs the term technically to refer to a dynamic of attitudes, perceptions and unconscious strategies that serves to consolidate and clarify identity, both individual and group. These dynamics are common to all group identity formation, and when they allow a transition into a more mature and fully-functioning identity they are creative and necessary. It is when they become detached from reality or resort to archaic defenses that they can become pathological.[1]

The elements of the paranoid process correspond to mechanisms we have already encountered at work in the early stages of object relations development, now operative in adult behavior. The process of group identity formation is analogous to the process of individual development, and involves the same processes of integration and differentiation. Human relationships are both positive and negative; they can be created and strengthened by positive feelings of affiliation and connectedness and they can be prevented or inhibited by feelings of hostility and aggression. The paranoid process provides several means for cementing relationships with those within the circle of positive relations and limiting affiliation with those outside.

In group formation, the most visible manifestations of the paranoid process are the idealization of the in group and projection of negative perceptions on outsiders. Meissner suggests that the cultic process serves as a means of bolstering members' self-esteem and enabling them to cope with a sense of vulnerability and powerlessness. The paranoid process enables adherents to deal with these feelings of inadequacy and inferiority by splitting them off and projecting them on the "other." "We" become the Children of Light; "they" are the Children of Darkness. These idealizations of the inner group

---

1. W. W. Meissner, *The Cultic Origins of Christianity: The Dynamics of Religious Development* (Collegeville, MN: The Liturgical Press, 2000).

and projections onto outsiders are consolidated and supported through a development of a belief system and ideology, often contrasted sharply with the beliefs of others.

When sacred texts develop to express and define group identity in a context of conflict, they often crystallize these idealizations and projections and preserve them in written form. While these formulations may be appropriate in the formative stages of the religious community, it sets the stage for future distortions. As Paul Ricoeur has observed, something significant happens when communication moves from speech to text. In dialogue, it is possible to clarify ambiguity by direct reference to the surroundings. Once a communication moves into text, however, the direct referential context is lost, and the multiple significances inherent in written language make a variety of interpretations possible.

Sacred texts that preserve the originating conflict through the expressions of the paranoid process can serve creatively to guide believers through present situations of conflict or persecution. The reader can project his situation onto the imagined world of the text, identify with those who were able to endure, and thus begin working through to a healthier and more integrated way in the world. In the case of individuals and groups whose sense of persecution is excessive or heavily shaped by archaic reaction mechanisms, it is a simple thing to project their present feeling of vulnerability and powerlessness onto the scriptural images, and to reframe the (now decontextualized) language of good and evil to fit their perceived situation. Indeed, what often happens in a violent religious movement is an insistence on recontextualizing the sacred text to fit a new situation. In its cultic formation, the new group not only rejects previously conventional interpretations of sacred text, it forms precisely around its claim that it understands the text better than anyone else.

Take for example the hostile characterizations of Jews in the Christian scriptures. In their struggle to define themselves over against Second Temple Judaism, Christians claimed that they had the correct interpretation of scriptures they shared with Jewish tradition. In the context of increasingly antagonistic relationships with other emergent Jewish groups, the Gospel writers cast the leaders of those other groups, Scribes and Pharisees, in the role of primary antagonists, ultimately laying the blame for the (Roman) crucifixion on "the Jews." In generation after generation these words, lifted out of their first century context and remapped into entirely different political, economic and social contexts, have served religious and political leaders as a justification for anti-Semitism, crusades, pogroms, and the Holocaust.

Does this lead us to the conclusion that scripture causes violence? Does a "toxic text" necessarily trigger paranoid reactions? Does it always support hostility and aggression? Which comes first, paranoia in the text or paranoia in the reader? Idealizations of the in-group and outward projections of aggression onto others developed during the beginnings of a religious movement provide only potential stimuli for violence. Scriptural justifications are far more likely to be secondary phenomena, mustered to support a worldview, attitude and ideology that are already hostile and aggressive.

Reading 13.3   Using the Bible in Pastoral Care and Counseling

HOWARD CLINEBELL

Howard Clinebell, a highly respected pastoral counselor, includes suggestions for how the Bible can be used therapeutically in his guidebook for pastoral counselors. Describing how the Bible can shape the therapeutic relationship both implicitly and explicitly, he nevertheless cautions that there can be a need to deal with pathological interpretations of the text as well. Note particularly his suggestion that a client's understanding of biblical stories can potentially function as a kind of Rorschach test, revealing more deeply the individual's issues and concerns.

Using the Bible Growthfully

There are a variety of valuable ways to use the Bible in pastoral care and counseling. The first is to *allow biblical wisdom to inform the process, spirit, and goals of caring/counseling relationships.* In chapter 3, I suggested why pastoral counselors need to stay in continuing dialogue with biblical images and insights. My friend and colleague John B. Cobb, Jr. says: "Pastoral counselors could experience their counseling not simply as in continuity with Christianity in its ultimate purposes but as informed by the Christian heritage in both form and substance." William B. Oglesby, Jr. has shown how biblical motifs can inform the goals and methods of pastoral counseling. He sees one unifying theological theme throughout the Bible — viz., that human beings are sinners needing

---

From Howard Clinebell, *Basic Types of Pastoral Care and Counseling: Resources for the Ministry of Healing and Growth*, rev. and enl. ed. (Nashville: Abingdon, 1984), pp. 124-27.

reconciliation and that God's action enables this reconciliation to occur. Various biblical subthemes — initiative and freedom, fear and faith, conformity and rebellion, death and rebirth, risk and redemption — all throw light on the complexities of the human issues encountered in counseling.[1]

A second and very common use of the Bible in pastoral care and counseling is *to comfort and strengthen people in crises.* Having a sense of the sustaining presence of God, as communicated for example in the familiar words of the twenty-third or the ninetieth Psalm can be a source of great strength for some people in handling shattering losses. They feel empowered as they walk through their shadowed valley, sustained by a sense of God's loving presence. Having such a source of support helps them deal with the new realities they must face, as well as with their agonizing feelings.

A third use of the Bible in counseling relationships is as *a means of diagnosis.* Wayne Oates's *The Bible in Pastoral Care* and Carroll Wise's *Psychiatry and the Bible* show how the Bible can illuminate the inner dynamics and problems of counselees.[2] Paul W. Pruyser in *The Minister as Diagnostician* recommends that basic theological-biblical themes — providence, repentance, faith, grace, vocation, communion, and awareness of the holy — be held in a minister's mind as unique guideposts for understanding theologically the issues in counseling.

A method I have found useful in diagnosing psychological, interpersonal, and spiritual growth issues is to invite clients to tell the Bible story they most like and the one they most dislike. One woman who had struggled with feelings of being trapped for years told the Exodus story as her favorite, adding, "I feel like I've been trying to escape from my own Egypt and, when I do, I end up wandering in the wilderness. It's the hope of finding the freedom of the promised land that keeps me going, I guess." The inner conflicts of church people may be expressed in the biblical characters with whom they identify. For example, many women today feel inwardly torn between the submissive, serving-others Martha side of themselves and the more liberated Mary side, wanting to participate fully as an equal in the "action." Donald Capps observes:

> While there is the danger that the diagnostic use of the Bible in counseling will be thought of as merely a clinical tool, diagnosis can mean using biblical insights to gain a more empathetic understanding of the coun-

---

1. John B. Cobb, Jr., *Theology and Pastoral Care,* ed. Howard J. Clinebell and Howard W. Stone (Philadelphia: Fortress Press, 1977), p. 61; see William B. Oglesby, Jr., *Biblical Themes for Pastoral Care* (Nashville: Abingdon Press, 1980).

2. See Wayne Oates, *The Bible in Pastoral Care* (Philadelphia: Westminster Press, 1953); see also Carroll Wise, *Psychiatry and the Bible* (New York: Harper & Brothers, 1956).

selee's struggles and conflicts. It can also mean evaluating the counselee's current difficulties from the perspective of biblical accounts of God's healing activity. . . . Jesus' parabolic vision is a particularly valuable biblical resource for this purpose.[3]

A fourth use of the Bible in pastoral care and counseling is *to help heal spiritual pathology and change pathogenic beliefs.* When a pastor senses that the Bible is being used to suppress anger, grief, guilt, or despair, a direct approach to correcting this distorted understanding of the Bible is needed. In dealing with a person who is suppressing anger, one may say, "My understanding is that anger is a gift of God to be valued and used constructively. Jesus seems to have gotten very angry on occasions. It's storing up anger — letting the sun go down on it — that makes it destructive to ourselves and others." Or in responding to repressed grief, "The New Testament says that it's a good thing — a blessed thing — to mourn. The story of Jesus' weeping when his friend died speaks to me when I try to avoid expressing the pain of a loss. . . ." Such statements by a minister may shake and challenge the comfortable but oppressive beliefs of the person. This cognitive dissonance may open such persons to explore in counseling alternative ways of understanding the biblical teachings about feelings.

When people ask questions in counseling about the Bible, it is important to resist the temptation to respond immediately with an answer. As David K. Switzer points out, when a person asks, "What does the Bible say about . . . (divorce, homosexuality, etc.)?," it is crucial to find out why this person is asking this particular question. "Usually the very simple question, 'Why do you ask?' will open the floodgates of a story that . . . will pour out, accompanied by a variety of emotions. Then we may move very quickly into the same type of pastoral conversation or even counseling that would have been initiated if the person had come and simply laid out a clearly delineated problem before us."[4] In the context of such counseling, the pastor's scholarly knowledge about the Bible can be useful in correcting destructive misunderstandings of biblical texts.

Beyond its use in helping people handle crises and problems, a fifth use of biblical wisdom is *as a key resource in the teaching and growth-nurturing dimension of pastoral care.* There are numerous ways of using the Bible as a growth resource. It can serve in counseling and growth groups to raise con-

---

3. Donald Capps, *Biblical Approaches to Pastoral Counseling* (Philadelphia: Westminster Press, 1980), p. 44.

4. David K. Switzer, *Pastor, Preacher, Person* (Nashville: Abingdon Press, 1979), p. 104.

sciousness about the Christian vision of life as a gift from God, a calling to serve those in need.[5] Switzer suggests:

> Persons may be taught, individually or in groups, to read selected passages in the Bible imaginatively and in such a manner that in a sense they move back into biblical times and into the life situation of the writer or the person being described, and then move again into their own present life-situation, accompanied by the particular Word they have received from their experience.[6]

Walter Wink's *The Bible in Human Transformation* and Karl A. Olsson's *Find Yourself in the Bible* describe ways to use the Bible for spiritual growth.

The Bible can be misused in wholeness-constricting ways in pastoral care. It can be quoted in a legalistic way by pastors to buttress their sagging authority, manipulate counselees to conform to rigid moralizing, and justify life-constricting attitudes toward issues such as sex and divorce. An example of the misuse of the Bible in pastoral counseling is the approach of Jay Adams.[7] He begins with a moralistic reductionism (similar to and apparently learned from O. Hobart Mowrer), which reduces the cause of all psychological problems to sin and irresponsible living. Psychological understandings of the human situation and psychotherapeutic methods are rejected as "humanistic" and "nonbiblical." All that a counselor needs, to be "more competent than a psychiatrist," is the Bible. The method is exclusively confrontational — confronting persons with their sin and then pushing them by the use of scripture, to conform to a legalistic and literalistic understanding of the teachings of the Bible.

There are three basic flaws in this approach. It is poor counselling because it does not integrate the biblical wisdom with contemporary wisdom from the human sciences and the psychotherapeutic disciplines. Second, Adams' approach encourages authoritarian advice giving, reinforced by biblical authority. This tends to increase counselees' dependency and block spiritual maturing. Third, the rigid biblicism of this approach tends to prevent people from discovering the Bible as the living Word that speaks to their particular situation in transforming ways. Hulme notes:

> In its misuse the Bible is converted into an ultimate authority — an end in itself. Converting a means into an end is basically what is meant by

---

5. William Edward Hulme, *Pastoral Care and Counseling: Using the Unique Resources of the Christian Tradition* (Minneapolis: Augsburg Publishing House, 1981), pp. 122-24.

6. Switzer, *Pastor, Preacher, Person*, p. 133.

7. See Jay Adams, *Competent to Counsel* (Grand Rapids: Baker Book House, 1970).

idolatry, and there are no means more susceptible to this distortion than religious symbols. When this happens to the Bible, the flexibility of the Holy Spirit is replaced by the rigidity of the Holy Book. The Bible's value to pastoral care depends on its mediatorial function: it is a means by which the Spirit bears "witness with our spirits that we are the children of God" (Rom. 8:16), that it is "profitable for teaching, for reproof, for correction, and for training in righteousness" (II Tim. 3:16).[8]

Reading 13.4   Biblical Stories for Psychotherapy and Counseling

MATTHEW B. SCHWARTZ AND KALMAN J. KAPLAN

Psychotherapists Schwartz and Kaplan express their concern that psychological theory and practice have long been dominated by a bias toward Greek mythology — for example, the myth of Oedipus, which became so central to Freud's model of psychological development. The Hebrew Bible, they argue, can be an important source for counseling. They suggest how specific stories might offer tools for dealing with different therapeutic issues and clients. In this reading, they consider what the stories of Jonah and Lot's wife might teach about taking responsibility and dealing with change.

Assuming Responsibility for Others: Jonah

Biblical Narrative

To act responsibly includes doing what is right even in opposition to one's own views or perceived interests. In biblical terms, right is defined as fulfilling God's commands and wishes. Whether based on selfish greed or altruism, one's own views must give way before God's. For the prophet Jonah, learning the true nature of responsibility was a perilous adventure, but God stayed

---

8. Hulme, *Pastoral Care and Counseling*, p. 113.

From Matthew B. Schwartz and Kalman J. Kaplan, *Biblical Stories for Psychotherapy and Counseling: A Sourcebook* (New York: Haworth Pastoral Press, 2004), pp. 49-52.

with him through a series of mistaken judgments until He was able to drive home to Jonah that God, not man, decides where man's responsibility lies.

Jonah was commanded by God to travel to Nineveh, capital of the mighty Assyrian Empire, and to urge the people to repent of their wicked way of life. Fearful, however, that his own people of Israel might look bad by comparison if the Ninevites repented, Jonah disobeyed God and instead fled by ship in the other direction. Jonah's concern for his own people and his lack of interest in the lot of the Ninevites was well-intentioned but inappropriate. He should have obeyed God. Certainly, he could have discussed with God any matters of doubt or disagreement as had Abraham, Moses, and other prophets before him. He should have even expressed his anger at God.

Although Jonah had disobeyed him, God still wanted to help Jonah both to fulfill his mission to Nineveh and to fulfill himself. God watched over him closely. He sent a storm, and Jonah responded by telling the sailors to throw him into the sea, almost an act of suicide. However, God still did not abandon Jonah, and He sent a large fish to swallow him and save him from drowning. From the fish's belly, Jonah prayed, and God had the fish spout him up onto dry land.

God sent Jonah again to Nineveh, where he was successful in persuading the people to mend their ways. Jonah, however, was still disgruntled and almost suicidal, and he sat outside Nineveh unsure what to do next. God had still not given up on Jonah. He caused a plant to grow overnight to give Jonah shade from the blazing Asian sun. Jonah felt much better. God then caused the plant to wither, again leaving Jonah without shade and feeling miserable. God already knew that it was important for Jonah to recognize and deal with the anger that he felt against God. Disturbed about the loss of the gourd, Jonah finally turned the direction of his anger from himself to God, "I am greatly angry even unto death" (Jonah 4:9). God as therapist could begin to deal with Jonah directly.

> You have had pity on the gourd for which you did not labor, nor did you make it grow; which came in a night and perished in a night. Shall I not have mercy on Nineveh that great city in which there are 120,000 people . . . ? (4:10-11)

God used the incident of the gourd to drive home to Jonah the immensity of God's care for mankind. Jonah had the right and indeed the obligation to understand both his own duties and God's intentions. Jonah was responsible to do what was right, i.e., what God required of him. He was so despondent at the failure of his own plans that on several occasions he expressed a wish to die. God wanted to salvage not only Nineveh but Jonah as well. Jonah had to learn that clarity of understanding and joy in life would come only by fulfilling the responsibilities that God placed on him and not by merely following his own plans.

Clinical Implications

The clinical message here is clear. Jonah is refusing to go to the people of Nineveh because he is disengaged from them. Perhaps he is afraid of being corrupted by them or that they will surpass him. In either case, Jonah's approach shows a lack of perspective and an inability to communicate with God. He is to be contrasted to Abraham who argued with God to save the city of Sodom. Individuals must learn that they can interact with people who are having problems in life without being overwhelmed by them. People in the helping professions need not be weighed down by their patients' problems. Therapists have a right, and indeed an obligation, to live their own lives.

Often, an individual's inability to help another emerges from a lack of mature perspective. One does not have to lose if the other one wins. One's success is not always measured against another's failure. Understanding this involves communication. Individuals locked into this underdeveloped perspective must be encouraged to communicate if they are able. If they are not able to communicate at a particular time they must be protected until they are able to. God does not give up on Jonah but shields him from self-destructive tendencies. Finally the message of compassion is transmitted not just intellectually, but experientially. Jonah only understands God's attachment to Nineveh when he experiences his attachment to the gourd.

Assuming Responsibility for Self: Lot's Wife

Biblical Narrative

A person faced with a new set of circumstances may well find it necessary to give up long-established patterns of behavior in order to survive and even to grow and improve. The name of Lot's wife is never mentioned in the Scripture, yet she figures in one of the Scripture's strangest and most remarkable episodes (Genesis 19). Two angels had come to Lot's home to warn him to take his family and escape that wicked city because God would destroy it with fire and brimstone that very night. Lot's wife was apparently reluctant to separate from Sodom and the family and friends that were not going with her. Even if she was not as evil as her fellow townspeople, she was too involved, too deeply enmeshed with them. Perhaps she was enamored of the lifestyle of Sodom. Alternatively, it may have been difficult for her to separate from something familiar.

Whatever her motivation, Lot's wife was ambivalent about leaving. Fiery destruction was already striking Sodom as Lot and his family fled the city. Lot's wife, however, was still unable to separate, for her heart was still in Sodom whether because she actively loved it or simply tolerated it. Impelled by misplaced loyalties, she turned for one more look at her beloved city, and she was caught in its destruction and turned into a pillar of salt. Lot's wife's self-definition seemed totally determined by her experiences with the people of Sodom. Therefore she was unable to see herself in any way other than as a Sodomite. Lot, however, with his experience of the family of Abraham and a self-definition independent of Sodom was able to break away.

Clinical Implications

Lot's wife preferred to continue familiar, if unsatisfactory, patterns of acting rather than change for the better, and she was trapped in the unfortunate results of that way of life. People may find themselves in situations where they are being abused or hurt, yet they seem unable to extricate themselves from this abuse as if they are receiving an unconscious sense of nurturance from it. Separating oneself from a familiar environment is not a simple task psychologically. It requires identifying with a transcendent force that provides a basis for self-esteem that is independent of the destructive environment. Consider a young boy from a highly abusive family. He is continually taunted by siblings and humiliated by parents. He unconsciously seeks the same punishment in adult relationships. He seems to feel that he deserves to be punished, and he cannot extricate himself from the destructive pattern. How can he? The very humiliation he receives so diminishes his sense of self that he thinks he deserves no better. Even if he summons the courage to leave, he will be confronted with severe criticism as he tries to leave. The job of the therapist is to provide a basis for self-definition that transcends his situation and enables him to withstand the criticism he will encounter when he leaves.

SUGGESTIONS FOR FURTHER READING

Therapeutic

Capps, D. *Biblical Approaches to Pastoral Counseling.* Philadelphia: Westminster, 1981.

Oates, W. E. *The Bible in Pastoral Care.* Philadelphia: Westminster, 1953.

Wink, W. *Transforming Bible Study: A Leader's Guide.* Nashville: Abingdon, 1980.

Pathogenic

Ellens, J. H., ed. *The Destructive Power of Religion: Violence in Judaism, Christianity, and Islam.* Vol. 1: *Sacred Scriptures, Ideology, and Violence.* Westport, CT: Praeger, 2004.

Greven, P. J. *Spare the Child: The Religious Roots of Punishment and the Psychological Impact of Physical Abuse.* New York: Knopf, 1991.

Weems, R. *Battered Love: Marriage, Sex and Violence in the Hebrew Prophets.* Minneapolis: Fortress, 1995.

CHAPTER 14

Biblical Psychology:
On the Nature and Habits
of the Soul

What Scripture says to us of cosmology, may certainly appear insufficient to originate a system of biblical cosmology; but assuredly it says to us infinitely more about man's soul and spirit than about Orion and the Pleiades. . . . There has never perhaps been a time more favorable to biblical psychology, as there has also never been a time that needed it more than the present.

Franz Delitzsch[1]

In 1855, one year before Sigmund Freud was born and twenty years before Carl Jung, one of Europe's premier biblical scholars, Franz Delitzsch, published a book that was as surprising in the nineteenth century as it is astonishing in the twenty-first. Its title was *A System of Biblical Psychology*. It opened with a remarkable statement: "Biblical Psychology is no science of yesterday. It is one of the oldest sciences of the church." To make his point, Delitzsch engaged in a survey of Western theology, beginning with Tertullian and Augustine, through Aquinas and the Reformation, to demonstrate "that the ancient church had a psychological literature that claims respect no less for its extent than for its substance."[2]

Delitzsch documented nineteen centuries of reflection and argumentation by Western theologians bent on comparing the biblical portrait of the human psyche/soul with that of Aristotle, Plato, the Stoics, and the Greco-Roman tradition.

---

1. Franz Delitzsch, *A System of Biblical Psychology*, trans. Robert Ernest Wallis, 2nd (1867) ed., Clark's Foreign Theological Library 13 (Edinburgh: T&T Clark, 1899), pp. 15 and 25.
2. Delitzsch, *A System of Biblical Psychology*, pp. 3 and 5.

Historians of psychology provide corroboration for the Greco-Roman half of the conversation. They remind us that "psychology" goes back as far as the fourth century B.C.E., tracing its origin in the West to the classic treatment of the human psyche by Aristotle in his *Peri Psyches* (English: *Concerning the Psyche*; Latin: *De Anima*). They identify Aristotle as the creator of the "first systematic psychology," having "laid down the lines along which the relationship between various manifestations of soul and mind were conceived" for two millennia.[3]

The evidence is overwhelming. Aristotle's research, in combination with that of Plato, Pythagoras, Anaxagoras, Empedocles, the Stoics, Plotinus, Hippocrates, and Galen, among others, produced a detailed psychological model of the self. They identified the parts and properties of the psyche in relation to the body *(soma)*, differentiating the elements of reason *(nous)*, spirit/will *(thymos)*, and desire *(epithymia)*. They itemized the various psychic functions: emotion, memory, learning, sensation, perception, socialization, imagination, and personality. They catalogued the four passions, the five senses, and the four humors. They studied epistemology and the relation of stimulus to sensation. They spoke of dreams as an expression of suppressed desire. They offered a taxonomy of psychological illness, ranging from mania and post-partum depression to melancholia, phobia, paranoia, and hysteria, proposing that "mental illness was a medical problem based on an organic dysfunction of the brain which could best be addressed by oral remedies."[4] In the second century C.E., Galen advanced a cure for psychic diseases that involved self-examination and counseling, a foretaste of Freud's "talking cure."[5]

But early church theologians believed that as insightful as the Greeks and Latins were in their description of the soul, the biblical tradition offered an even higher vision. Thus a biblical psychology emerged as a significant part of systematic theology, researching the biblical perspective on the nature, origin, powers, health, and destiny of the soul. By the eighteenth and nineteenth centuries it generated a school of opinion, reflected in Delitzsch's work, that was willing to learn from the "new psychology" emerging in the academic world, but was rooted in the conviction that biblical psychology had something significant to add to the picture.

---

3. R. S. Peters and C. A. Mace, "Psychology," in *The Encyclopedia of Philosophy*, ed. Paul Edwards (New York: Macmillan, 1967), pp. 1, 4.

4. A. Solomon, review of *Out of Its Mind, Psychiatry in Crisis: A Call for Reform*, by J. Allan Hobson and Jonathan A. Leonard (Cambridge, MA: Perseus), in *New York Times Book Review*, October 7, 2001, p. 15.

5. Wayne G. Rollins, *Soul and Psyche: The Bible in Psychological Perspective* (Minneapolis: Fortress, 1999), pp. 9-12.

Although the phrase "biblical psychology" is in the singular, it represents a diversity of "psychologies" within the spectrum of biblical writings, as will be evident in the readings that follow. The first reading proposes a threefold agenda for the study of biblical psychology. The second compares the psychological descriptions of the self in the Hebrew Bible and Paul. The third postulates powerful archetypal realities at work in the various permutations of the "son-of-the-man" imagery implicit in Paul and John and in other early Christian, Judaic, and Gnostic visions of "the human being."

Reading 14.1   What Is Biblical Psychology?

WAYNE G. ROLLINS

In the section of his book that precedes this reading, Rollins explains that most "biblical psychology" was written prior to the 1920s, before the "blackout" in communication between biblical scholars and psychologists, a standoff that lasted for half a century. Since the 1970s, however, articles, books, and essays reemerged as biblical scholars began to realize their need to think psychologically about the Bible and as psychologists began to realize that the Bible provides insight into the nature and dimensions of the self. In the present section, Rollins proposes an agenda for a contemporary biblical psychology.

The goal of research in biblical psychology can be defined in terms of a threefold agenda: descriptive, prescriptive, and comparative. The *descriptive agenda* for biblical psychology is virtually spelled out in the chapter headings of the "biblical psychologies" of Delitzsch, Fletcher, and Robinson.[1] But these need refinement in terms of new psychological theories that have emerged since the

---

1. Franz Delitzsch, *A System of Biblical Psychology,* trans. Robert Ernest Wallis, 2nd (1867) ed., Clark's Foreign Theological Library 13 (Edinburgh: T&T Clark, 1899); M. Scott Fletcher, *The Psychology of the New Testament,* 2nd ed. (New York: Hodder & Stoughton, 1912); H. Wheeler Robinson, *The Christian Doctrine of Man* (Edinburgh: T&T Clark, 1911).

From Wayne G. Rollins, *Soul and Psyche: The Bible in Psychological Perspective* (Minneapolis: Fortress, 1999), pp. 140-44.

early twentieth century and the new questions and perceptions of the self they introduce. This requires identification, description and analysis of the Bible's perspective on a wide range of aspects of the psyche, both in its individual and social manifestations. These include, for example, the constituent elements of the self (soul, heart, mind, body, flesh, spirit, "bowels"), psychic functions (intelligence, reason, free will, desire, conscience, imagination, dreaming), the substance of the "inner" and "outer" self of which the Bible speaks (language that suggests recognition of an unconscious dimension of the self),[2] the biblical understanding of human drives and emotions in the life of the psyche (affect, appetite, libido, love, hate, anger, ecstasy, fear, anxiety, terror, grief, joy, sorrow), and biblical perceptions on the psychology of behavior (work, play, sexuality, socialization, war, crime and punishment). In summary, the descriptive agenda of biblical psychology is to identify, catalogue, and analyze the complex of entities, functions, faculties, and behavioral patterns — along with the typical predicaments, problems, and possibilities — that the Bible understands as constitutive of the life of the human psyche, individually and collectively.

The *prescriptive agenda* for biblical psychological research turns to another fundamental feature of the Bible's interest in the human psyche: its concern with the question not only of what a human *psyche*/soul is, and perhaps more fundamentally, with what a human *psyche*/soul can be. Accordingly the prescriptive agenda of a "biblical psychology" will focus on what the Bible teaches about the care, nourishment, proper development, and goal of the human *psyche,* elaborating its views of health and sickness, physically, morally, and spiritually (sin, suffering, death, demonic possession, fallenness, salvation, grace, rebirth, transformation, reconciliation); on its perceptions and models of human development (concepts of maturity and immaturity, the *psychikos* vs. the *pneumatikos* [the biological and the spiritual], the laws governing successful human behavior), and the role of spirituality in the life of the soul (prayer, piety, God-consciousness, obedience to the law, faith, hope, love, vice and virtue, and images of the holy forged by the *psyche*).

The data for constructing such a "biblical psychology" are in two sources. The most obvious is the catalogue of biblical passages that speak explicitly of the nature, habits, and destiny of the human soul. A second source, however, would be biblical passages in which the perspective on the nature and habits of the soul is implicit, but not consciously explicated. A negative exam-

---

2. Gerd Theissen, in *Psychological Aspects of Pauline Theology,* trans. John P. Galvin (Philadelphia: Fortress, 1987), makes a convincing case for biblical acknowledgement of the unconscious in his section on "The Secrets of the Heart: The Disclosure of Unconscious Motives Through Pauline Theology," especially pp. 81-114.

ple would be the "texts of terror" noted by Phyllis Trible, stories of awesome violence that seem to leave the biblical mind and the textual authors unfazed. Such stories bear witness to enigmatic, and even neurotic, obsessively destructive, or psychotic qualities that are so operant in the biblical conception of what constitutes "normalcy," they are not explicitly commented on or acknowledged.[3] A "positive example" would be the apocalyptic visions of the survivors of the "great tribulation" in Revelation, the Gospel parable images of the good Samaritan, the prodigal and the publican, the portrait of the "poor in spirit" in the Beatitudes, the legends of the patriarchs as "example stories," and the soliloquies of Jeremiah. All these bear witness implicitly to a vision of the nature, mettle, and developmental potential of the human soul.

The *comparative agenda* for biblical psychological research turns attention to a critical comparison of the biblical perspective on the self and that of contemporary psychology. The task can be framed as two questions, "What has the Bible to learn from psychology?" and "What has psychology to learn from the Bible?" Though the apparent incongruity between biblical and psychological scholarship has always seemed sufficient to preclude meaningful exchange, there are signs . . . of a thaw in the relationship and of the possibility of mutual learning taking place.[4]

With respect to the question, "What has the Bible to learn from psychology?" it is evident from the growing corpus of work in the field of psychological biblical criticism that, despite the pronouncement of psychoanalyst-theologian Dominique Stein that "exegesis has nothing to expect from psychoanalysis," exegesis has had something to learn from psychology. . . . William Meissner's observation on the contribution of psychological insight to the study of religion characterizes its parallel contribution to biblical studies. He notes that psychology helps us see "the religious belief system and its tradition" in "increasingly realistic terms," affirming "their inherent tensions and ambiguities," and accepting "the relativity, partiality, and particularity of the beliefs, symbols, rituals and ceremonials of the religious community."[5]

---

3. Phyllis Trible, *Texts of Terror: Literary-Feminist Readings of Biblical Narratives* (Philadelphia: Fortress, 1984).

4. J. Harold Ellens, founding editor of the *Journal of Psychology and Christianity*, has been a consistent advocate of "mutual illumination" between psychology and religion, and most recently between psychology and biblical studies. See Ellens, "Biblical Themes in Psychological Theory and Practice," in *Christian Counseling and Psychotherapy*, ed. D. G. Benner (Grand Rapids: Baker, 1987), pp. 23-33; *God's Grace and Human Health* (Nashville: Abingdon, 1982); "The Bible and Psychology, an Interdisciplinary Pilgrimage," *Pastoral Psychology* 45, no. 3 (1997): 193-208.

5. Dominique Stein, "Is a Psycho-Analytic Reading of the Bible Possible?" in *Conflicting Ways of Interpreting the Bible*, ed. Hans Küng and J. Moltmann (New York: Seabury; Edinburgh:

"What does psychology stand to learn from the Bible?" In his essay on "Biblical Psychology," theologian Emil Brunner comments on the relation between two approaches to the soul — one scientific-psychological; the other, "biblical psychological." Concerning the first he writes:

> Empirical psychology, which takes as its model the freedom from prejudice of the natural sciences, has without doubt brought to light a great store of important knowledge which we should be loath to do without. But we must from the beginning draw attention to the fact that this psychology, like every psychology, is based on a definite world-view as its axiomatic presupposition.

He identifies the world-view of scientific psychology as "naturalistic positivism," which "conceives of the soul and psychological realities as objects among objects," rather than as subjects that constitute the observer-self. He goes on to suggest that the biblical forms — story, legend, myth, parable, saga, psalm, proverb, letter and apocalypse — capture dimensions of the self not susceptible to scientific observation but quintessential to a full portrait of the human *psyche*/soul.[6]

A number of researchers in the field of biblical psychology have suggested specific dimensions of the soul that do not submit to rigorous scientific description, but that are identified and addressed in biblical literature as fundamental features of the self. Psychology would do well to reflect upon these qualities.

In speaking of the contribution of "biblical psychology" to counseling, for example, J. Harold Ellens identifies eight insights from the Bible that are important for fully understanding "the living human document." He calls these "the biblical theology of (a) human personhood, of (b) alienation, of (c) sin, of (d) discipline, of (e) grace, of (f) wounded healer, of (g) mortality, and of (h) celebration.[7] Similar views have been expressed by Karl Menninger and D. Andrew Kille. Menninger has recommended reappreciation of the concept of "sin" from a psychological perspective.[8] Kille

---

T&T Clark, 1980), pp. 24-32; William Meissner, in *Psychoanalysis and Religious Experience* (New Haven: Yale University Press, 1984), p. 157. See Dan Merkur, "Freud's Atheism: Object Relations and the Theory of Religion," *Religious Studies Review* 16, no. 1 (January 1990): 14.

6. Emil Brunner, "Biblical Psychology," in *God and Man: Four Essays on the Nature of Personality* (London: SCM Press, 1946), p. 138.

7. J. Harold Ellens, "The Bible and Psychology, an Interdisciplinary Pilgrimage," *Pastoral Psychology* 45, no. 3 (1997): 200.

8. Karl Menninger, *Whatever Became of Sin?* (New York: Hawthorn Books, 1973).

has recommended probing the psychological value of the biblical concepts of the fall, repentance, redemption and grace, and eschatological consciousness. He states that "each of these themes highlights an issue that might be used to critique aspects of modern psychology." The doctrine of creation, for example, avoids both the apotheosization and degradation of humans; the doctrine of the fall crystallizes the reality of the brokenness and incompleteness of life; repentance critiques psychological determinism and attests to the possibility of transformation; the theology of redemption and grace contravenes the theory of a directionless and purposeless universe.[9]

Contemporary psychological biblical critics have joined M. Scott Fletcher who in 1912 identified the biblical concept of the "spirit" — with its attendant experiential categories of new creation, transformation, and rebirth — as a psycho-anthropological element meriting consideration in understanding the life and experience of the psyche.[10] In 1946, Brunner referred to the Spirit as the "theologian's stepchild," implying that the empirical positivism of the mid-nineteenth century had even affected theology.[11] Perhaps the most eloquent apologia for reclaiming a sense of "spirit" is voiced by Carl Jung:

> We moderns are faced with the necessity of rediscovering the life of the spirit; we must experience it anew for ourselves. It is the only way in which to break the spell that binds us to the cycle of biological events. . . . The wheel of history must not be turned back, and man's advance toward a spiritual life, which began with the primitive rites of initiation, must not be denied. . . . Scientific thought, being only one of the psyche's functions, can never exhaust all of its potentialities. The psychotherapist must not allow his vision to be colored by pathology; he must never allow himself to forget that the ailing mind is a human mind and that, for all its ailments, it unconsciously shares the whole psychic life of man. He must even be able to admit that the ego is sick for the very reason that it is cut off from the whole, and has lost its connection not only with mankind but with the spirit. . . . For thousands of years, rites of initiation have been teaching rebirth from the spirit; yet, strangely enough, man forgets again and again the meaning of divine procreation. Though this may be poor testimony to the strength of the spirit, the penalty for misunderstanding

9. Kille, in personal communication in the course of his doctoral work at the Graduate Theological Union, Berkeley, California.

10. Fletcher contends that the Bible contains "psychological material of the highest value" providing a "new view of human personality." A chief feature of this new view is its doctrine of the spirit as a distinctive feature of regenerate humans; *Psychology,* pp. 10, 146, 287.

11. Brunner, "Biblical Psychology," p. 113.

is neurotic decay, embitterment, atrophy, and sterility. It is easy enough to drive the spirit out of the door, but when we have done so the meal has lost its savor — the salt of the earth.[12]

Biblical psychology needs to be reclaimed as a legitimate and significant rubric within biblical scholarship. For readers of the Bible it can shed new light on human self-understanding. For professional psychologists it can engender a deeper and broader understanding of the nature, origin, habits, powers, possibilities, and purpose of the human psyche. . . .

The above threefold agenda — descriptive, prescriptive, and comparative — represents the beginnings of what psychological criticism might contribute to biblical exegesis. The ultimate goal of such criticism, indeed of the entire apparatus of critical biblical scholarship, is, in the words of Carl Jung, "to create more and more consciousness."[13] Psychological criticism can contribute to that goal by heightening awareness of the text as an expression of a psychic as well as historic process. In doing so, it will build on the promethean achievements of historical and literary criticism, and join the host of other critical disciplines that have emerged during the past two decades. As Gerd Theissen has observed with respect to New Testament scholarship:

> We do not yet grasp what historical forces brought forth and determined early Christianity. But beside and within this external history there is an inner history. . . . Anyone who thinks that this religion can be illumined historically and factually without psychological reflection is just as much in error as one who pretends that everything about this religion can be said in this fashion.[14]

---

12. Carl Gustav Jung, *The Collected Works of C. G. Jung*, trans. R. F. C. Hull, ed. Gerhard Adler et al., Bollingen Series 20 (Princeton: Princeton University Press, 1953-78), vol. 4, par. 780-83.

13. Carl Gustav Jung, *Memories, Dreams, Reflections*, trans. Richard Winston and Clara Winston (New York: Vintage Books, 1963), p. 326.

14. Theissen, *Psychological Aspects*, p. 398.

Reading 14.2   Biblical Psychology in Paul
and the Old Testament

H. Wheeler Robinson

H. Wheeler Robinson was one of the primary figures in the early 1900s engaged in the descriptive task of biblical psychology. His book *The Christian Doctrine of Man* explores Old Testament, New Testament, and patristic perspectives on the nature of the human psyche or soul. In treating each of these bodies of literature, Robinson includes a sub-section on psychology. He analyzes the vocabulary employed by each to tell us "who we are" — *mind, spirit, soul, heart, conscience, body, flesh,* etc. (but also *kidney, heart, liver,* and *bowels,* each of which was thought to exercise a psychological function, such as will, emotion, intellect, or consciousness). In this section Robinson focuses on the psychology of Paul's view of humankind (anthropology), emphasizing its roots in classical Hebrew "psychology."

The psychological vocabulary of Paul is the most elaborate in the New Testament; this is the result of his characteristic emphasis on personal experience. In regard to details the problems are many, and the controversy has been great; but, for our present purpose, the main lines are sufficiently clear. The Pauline psychological vocabulary, in most of its elements, is drawn from that of the Old Testament (mediated by the usage of the Septuagint); but it has been much discussed whether the change from Hebrew into Greek corresponds with deeper changes of attitude in the use of these terms, and, in particular, whether Paul's conception of the flesh as the seat and immediate source of sin points to the influence of "Hellenistic dualism."

The view here maintained is that Paul, in spite of the use of some Greek terms ("inner man," "mind," "conscience"), remains psychologically what he calls himself, a Hebrew of the Hebrews; the advances he makes on the conceptions of the Old Testament are a natural Jewish development, while their originality can be shown as compared with Palestinian Judaism, as well as with the Hellenistic thought of Alexandria; his modifications of current Jewish thought are primarily due to his personal experience, and such Hellenistic influences as were inevitable in his period were un-

From H. Wheeler Robinson, *The Christian Doctrine of Man* (Edinburgh: T&T Clark, 1911), pp. 104-11. Several of the author's archaic expressions have been changed: "whilst" to "while"; "shewn" to "shown"; and "amongst" to "among." Also, his older-style transliteration of the Greek word, "psuche," has been replaced with the modern transliteration, "psyche."

consciously imbibed by Paul and subordinated or assimilated to his Jewish Psychology.[1]

We have already seen that the psychological vocabulary of the Old Testament came into existence along more or less independent and parallel lines, a fact which explains its evident want of system. By the close of the Old Testament period, however, this development had resulted in four principal terms, namely, "heart" [Hebrew, *leb*], *nephesh* [soul], and *ruach* [spirit], to denote different aspects of the inner life, and "flesh," to denote man's visible personality. These four terms, in their Greek equivalents, form the basis of Paul's vocabulary, namely, *kardia* [heart], *psyche* [soul], *pneuma* [spirit], and *sarx* [flesh]. But the tendency already seen in the Old Testament to make *nephesh* predominantly emotional is carried further by Paul, who connects *psyche* [soul] and its adjective *psychikos* [soul-like] specially with the life of the flesh, in contrast with *pneuma* and its adjective *pneumatikos* [spirit-like] used of the "spiritual" and higher life. . . . This contrast, which is of fundamental importance for Pauline thought in general, is further emphasized by the introduction of the antithetical terms, the "inner" and "outer" man, while a general term occurs for "body" *(soma)*, for which, also, there is no Old Testament equivalent. . . .

On the other hand, Paul's detailed references to the present inner life called for something more exact than the general and inclusive term "heart," which was sufficient for the Old Testament; consequently, we find him using two other Greek terms, *nous* and *suneidesis* ("mind" and "conscience") to denote special groups of psychical phenomena which, among others the Old Testament ascribes to "heart." . . .

We may begin with the general and central term "heart," which Paul uses in 52 instances. (1) He makes no use of "heart" in a purely physical or simply figurative reference. (2) In 15 cases, "heart" denotes personality, character, or the inner life in general; e.g. 1 Cor. xiv.25: "The secrets of his heart are made manifest." (3) In 13 cases, it is the seat of emotional states of consciousness; e.g. Rom. ix.2: "I have great sorrow and unceasing pain in my heart." (4) In 11 cases, it is the seat of intellectual activities; e.g. Rom. i.21: "They were made foolish in their reasonings and their stupid *kardia* was darkened." (5) In 13 cases, it is the seat of volition; e.g. Rom. ii.5: "According to thy stubbornness and impenitent *kardia* thou art storing up for thyself anger against the day of anger." . . .

The term *nous* (occurring 21 times) denotes the intellectual faculty of

1. This thesis is argued by the present writer in Mansfield College Essays, pp. 267-86: "Hebrew Psychology in relation to Pauline Anthropology." For the whole section see Peake's excellent article, "The Quintessence of Paulinism" in *Bulletin of the John Rylands Library*, Manchester, iv. 2, pp. 285f. (1918).

the natural man (1 Cor. xiv.14; Phil. iv.7), and is also applied to the "mind" of God or Christ (Rom. xi.34; 1 Cor. ii.16). This faculty is employed in theistic argument from nature (Rom. i.20, verb corresponding to *nous*) or in practical moral judgment (Rom. xiv.5). In a particular individual, its moral quality may be good or bad; the *nous* of Paul comprehends or contains that law of God in which he delights, and of which he approves (Rom. vii.23, 25); on the other hand, the *nous* may be immoral, vain, fleshly, corrupt, defiled (Rom. i.28; Eph. iv.17; Col. ii.18; 1 Tim. vi.5; 2 Tim. iii.8; Tit. i.15); in the Christian, its renewal works the transformation of the life (Rom. xii.2).

The Greek term for "conscience" *(syneidesis)* is used 20 times by Paul, and its use covers the consciousness of rectitude within one's own heart (Rom. ii.15), the appeal to similar moral judgment in the consciousness of others (2 Cor. iv.2; cf. 1 Cor. x.23f.), and the characterization of this faculty for moral judgment as either "defiled" (1 Cor. viii.7) or "pure" (1 Tim. iii.9). It will be noticed that the term is not used by Paul, any more than by the Greeks, to denote the source of ethical knowledge, but, in a sense near to "consciousness," of judgment upon the moral quality of an action. The moral law itself is "the law of the *nous*" (Rom. vii.23), or is "written in the heart" (Rom. ii.15). . . .

The most significant point in regard to *psyche* is Paul's very limited use of the term, which occurs only 13 times. In 6 cases, it denotes "life," without psychological content; thus, Epaphroditus "for the work of Christ came nigh unto death, hazarding his *life*" (Phil. ii.30; cf. Rom. xvi.4; 2 Cor. i.23; 1 Thess. ii.8; in quotations from the Old Testament, Rom. xi.3; 1 Cor. xv.45). In 3 cases, *psyche* denotes [the] "individual" *(pasa psyche = kol nephesh* ["every soul"] Rom. ii.9, xiii.1) or the strong personal pronoun (2 Cor. xii.15) exactly like *nephesh*. In 3 psychical cases, the special Old Testament sense of "desire" reappears (Eph. vi.6; . . . Phil. i.27; Col. iii.23, . . .). There is left one case only on which to rear the stately and wholly artificial structure of Pauline "trichotomy," namely, the well-known passage, 1 Thess. v.23: "And the God of peace Himself sanctify you wholly: and may your spirit *(pneuma)* and soul *(psyche)* and body *(soma)* be preserved entire without blame at the coming of our Lord Jesus Christ."

But this is not a systematic dissection of the distinct elements of personality; its true analogy is such an Old Testament sentence as Deut. vi.5, where a somewhat similar enumeration emphasizes the totality of the personality: "Thou shalt love the Lord thy God with all thine heart *(leb),* and with all thy soul *(nephesh),* and with all thy might." In both cases, the inner life is viewed under the two aspects of intellect (with volition) and emotion. . . .

It is far otherwise with *pneuma* [spirit], the most important word in Paul's psychological vocabulary, perhaps in his vocabulary as a whole. It occurs 146 times, and its usages are here classified on the same lines as those of *ruach* [Heb. "spirit"], which it continues and develops. (1) In the natural sense of "wind," it is not used by Paul, who employs *anemos* [wind] in this sense (Eph. iv.14). (2) Most of the cases (116) fall into the second class, namely, "supernatural influences." . . . (3) The use of *ruach* to denote the principle of life, or breath (in man), is hardly represented among the usages of *pneuma*. This connotation, like that of "wind," has been displaced by the higher associations of the term. (4) There remain 30 cases of the psychical use of *pneuma* in the narrower sense, of which 14 refer to the higher nature of a Christian man, and are hardly to be distinguished from the result of the divine *pneuma*, while 16 denote a normal element in human nature. . . .

But the very fact of its presence shows that we are on the right track in claiming a central place for Hebrew psychology in the interpretation of Paul's thought; the same ambiguity already exists in the Old Testament in the double use of *ruach* (after the exile) to denote both a supernatural influence and a natural element in human nature. To Paul, doubtless, this double use did not appear as a confusion at all; it supplied a point of contact in human nature for the regenerative action of the Spirit of God.

Reading 14.3 The Human Being: Jesus and the
Enigma of the Son of the Man

WALTER WINK

"Son of Man" is one of the first "titles" of Jesus that one encounters in a course on the Gospels. One learns at the outset that in the Gospels the "Son of Man" phrase is voiced only by Jesus, suggesting to biblical scholars that this was his preferred self-designation. In addition, unlike other titles that gradually emerged in the faith of early Christians, such as "Lord," "Messiah," "Savior," "King," and "Son of God," the term "Son of Man" virtually disappeared after the first century c.e. This suggests again that it was a phrase associated with the historical Jesus, but never fully understood by the early church.

Generations of biblical scholars have tried to determine where Jesus may have gotten the phrase and what he meant by it. Was it the Son of Man we hear of

From Walter Wink, *The Human Being: Jesus and the Enigma of the Son of the Man* (Minneapolis: Fortress, 2002), pp. 208-9, 201-3, 323-24.

in Ezekiel when God called him to his prophetic task? Or was it simply a commonly known Aramaic phrase, meaning "human being"? Or did it derive from the apocalyptic figure in Daniel 7:13 who appears at the end of time to receive kingship and sovereignty?

Wink proposes a fourth option that takes into account the others. Wink's thesis is that the term "son of the man" (the literal translation of the phrase in the original Greek) is a term for an archetypal image that was emerging in popular consciousness in generations preceding Jesus. It was a consciousness that filled the imagination of Jesus himself, and that continues in its archetypal effect today.

Wink writes: we can observe "around the beginning of the first millennium, the explosion of a massive archetypal mutation: an inner Anthropos ['man'], a divine child, born of the divine Human — a homing device orienting us toward our true selves." "This revelation had steadily been asserting itself from the time of Ezekiel forward, and was now affecting everything in its path. It not only dominated Christian and Jewish theology and mystical practice, but manifested itself in a novel way in Gnosticism, and within the bosom of Islam, in Sufism." "This new spiritual understanding burst onto the scene with incomparable power." And within the life of Jesus if "'the son of the man' is the name Jesus gave to the dawning reality he was incarnating in his life, work, and being, then the entire gospel is the content of the son of the man."[1]

Wink's book places the discussion of "Son of man" in a totally new context — namely, the process in which and out of which the Son-of-the-man image emerges as a heuristic, archetypal force within the human psyche.

What follows are excerpts demonstrating Wink's "biblical psychology," an approach that does not limit itself to the exegesis of biblical words and phrases, but considers the broader, powerful psychic realities that are mediated through them, that were at work in the lives of their authors, and that continue to incarnate in the readers "in front of the text."

The first reading focuses on the concept of the "inner man" in Paul. The second, on John's Gospel, captures the essence of Wink's attempt to get at the psychological realities at work in the experience and language of the biblical authors and in those communities whose consciousness was catalyzed by the "original impulse of Jesus," a key phrase in Wink's book.

---

1. Wink, *The Human Being*, pp. 247, 229, 246, and 253, citing Delbert Burkett, *The Son of Man Debate: A History and Evaluation*, Society for New Testament Studies Monograph Series (Cambridge: Cambridge University Press, 2000), pp. 92-93.

A. Paul: The Inner Anthropos

Paul and his lieutenants used *anthropos* [man] eight or so times in a way that not only was continuous with the Gospels' use of "the son of the man," but that also created a vocabulary on which the Gnostics later would seize. "Clothe yourselves with the new self [literally, 'new *anthropos*' — *kainon anthropon*], created according to the likeness of God in true righteousness and holiness" (Eph. 4:24). This sense of a radical new inwardness at the core of a person's being — a being lived forward into history — is one of the most significant innovations of that era. The idea was fully articulated by Augustine in his new notion of the individual personality. In the New Testament, however, the idea is still an emergent intuition. "We know that our old self [literally, "old *anthropos*"] was crucified with him (Christ) so that . . . we might no longer be enslaved to sin" (Rom. 6:6). "Our outer nature [literally, "outer *anthropos*"] is wasting away, our inner nature ("*anthropos*" implied) is being renewed day by day" (2 Cor. 4:16). "You have stripped off the old self ("*anthropos*") with its practices and have clothed yourselves with the new self ("*anthropos*" implied) . . . according to the image of its creator" (Col. 3:9-10). "Be strengthened in your inner being ["inner *anthropos*"] with power through his Spirit . . . that Christ may dwell in your hearts through faith, as you are being rooted and grounded in love" (Eph. 3:16-17). This last text indicates that this inner self — what 1 Peter 3:4 calls "the hidden *anthropos* at the center of your being" — is in development; it is not yet complete. The same idea is expressed by Eph. 4:13 — "until all of us come to the unity of the faith and of the knowledge of the Son of God, to maturity [*eis andra teleion*, lit., "into the finished/completed/perfect Human Being"], to the measure of the full stature of Christ."

Further evidence that Paul equates the son of the man with the inner *anthropos* is provided in reverse by Matt. 9:8, in which Matthew concludes the healing of the paralytic story with the words, "and they glorified God, who had given such authority to human beings *(anthropois)*." . . .

But this radical inwardness is even more radically social. Psalm 80 and Daniel 7 had spoken of Israel as the collective Human Being. Ephesians now extends it to encompass all peoples. Thus Eph. 2:15-16 can speak of Christ creating "in himself one new *anthropos* in place of the two [Jew and Gentile]" and of reconciling "both groups to God in one body through the cross." First Corinthians 15:47-49 compares the first and second Adams: "The first *anthropos* was from the earth, a man of dust; the second *anthropos* is from heaven. As was the *anthropos* of dust, so are those who are of the dust; and as is the *anthropos* of heaven, so are those who are of heaven. Just as we have borne the image of the *anthropos* of dust, we will also bear the image of the *anthropos* of heaven" — the latter an unmistakable allusion to the ascended Human Being of the Gospels. Second Adam ("second man"), of course, is a pun on "the son of the man."

The new Adam = second Adam = son of Adam = son of the Man typology is set forth in greatest detail in Rom. 5:12-21, in which all humanity is incorporated into the first Adam and his fallen estate, or into the second Adam and the fellowship of those being redeemed. No one grasped more profoundly the corporate dimension of the "inner *anthropos*" than Paul, who saw it embracing humanity as a single Human Being.

B. The Human Being in John

. . . Contrary to a dogma tenaciously held, Jesus does not exhaust the possibilities of incarnating God. As Tom F. Driver notes, Jesus is neither the sole incarnation of God nor the perfect incarnation. As a male, he does not provide a definitive picture of what incarnation might look like for a woman. But neither does he provide a definitive picture for a man. Jesus did not experience marriage, child rearing, long life, debilitating illnesses, and a host of other things commonly experienced by human beings. Jesus' incarnation is complete from the point of view of his own life, but not from the point of view of others' lives.[1] Put more positively, Jesus is not the incarnate God, but a human being who incarnated God and who taught us how to do the same, through the working of the divine Spirit within us. That is what it means to incarnate God. . . .

The son of the man is God's ultimate statement about the goal of the human enterprise. Yet Jesus' followers are not excluded from the reality that the Human Being represents. In ways that go far beyond the Synoptic Gospels, Jesus the Human Being incorporates his disciples into union with himself in God. He gives them "power to become children of God," as he is (John 1:12). They are not just born of earthly parents, but of God, as he is (1:13). Jesus ascends to heaven (3:13); so, in apparent contradiction, will his disciples (14:2). Jesus testifies to what he has seen and heard from God (3:32); the disciples do likewise (12:17). Jesus judges and forgives (3:17-21); the disciples will also (20:23). Jesus does the works of God; his followers do as well (6:28-29; 9:4), and greater works (14:12). Jesus is God's son; his followers are "gods" and "children of the Most High" (Ps. 82:6; John 10:34-35). Where Jesus is, his disciples will be also (14:3). Jesus alone sees and knows the Father, but the disciples do as well (14:6-7, 9). He is the vine, they are the branches, and the Father is the vinedresser (15:1-11). Nothing could express more completely the collective, corporate nature of the Johannine Human Being than 14:20 — "you will know that I am in my Father, and you in me, and I in you." John has, in short, not only preserved the collective aspect of the Human Being, but raises it to its apogee.

Wink adds the following note to the preceding paragraph:

The rabbis also grasped that the believer is to perform the same acts as God:

> The righteous have power over the same things as God, if one may say so. In which way? Everything that God does, the righteous do. How? God remembers barren women; Elisha, too, remembered the Shunammite woman. . . . God quickens the dead; and Elisha, too, brought back to life the son of the Shunammite woman. God parts the seas; Elijah and Elisha, too, parted seas. . . . God heals without emollients, and Elisha healed Naaman without emollients. God sweetens the bitter waters, and Elisha sweetened the bitter waters. . . . God withholds the rain, and Elijah withheld the rain. . . . God causes rain to fall, and Samuel caused rain to fall. . . . God sends down fire, and Elijah brought down fire [from heaven] . . . (Deut. Rab. 10.3; Soncino edition, 166-67).

The Jewish Christians were not innovating as much as extending a notion shared by their Jewish compatriots when they called themselves Christoi, the Anointed Ones. They did not mean to imply that they resembled the Messiah in every respect, but they believed that, in imitation of him, they were anointed with the Holy Spirit. The Spirit that descended on Jesus at his baptism has continued to fill initiates ever since.[2]

———————

1. Tom F. Driver, *Christ in a Changing World: Toward an Ethical Christology* (New York: Crossroad, 1981), p. 44.

2. Gilles Quispel, *Gnostic Studies I* (Istanbul: Nederlands Historisch-Archaeologisch Instituut, 1974), p. 235.

SUGGESTIONS FOR FURTHER READING

Bloom, Paul. "The Duel Between Body and Soul." *New York Times*, September 10, 2004, A25.

Bultmann, Rudolf. "The Anthropological Concepts [of Paul]." In *Theology of the New Testament*, translated by Kendrick Grobel, vol. 1, 190-269. New York: Charles Scribner's Sons, 1951.

Burrows, Millar. *An Outline of Biblical Theology*. Philadelphia: Westminster Press, 1946, particularly pp. 134-41.

Delitzsch, Franz. *A System of Biblical Psychology*, translated by Robert Ernest Wallis, 2nd (1867) edition. Clark's Foreign Theological Library 13. Edinburgh: T&T Clark, 1899.

Fletcher, M. Scott. *The Psychology of the New Testament*. 2nd edition. New York: Hodder & Stoughton, 1912.

Green, Joel B. "'Bodies — That is, Human Lives': A Re-Examination of Human Nature in the Bible." In *Whatever Happened to the Soul? Scientific and Theological Portraits of Human Nature*, edited by Warren S. Brown, Nancey Murphy, and H. Newton Malony, 149-74. Minneapolis: Fortress, 1998.

Hopkins, D. D. "Biblical Anthropology, Discipline of." In *Dictionary of Pastoral Care and Counseling*, edited by R. Hunter, 85-88. Nashville: Abingdon, 1990.

Wink, Walter. "The Original Impulse of Jesus." In *Psychology and the Bible: A New Way to Read the Scriptures*, edited by J. Harold Ellens and Wayne G. Rollins, vol. 4, 209-22. Westport, CT: Praeger Publishers, 2004.

Glossary

Alchemy (Jungian psychology)   An ancient (500-1500 C.E.) body of knowledge devoted to the effort to transform base elements into gold. This task, or opus, was carried out on the prima materia (Latin: "first matter"), with the help of the *philosopher's stone,* which served as a catalyst. Jung believed that alchemy concerned not an external transformation process, but an internal one — the transformation of the psyche — and its principles and methods were symbolic expressions of *archetypal* processes.

Analytical psychology (Jungian psychology)   Carl G. Jung's name for his therapeutic approach, distinguished from Freud's *psychoanalysis.*

Anima/animus (Jungian psychology)   The unconscious archetype of the opposite gender. The feminine element in men is the *anima;* the masculine in women is the *animus.* These unconscious elements exert significant influence over one's relationships with the opposite sex.

Apologetics   The branch of Christian theology devoted to defending the truth of the Christian faith.

Apotheosization   The act of glorifying someone or something to the highest degree, deification. From Greek, "to deify."

Apotropaic   Having the power to avert evil or misfortune. From the Greek "to turn away."

Archetype/archetypal image (Jungian psychology)   An unconscious structure or patterning tendency in the psyche that is part of the common inheritance of all human beings. Archetypes cannot be observed directly; they express themselves through archetypal images in dreams, symbols, and myths.

Behavioral psychology   A branch of psychology that considers only observable behavior appropriate for study. Key concepts in behaviorism include the relationship of stimulus to response and how specific stimuli can condition behavior. See also *Operant conditioning, Reinforcement.*

Biblical criticism   An inclusive term covering a variety of approaches to understanding the text, history, origins, structures, and meanings of the Bible. "Criticism" does not imply a negative judgment, but a careful and evaluative study. Biblical criticism in its modern form began in the mid-nineteenth century and includes, among many others, textual, historical, editorial, rhetorical, feminist, ideological, and psychological criticism.

Charism/charismatic   A spiritual gift, especially one involving an unusual or ecstatic experience or capability such as prophecy or speaking in tongues. From the Greek for "gift" or "grace."

Canon   From the Greek "kanon," a measuring stick, a canon is the officially approved collection of writings within a religious tradition. The biblical texts include the Jewish canon (Old Testament) and the Christian canon (Old and New Testaments). Roman Catholics and Orthodox canons also include the *Deuterocanonical* texts.

Cognitive dissonance (cognitive psychology)   The tension between one's expectations of reality and one's actual experience. The greater the difference, the stronger the need to reduce the dissonance. This can be achieved through reformulating one's expectations, denial, or reframing one's perceptions.

Cognitive psychology   A branch of psychology that focuses on the structures and mental processes of thinking (cognition). Cognitive studies may, for example, examine memory, perception, learning, reasoning, and problem-solving.

Collective unconscious (Jungian psychology)   The deepest part of the psyche, inherited and shared by all human beings. The collective unconscious is the source of many of the *archetypes* and explains the commonality of myths and symbols across time and space.

Compulsive behavior   A *defense mechanism* that uses ongoing actions over which an individual does not have conscious control in an attempt to reduce anxiety. Also known as obsessive-compulsive behavior.

Conscious/consciousness   That part of the mind or intellect of which the individual is aware. It is the "I" or "me" that we speak of when referring to ourselves.

Cura animarum Latin term meaning "the cure of souls." It has been used both in religious and in psychological contexts to refer to the healing work of the church or therapy.

Defense mechanism (depth psychology) A variety of unconscious methods by which the conscious ego can protect itself from stressful or threatening situations. Defense mechanisms can serve to deny the issue (*denial, repression,* suppression), blame someone else *(transference, displacement, projection),* or channel the reaction in a different way *(compulsive behavior,* sublimation, *reaction formation).*

Demythologization (biblical criticism) Looking beyond the mythical qualities of the Bible in order to recover the original experience and meaning that lie behind the text. The term was introduced into biblical studies in the 1950s by prominent New Testament scholar Rudolf Bultmann.

Denial A *defense mechanism* by which an individual refuses to acknowledge consciously a disturbing thought, feeling, or situation. Less strong than *repression.*

Depth psychology A branch of psychology that deals with the effect of unconscious (depth) factors on behavior. Depth psychology includes *psychoanalytic psychology* (Freud), *analytical psychology* (Jung), and *object relations* theory, among others.

Deuterocanonical Literally "Second Canon," it refers to those biblical books that were originally written in Greek before the New Testament. These books are not recognized by the Jewish or Protestant *canons,* but are accepted by Roman Catholics and Orthodox Christians.

Developmental psychology A branch of psychology that deals with the psychological development of the individual from childhood through adulthood.

Displacement A *defense mechanism* in which one directs one's feelings from the true target to one that is "safe." It may involve getting angry at the dog instead of dealing with the boss, or, more constructively, punching a pillow instead of a co-worker.

Dissociation A process in which the ego splits some aspect of the *conscious* mind (memory, feeling, idea), making it inaccessible. Dissociation can range from the mild (daydreaming), to the severe (multiple personality disorder). It can be a normal way of dealing with trauma or a *defense mechanism.*

Ego (depth psychology) The conscious center of the personality; the sense of

"I." In Freudian psychology, one of three components of the psyche (with *super-ego* and *id*). In Jungian psychology, the ego is the means for relating to the unconscious *archetypes*. From the Latin word for "I."

Eisegesis (biblical studies)   From the Greek, meaning "to lead in." It involves imposing one's own interpretation on a text, forcing the text to fit one's preconceived notions. The opposite of *exegesis*.

Exegesis (biblical studies)   From the Greek, meaning "to lead out." The process of analyzing the language, structure, and historical context of a biblical text in order to understand "what it says." Paul Ricoeur calls this the "explanation" of the text, in contrast to the "appropriation" of the text *(hermeneutics)*.

Feminist criticism (biblical criticism)   A way of reading the biblical text that is sensitive to the historical, contextual, and ideological issues in the text that affect women. Several forms of feminist criticism have been used, ranging from those who highlight the significant role of women in the Bible to those who find biblical themes that condemn all oppression, including that of women, to those who find the Bible irredeemably patriarchal and male-oriented.

Forschungsgeschichte   From the German, "history of research." It is a process of collecting and reviewing the research in a given field of study.

Freudian psychology   See *Psychoanalysis*.

Functions (Jungian psychology)   See *Psychological types*.

Hellenistic world   The culture and religion that developed throughout the Mediterranean following the conquests of Alexander the Great in the second century B.C.E. The *Septuagint* (Greek translation of the Hebrew scriptures), the *Deuterocanonical* books, and the Hellenistic context significantly shaped the books of the New Testament.

Hermeneutics (biblical criticism)   Derived from the name of the Greek god Hermes, the messenger of the gods, hermeneutics is the study of the process of interpretation. Paul Ricoeur describes it as the task of "appropriation," in contrast to the task of "explanation" *(exegesis)*. Hermeneutics considers not only the text but also the reader and the context for interpretation, all of which contribute to understanding.

Hermeneutics of suspicion (biblical criticism)   Reading a text with careful attention to hidden factors that may affect the text and/or its interpretation, such as unconscious motivations, ideologies, or hidden agendas. Paul Ricoeur used the term to apply to interpretation after Freud's theories led to questioning consciousness as the rule of meaning.

Heuristic   Referring to a model, hypothesis, or process used to test a theory and develop it further. From the Greek word "to find."

Historical criticism (biblical studies)   A way of reading the biblical texts that seeks to uncover their original historical context and meaning. Historical criticism dominated biblical studies from the mid-nineteenth century until the latter part of the twentieth.

Homeostasis   The tendency of a complex system (such as the *psyche*) to maintain stability and equilibrium within itself. From the Greek roots "homeo" (the same) and "stasis" (standing).

Humanistic psychology   A branch of psychology emphasizing the study of the whole person, including subjective experience and the potential for growth and development of one's human potential. Humanistic psychology is sometimes known as the "Third Force," alongside *behaviorism* and *depth psychology.*

Id (Freudian psychology)   Together with the *ego* and the *superego,* the third part of the *psyche.* The id is the instinctual drive of the personality; it is irrational and pleasure-driven. From the Latin word for "it."

Individuation (Jungian psychology)   The process of becoming the unique individual that one is created to be. A lifelong process of development, it involves the integration of conscious and unconscious elements of the psyche into a relational whole.

Inferior function (Jungian psychology)   See *Psychological types.*

Jungian psychology   See *Analytical psychology.*

Kerygma (biblical studies)   The proclamation of the Christian message, especially as described in the New Testament. From the Greek for "proclamation."

Myth   Despite its common use as a synonym for "untruth," in religious and psychological studies it refers to a story that is integral to a culture or tradition and serves to explain "the way things are." Myths serve to shape a culture's view of the world and its meaning and the place of human beings in it, to demonstrate the proper attitudes, relationships, and actions in that world, and to warn of common dangers or pitfalls.

Neurosis/neurotic (psychological theory)   A generic term for a mild form of disturbance of feeling, thinking or behavior, such as depression, anxiety, or *compulsive behavior*. In depth psychology, neuroses are understood as symptoms of deeper unconscious conflicts.

Object relations theory (psychoanalytic theory)   A branch of *psychoanalysis* that focuses on the development of personality through internalized representations (internal objects) of significant others (e.g., parents).

Obsessive-compulsive   Related to a psychological anxiety disorder in which an individual is driven to perform specific acts or rituals to ward off the anxiety.

Oedipus complex (Freudian psychology)   The developmental crisis (for boys; in girls it is called the Electra complex) in which a boy develops sexual attraction to his mother, accompanied by a sense of rivalry with his father.

Operant conditioning (behavioral psychology)   A process of modifying behavior through *reinforcement*.

Opus (Jungian psychology)   See *Alchemy*.

Pathogenic   Something that is capable of causing physical or psychological disease or dysfunction. The opposite of *therapeutic*.

Persona (Jungian psychology)   From the Latin word for the mask worn on stage by ancient actors, the persona is the public face that one presents to the outside world. It is who others think one is, and it may be more or less consistent with one's inner *psyche*.

Personal unconscious (Jungian psychology)   The unconscious dimension of the *psyche* that is specific to the individual, as distinct from the *collective unconscious*. The personal unconscious contains elements from the individual's unique life-experience.

Personality   A cluster of relatively stable attributes, attitudes, and behaviors that distinguish one person from another.

Philosopher's stone (Jungian psychology)   See *Alchemy*.

Prima materia (Jungian psychology)   See *Alchemy*.

Projection   A *defense mechanism* in which an individual attributes his or her own unconscious motives or qualities to another person without acknowledging them in him- or herself. Projections can be either positive or negative.

Psyche The Greek word for life, breath, or soul, used in early Christian writings to denote the soul or spiritual dimension of the human being. It is used in *depth psychology* to refer to the totality of an individual's mental processes, including both conscious and unconscious dimensions.

Psychoanalysis/psychoanalytic psychology (Freud)   Sigmund Freud's name for his psychological approach, which focused on analyzing, understanding, and integrating the unconscious motivations or reactions of an individual.

Psychodynamics   The interaction of psychological factors, especially unconscious factors, in shaping both internal and external behavior.

Psychological biblical criticism   A way of reading the biblical text that is sensitive to psychological factors and dynamics active in all aspects of the creation, transmission, and interpretation of the Bible.

Psychological types (Jungian psychology)   A system of personality types based on Jung's four functions of sensing, intuiting, thinking, and feeling, and the orientations of introversion and extraversion. The superior function is the one that is easiest for an individual to exercise; the inferior function remains relatively undeveloped. The Myers-Briggs Temperament Indicator adds another category: judging and perceiving.

Psychologizing   Explaining phenomena exclusively in terms of psychological factors, without regard for other potential influences.

Quaternity (Jungian psychology)   A cluster of four things that together make a unity. For Jung, patterns of quaternity that recur in symbols, myths, art, and dream images express the *archetypal* four dimensions of psychological experience.

Reaction formation   A *defense mechanism* in which an individual develops a characteristic response to a situation and then unconsciously transfers that response to a new situation.

Reader response criticism (biblical criticism)   A way of reading the biblical text that is sensitive to the way a reader interacts with the text in the creation of meaning. It focuses on how the reader's expectations, preconceptions, context, and reading process affect interpretation.

Reinforcement (behavioral psychology)   A stimulus following a given behavior that affects whether that behavior will be repeated. Positive reinforcement rewards the behavior and encourages it; negative reinforcement punishes the behavior and discourages it.

Repression A *defense mechanism* in which disturbing memories, feelings, or reactions are unconsciously kept out of an individual's awareness. Repression is deeper and more unconscious than *denial.*

Self (Jungian psychology) The *archetype* of wholeness within the *psyche.* As one moves further along in the process of *individuation,* the individual *ego* ceases to be the sole center of conscious life and is more and more related to the Self. Encounters with the Self have a sacred quality, and images of the divine are often closely related to the archetype of the Self.

Self psychology A branch of psychology developed by Heinz Kohut, which is essentially psychoanalytic, but differs in that it focuses especially on the healthy development of the individual self (or ego) through supportive relationships with others.

Septuagint A collection of translations of the Hebrew scriptures into Greek with some additional material, compiled in about the third century B.C.E.

Shadow (Jungian psychology) The unconscious dimension of the *psyche* that contains all the aspects of an individual's personality that he or she does not consciously acknowledge. It is generally the opposite of the *persona.*

Superego (Freudian psychology) One of the three components of the *psyche* (with the *ego* and the *id*), it represents the authority of parents, values, and culture that have been internalized and exert control over the individual's attitudes and actions.

Superior function (Jungian psychology) See *Psychological types.*

Symbol Something that stands for or represents something else. In *depth psychology,* symbols in dreams, myths, and art are considered expressions of the *unconscious* and can help in understanding unconscious dynamics.

Tetragrammaton From the Greek for "four letters." The proper name of God in the Hebrew scriptures, consisting of the Hebrew letters YHWH. It is represented in English as YHWH, Yahweh, Jahweh, or (incorrectly) Jehovah. Since many consider it improper to pronounce the name, "the Lord" is often substituted in English translations.

Theophany   The visible manifestation or appearance of God. From Greek, "appearance of God."

Therapeutic   Contributing to health or healing; the opposite of *pathogenic.*

Transference (depth psychology)   An unconscious process in which an individual's interactions with another person are reenacted in relation to a different person, usually the therapist.

Transitional space (object relations)   An imaginary relational space that is neither entirely internal nor entirely external where people interact with each other. Transitional space is where art, culture, and religion are shaped and developed.

Unconscious (depth psychology)   That part of the psyche that is not immediately accessible to the conscious mind or *ego.* Jung further distinguished between the *personal unconscious* and the *collective unconscious.*

Wirkungsgeschichte   From the German "history of effects," it is the study of the impact of the Bible on individuals and communities through time.

Yahweh   See *Tetragrammaton.*

Yahwistic (biblical studies)   Pertaining to the religious and theological traditions that developed in the southern kingdom of Judah, which used the name YHWH to refer to God. See *Tetragrammaton.*

Acknowledgments

The editors and publisher gratefully acknowledge permission to include material from the following sources:

Chapter 2

Excerpts from Prologue from *Soul: An Archaeology: Readings from Socrates to Ray Charles*, Compiled and Edited by Phil Cousineau. Copyright © 1994 by Phil Cousineau. Reprinted by permission of HarperCollins Publishers.

Ray S. Anderson, "On Being Human: The Spiritual Saga of a Creaturely Soul." In *Whatever Happened to the Soul? Scientific and Theological Portraits of Human Nature*, edited by Warren S. Brown, Nancey Murphy, and H. Newton Malony (Minneapolis: Fortress, 1998). Used by permission of Augsburg Fortress Publishers.

Chapter 3

Wayne G. Rollins, adapted and revised version of "The Bible in Psycho-Spiritual Perspective: News from the World of Biblical Scholarship," *Pastoral Psychology* 51, no. 2 (2002). Used with kind permission of Springer Science and Business Media.

Ilona Rashkow, *Taboo or Not Taboo: Sexuality and Family in the Hebrew Bible* (Minneapolis: Fortress, 2000). Used by permission of Augsburg Fortress Publishers.

Ilona Rashkow, *The Phallacy of Genesis: A Feminist-Psychoanalytic Approach*

(Louisville: Westminster/John Knox Press, 1993). Copyright © Ilona Rashkow. Used by permission.

Michael Willett Newheart, *My Name Is Legion: The Story and Soul of the Gerasene Demoniac,* Interfaces (Collegeville: Liturgical Press, 2004). Used by permission.

Chapter 4

Edward P. Bolin and Glenn M. Goldberg, "Behavioral Psychology and the Bible: General and Specific Considerations," *Journal of Psychology and Theology* 7, no. 3 (1979). Used by permission.

Gerd Theissen, *Psychological Aspects of Pauline Theology,* translated by John P. Galvin (Philadelphia: Fortress, 1987). Used by permission of Augsburg Fortress Press.

Ralph Underwood, "Winnicott's Squiggle Game and Biblical Interpretation," in J. Harold Ellens and Wayne G. Rollins, *Psychology and the Bible.* Copyright © 2004 Praeger Publishers. Reproduced with permission of Greenwood Publishing Group, Inc., Westport, CT.

Lyn Bechtel, "Developmental Psychology in Biblical Studies," in J. Harold Ellens, *Psychology and the Bible.* Copyright © 2004 Praeger Publishers. Reproduced with permission of Greenwood Publishing Group, Inc., Westport, CT.

Chapter 5

Excerpt taken from *Psychology of Biblical Interpretation* by Cedric B. Johnson. Copyright © 1983 by Zondervan Corporation. Used by permission of The Zondervan Corporation.

Excerpt from *Viewpoints: Perspectives of Faith and Christian Nurture.* Copyright © 1998 by H. Edward Everding Jr., Mary W. Wilcox, Lucinda A. Huffaker, Clarence H. Snelling Jr. Used by permission of Continuum International Publishing Group.

Leslie J. Francis, *Personality Type and Scripture: Exploring Mark's Gospel* (London: Mowbray, 1997). Used by permission.

Chapter 6

Patrick Henry, "Water, Bread, Wine: Patterns in Religion," from *New Directions in New Testament Study* by Patrick Henry. © 1979 The Westminster Press. Used by permission of Westminster John Knox Press.

Elizabeth-Anne Stewart, *Jesus the Holy Fool* (Franklin, WI: Sheed & Ward, 1999). Used by permission of Sheed & Ward, an imprint of Rowman & Littlefield Publishing, Inc.

Chapter 7

David J. Halperin, *Seeking Ezekiel: Text and Psychology*, University Park: Pennsylvania State University Press, 1993, pp. 207-15. Copyright 1993 by the Pennsylvania State University. Reproduced by permission of the publisher.

Terrence Callan, *Psychological Perspectives on the Life of Paul*, published by Edwin Mellen Press. Used by permission.

Chapter 8

Excerpts from Edward Edinger, *The Bible and the Psyche: Individuation Symbolism in the Old Testament* (Toronto: Inner City Books, 1986). Used by permission.

John W. Miller, *Jesus at Thirty: A Psychological and Historical Portrait* (Minneapolis: Augsburg/Fortress, 1997). Used by permission of Augsburg Fortress Publishers.

Chapter 9

Excerpts from *The Man Who Wrestled with God*, by John A. Sanford. Copyright 1987, Paulist Press, Inc., New York/Mahwah, NJ. Used with permission of Paulist Press.

André Lacocque, "A Psychological Approach to the Book of Jonah," in J. Harold Ellens and Wayne G. Rollins, *Psychology and the Bible*. Copyright © 2004 Praeger Publishers. Reproduced with permission of Greenwood Publishing Group, Inc., Westport, CT.

Excerpts from Edward Edinger, *The Bible and the Psyche: Individuation Symbol-*

ism in the Old Testament (Toronto: Inner City Books, 1986). Used by permission.

Chapter 10

Charles T. Davis III, "Revelation Seventeen," in J. Harold Ellens and Wayne G. Rollins, *Psychology and the Bible.* Copyright © 2004 Praeger Publishers. Reproduced with permission of Greenwood Publishing Group, Inc., Westport, CT.
Robin Scroggs, "Psychology as a Tool to Interpret the Text: Emerging Trends in Biblical Thought." Copyright 1982 Christian Century. Reprinted with permission from the March 24, 1982, issue of the *Christian Century.*

Chapter 11

Pages 77-79, 93-96 from *Dreams: God's Forgotten Language* by John Sanford. Copyright © 1968 by John Sanford. Reprinted by permission of HarperCollins Publishers.
Max Weber, "Judaism: The Psychology of the Prophets," in *The Symbolic Instrument in Early Times,* vol. 1 of *Propaganda and Communication in World History,* ed. H. D. Lesswell, D. Lerner, and H. Speier (Honolulu: University of Hawaii Press, 1967). Used by permission.
The Surprising Gospel: Intriguing Psychological Insights from the New Testament, by Wilhelm H. Wuellner and Robert C. Leslie, Nashville: Abingdon Press, 1984. Used by permission.

Chapter 12

Jesus and Logotherapy: The Ministry of Jesus as Interpreted through the Psychology of Viktor Frankl, by Robert C. Leslie, Nashville: Abingdon Press, 1965. Used by permission.
Gerd Theissen, *Psychological Aspects of Pauline Theology,* translated by John P. Galvin (Philadelphia: Fortress, 1987). Used by permission of Augsburg Fortress Publishers.

Chapter 13

Charles T. Davis III, "The Evolution of a Pauline Toxic Text," in J. Harold Ellens, *The Destructive Power of Religion.* Copyright © 2004 Praeger Publishers. Reproduced with permission of Greenwood Publishing Group, Inc., Westport, CT.

D. Andrew Kille, "'The Bible Made Me Do It': Text, Interpretation and Violence," in J. Harold Ellens, *The Destructive Power of Religion.* Copyright © 2004 Praeger Publishers. Reproduced with permission of Greenwood Publishing Group, Inc., Westport, CT.

Basic Types of Pastoral Care and Counseling: Resources for the Ministry of Healing and Growth, by Howard Clinebell. Nashville: Abingdon Press, 1984. Used by permission.

Excerpts from Matthew B. Schwartz and Kalman J. Kaplan, *Biblical Stories for Psychotherapy and Counseling: A Sourcebook* (New York: Haworth Pastoral Press, 2004). Reprinted with permission.

Chapter 14

Walter Wink, *The Human Being: Jesus and the Enigma of the Son of the Man* (Minneapolis: Fortress, 2002). Used by permission of Augsburg Fortress Publishers.

Index of Authors

Index of Subjects

Abraham, 197
Adam and Eve, 160-65
Affiliation, 237
Aggression, 237
Ambivalence, 246
Angels, 196
Anger, 169, 241
Antichrist: "antichristology," 187; projection of, 181-88; as stereotype, 184-85
Anti-Judaism, 238
Archetypes and archetypal images, 99-115, 171, 174, 183; biblical, 101-2; of the cosmos, 108; cross, 115; death and resurrection, 110-11; divine child, 146; God as archetypal image, 108-9; good and evil, 110; the hero, 107, 185-86; the holy, 108-9; "Holy fool" as archetype, 113-15; masculine and feminine, 107; persons, places, and things, 107-10; processes, 110-11; the self, 107-8, 111-13; 186-87; "Son-of-the-man," 259-63; types of, 101. *See* Jung; Symbols
Aristotle: on the psyche, 26; *Peri Psyches (De Anima),* 249
Attribution, 130
Authority, 85
Autobiographical criticism, 53

"Bad mother," 122
Baptism: symbolism of, 103-6

Behaviorism, 27-28, 56, 57, 58-63; applied to biblical figures, 116-18
Bible: and psychology, 24; on the soul, 25; and soul-making, 24, as therapeutic, 47. *See* Biblical psychology
Biblical criticism. *See* Autobiographical criticism; Historical-critical method; Narrative criticism; Psychoanalytic literary theory; Psychological biblical criticism; Reader-response criticism
Biblical personality portraits, 45-46, 138-59
Biblical psychology, 3, 5, 6, 11, 14, 248-63; on childhood trauma, 122; in conversation with modern psychology, 252-55; psychological vocabulary of the Bible, 250-55; threefold agenda, 250-55
Biblical religious phenomena, 45

Christ: as archetype of the self, 113, 115, 173-74; blood of, as amulet, 145-46; and the Beast of Revelation, 181-82; Christ-antichrist motif, 182-88; Christ figure, 46; Christ mysticism, 190. *See* Jesus
Cognitive dissonance, 176, 241
Cognitive orientation, 86
Cognitive psychology, 57, 60, 189
Collective unconscious, 44
Compensatory function of texts, 45
Consciousness, 161. *See* Jung; Freud

37n.4, 253; body and soul, 38; history of, 29-31; in Jung's thought, 24-25; loss or death of, 22, 30; reality of, 35; reclaiming a sense of, 30-31, 36-38; in scripture, 37n.4; "soul-making," 23; soul-sickness, 34-35; soul and spirit, 37-38; terms for, in world cultures, 29, 33-35. *See also* James Hillman; Psyche; Self
Speaking in tongues. *See* Glossolalia
Spirit, 254-55; "in the spirit," 196; as healer, 206. *See* Holy Spirit
Splitting, 237
"Squiggle game," 69-72. *See* Object relations
Suffering: in Freud and Jung, 62
Symbols, 72, 99-115; fire, 143; light, 146-47; the number forty, 146; Marah (bitterness), 147-48; Passover symbolism, 145-46; and signs, 100; types of, 100-101, water, 103-6; wilderness, 146. *See* Archetypes and archetypal images

Teaching, 241
Ten Commandments, 171-74
"The Other," 234, 235

"The Same," 234
Therapeutic texts, 46-48; therapeutic effects, 231, 247
Third force psychology. *See* Humanistic psychology
"Toxic text," 231, 232, 232-36
Transference, 84-86
Transitional space, 69, 72

Unconscious, the, 41, 48-50, 53-55, 70, 82, 159, 171, 197, 198; in the Bible, 43-44

Visions, 194-99, 200. *See* Unconscious
Voice of God, 200, 202

Wedding at Cana: in psychological perspective, 177-80
Wirkungsgeschichte, 20
Wisdom, 66, 239
World behind the text, 117, 194, 231
World in front of the text, 81, 117, 139, 194, 231
World of the text, 117, 140, 231

YHWH, 144

Index of Scripture References